MOON OVER
OVER
MARTINBOROUGH

MOON
OVER
MARTINBOROUGH

From Michigan to the Wairarapa . . . How an
American city boy became a Kiwi farmer

Jared
Gulian

RANDOM HOUSE
NEW ZEALAND

A RANDOM HOUSE BOOK published by Random House New Zealand
18 Poland Road, Glenfield, Auckland, New Zealand

For more information about our titles go to www.randomhouse.co.nz

A catalogue record for this book is available from the
National Library of New Zealand

Random House New Zealand is part of the Random House Group
New York London Sydney Auckland Delhi Johannesburg

First published 2013

© 2013 text Jared Gulian; photographs Mike Heydon unless
otherwise credited to Jared Gulian; illustrations Greg Keith

The moral rights of the author have been asserted

ISBN 978 1 77553 005 3
eISBN 978 1 77553 256 9

Design: Carla Sy
Illustrations: Greg Keith www.wolfies.co.nz
Cover photograph: Mike Heydon

Printed in New Zealand by Printlink

This publication is printed on paper pulp sourced from sustainably
grown and managed forests, using Elemental Chlorine Free (EFC)
bleaching, and printed with 100% vegetable-based inks.

Author's note

THE EVENTS, PEOPLE AND ANIMALS in this book are real. I believe in poetic licence and I use it from time to time, although never so much as to alter the essential truth of the story.

My neighbours' names are changed out of respect for their privacy. I shifted the timeline of some minor events to fit the story arc, such as when the chickens and pigs first arrived on our tiny olive farm, and when I tasted certain wines.

I glossed over some tedious details, such as exactly where the Martinborough olive press was located the first time we went there and who owned it. (It changed hands and moved a few streets over.)

And I hereby confess that I blatantly made up the quotes that I attributed to the chickens.

TO CJ

Contents

The Second Year

The Third Year

The Fourth Year

Getting intimate with a cast sheep

'**T**here's a sheep down in your paddock,' Jim the Mad Welshman says over the phone. Jim's our neighbour on the eastern boundary. He was working along the fenceline when he saw the sheep. 'It looks pretty sick,' he says.

I IMMEDIATELY CALL HAMISH, who leases our paddocks. The sheep are his.

'Probably cast,' Hamish says. 'Might just need propping back up, then she'll be right.'

'Cast?' I say.

'Yiece.' This, I had already learned, is what many Kiwis say when they mean 'yes'. It rhymes with 'niece'.

Then Hamish mumbles, 'Cast sheep.'

'Of course,' I say, having absolutely no idea what he's talking about. I figure that a 'cast sheep' can only mean one of two things. Either the animal is recovering from a broken leg, or it just got a part in a movie. Neither seems entirely likely.

'Um, just what exactly is a cast sheep?' I ask.

'Can't get up.'

'Oh?'

'Yiece.'

'Why can't it get up?'

'She's cast.'

It takes some time before Hamish realises that he's speaking to a man who has somehow made it into adulthood without ever having come across a cast sheep. Then he provides an explanation. A cast sheep is a sheep that has lain down and can't get up because its centre of gravity is off — sometimes because it's pregnant or simply because it has a full fleece. Hamish had put a ram in with the ewes, and some of them were pregnant, so that increased the risk. Once cast sheep are down, gases start to build up in their abdomens and they can die in a matter of hours. If you get them back up on their feet, then they're fine.

'Could you prop her up?' Hamish asks. 'It'd save me a trip over. If it doesn't work, I'll come by. You mind?'

Hamish knows I could say no, since they *are* after all his sheep. But this is the country, and if there's one thing I've learned in the country it's that people help each other. Besides, how often do you get the chance to prop up a cast sheep?

'Sure,' I say. 'But you have to tell me how.'

He says I should straddle the sheep, putting one leg on either side of it, and bend down. It already sounds dodgy to me. Then I have to pull the sheep up by the wool and hold it up while the circulation gets back into its legs. After that, I can let go and, in Hamish's words, 'she'll be right'. I am certain that Hamish is lying through his teeth. He just wants to trick an ignorant American city boy. He probably has a camera hidden in the shelterbelt. Soon there'll be an image of me in a compromising position with a sheep on the front page of the *Martinborough Star*.

But Hamish assures me that it is all true and I agree to 'give it a go', as the Kiwis say. CJ isn't home, so I'm on my own. There is one problem. I don't want our neighbour Jim to see me standing astride a sheep without a clear explanation in advance, so I call him and tell him what I'm about to do.

He just laughs. 'Now I've heard it all. That sheep's sick. Propping her up won't help.'

It's September and the paddocks everywhere are the intense, vibrant green of spring. I find the sheep lying on her side between the hay shed and the olive grove. Her back is covered in poop and she doesn't look at all well. I have serious doubts about Hamish's clever plan. But I straddle the poor, sick sheep anyway. I figure it would really hurt to be yanked up by your wool, so I try to wrap my arms around her. I feel everywhere under her belly, but I can't get a good hold. There are no handles. In the end I resort to grabbing fistfuls of wool and pulling her up the way Hamish said. The sheep immediately pushes her legs down and tries to run forward. I hold on tightly, leaning back and straddling her in such a way that were I in a public spot I would surely be arrested.

Very quickly the sheep breaks free and tries to run. After only a few steps, she falls down again. I walk over and straddle the pathetic creature a second time, pull her up by her wool, and hold on again. I manage to hang on longer this time, but once more she breaks free, runs, and falls. It seems pointless. I'm just torturing the poor animal. But I decide to try one last time. I straddle her and pull her up again, and this time something strange happens. She doesn't struggle or try to run. She stands perfectly still, as though she now understands I'm trying to help.

I hold on tight and wait. It's ridiculous. Here I am, standing in a grassy paddock in New Zealand with a sick, poop-stained sheep between my legs. Oh, if only my friends and family back in the States could see me now! What a glamorous life I lead! All of a sudden, I start laughing. Between the hay shed and the olive grove, as the sun beats down, I stand, straddling a sheep, laughing.

In the end I wait a good three or four minutes before I finally let go. The sheep does not run. She does not fall. She stands perfectly still beneath me. I swing my right leg over her and step away. She starts to nibble at the grass. After a minute or so, she takes one tentative step and stops. She eats some more. I walk back to the fence and watch. She eats slowly. She takes a couple more cautious steps, then starts eating again.

Jim comes up to the other side of the fence. 'Look at that,' he remarks. 'She's up.'

'Yes, look at that,' I say proudly. 'I did a little bit of laying on of hands. I healed her.'

Jim smiles. 'So you'll be opening up your own church then?'

We watch the sheep for a while, and then she finally wanders off, looking perfectly fine.

Back in the house, I call Hamish again to report my success.

'You're practically a professional shepherd now,' Hamish jokes.

'That's right,' I say. 'From now on every time I come across a dead sheep, I'm going to prop it up and see if it walks.'

Hamish laughs. 'Yiece. You let me know how you get on with that.' Then he says something I've come to hear often here, an expression I especially like: 'Good as gold, mate. Thanks heaps.'

SO HOW DOES AN American city boy go from living in a tiny urban apartment to straddling sheep in rural New Zealand? Well, let me tell you how it all began . . .

The
Firs
Yea

Chapter 1

The first time I saw the trees

It was a gorgeous September spring morning in 2006, and CJ and I were climbing into our car for a day trip to Martinborough.

I THREW SOME APPLES into the back seat to snack on later, and I placed two travel mugs full of hot coffee in the cup holders between us. The morning light was pale blue as CJ started the engine and pulled out of our driveway.

In 2006 we were living in Wellington. Somewhere along the course of our lives we'd accidentally become itinerant Americans, moving first from the North Side of Chicago together to northern Japan, then down to the bright lights of Tokyo, and most recently all the way to the bottom of the planet, here to New Zealand. We were in our early forties, and we'd been together 12 years. But we were hopeless nomads. In the two previous years alone, we'd lived in four different spots in Wellington. Our running joke was that as soon as we hung pictures on the wall, it was time to move.

Although this was just a day trip, there was something bigger behind the drive to Martinborough. We were going because CJ had proposed something radical. He had proposed we settle. We were off to look at CJ's Fantastic New Idea. I was extremely sceptical.

To get to Martinborough from Wellington, you pass the clustered office buildings of Wellington's central business district, get on State Highway 1 and head out of the city along the edge of the harbour.

That morning the harbour was calm and Matiu/Somes Island in the middle looked green and peaceful. Across the blue stillness we could see the Rimutaka Ranges, the mountains that form a massive wall separating Wellington from the Wairarapa valley, and that was where we were headed.

The Saturday morning traffic was light. We cracked the windows and balmy spring air filled the car. Eventually Wellington's wooden hillside houses disappeared behind us, and then we left the harbour behind as well. We passed suburbs dotted with green lawns and drove alongside the Hutt River. There were hills above us on either side. Then the suburbs gave way to farms and open spaces, fields with horses and cattle — only of course they are called 'paddocks' here, not fields.

As we approached the foothills of the Rimutakas, the road began to wind back and forth and up and down. In front of us, the mountains loomed.

I have always been amazed that New Zealanders call the stretch of road over these mountains the 'Rimutaka Hill Road', and that whenever they're travelling it they say they're just 'heading over the hill'. I assure you, the Rimutakas are no hill. With the tallest peak reaching 949 metres above sea level and the entire range stretching 55 kilometres long, referring to those mountains as 'the hill' is, to my mind, a classic example of Kiwi understatement. It's this same low-key spirit that makes Kiwis refer to travelling to Australia — a trip involving a three-hour flight over 2223 kilometres of turbulent, shark-infested waters — as simply 'crossing the ditch'.

The fact is that the Rimutaka Hill Road is notoriously bad. When the weather turns nasty, surface flooding, slips and high winds close the road. This kind of thing happens all the time, and it's so challenging that the transit authorities have erected a sign near the approach to the Rimutakas informing motorists whether or not the road is open that day.

The local news is regularly peppered with stories of drivers disappearing over the road's steep drop-offs — even when the weather is good. Crashed cars are quickly swallowed by the thick tangle of native tree ferns and thorny gorse. In one gruesome case, the car of a missing local businessman was discovered down one of the banks a full two months after he'd disappeared. His body was still there in the driver's seat, slowly decomposing.

I heard the change in the engine as CJ stepped on the gas and the car began to climb. Our car is a Nissan Pulsar, a little burgundy two-door hatchback. It's a city car, and it's fine for zipping around Wellington. It is not meant for crossing mountains. As the road grew steeper, the little car huffed and puffed, and I felt my stomach sink.

I'd insisted that CJ drive because there was no way I was driving that road. When I was a kid I was afraid of heights. I'm mostly over that now, but it comes back sometimes. Like when I'm in a car alongside a steep drop-off, and there's something like a metre between the wheels of the car and my death. Call me silly.

In most spots the fence along the Rimutaka Hill Road is just a line of little stakes with a few white wires strung along between them. I can't imagine such a fence would ever stop a car from going over the edge.

'The fence looks like toothpicks and dental floss,' CJ said, and my stomach sank some more.

Somehow, in spite of my firm convictions that we were going to die, we made it over the hill with no troubles that day. There's a spot as you're coming down the northern side when suddenly the view opens up and you're looking out across the entire Wairarapa valley, over its hills and quilted squares of green, grassy paddocks. The beauty is astonishing. Even I, sweating at the certainty of my impending doom, could see that.

When we finally reached the foot of the Rimutakas on the other side, I breathed a sigh of relief. In the little town of Featherston, we left the main road and veered off to the south-east toward Martinborough. Suddenly we were surrounded by flat farmlands dotted with cows and sheep. Big rows of trees made massive hedges.

There weren't many people to be seen. The entire South Wairarapa has a grand total population of 9000 people, 468,000 sheep and almost 100,000 cows.

At one point we came to a T in the road, and that's where I first saw the gorgeous Martinborough basin. It's like a giant, hill-encircled bowl with a dot of a village in the middle. This basin, they say, gives Martinborough its special weather — hot in the day and cool at night. The grapes and people love it. We drove down the escarpment and into the giant, green bowl.

IN THE WEEKS BEFORE, CJ had been spending time in the Wairarapa for work. In the process he'd come across a property that he adored, and one day he came home and said, 'Let's move to Martinborough.'

I just looked at him and laughed. He may as well have said, 'Let's paint ourselves blue and live in the trees.'

For some strange reason, however, CJ didn't laugh with me. He just said, 'I mean it. Let's move there.'

I was astonished. 'What? Martinborough is in the middle of nowhere!'

CJ and I are city boys. We thrived in Chicago and Tokyo, loved visiting Shanghai and Bangkok. When we moved to Wellington, our biggèst concern was that — with only 390,000 people — it might feel too small. Now, how could CJ possibly want to move out to the country? What was he thinking?

'Just come and see the property,' he said. 'It's a lifestyle block.'

'A lifestyle block? You want us to go live on a *lifestyle block*?' I shook my head. 'You're insane.'

'There's twenty acres and an olive grove,' CJ said. 'It's paradise.'

I began to wonder if CJ was entirely well.

'CJ, we know nothing about olive trees,' I explained. I spoke slowly and clearly, as though I were talking to some sort of mental patient. 'We know nothing about agriculture *at all*. We've never even had a *garden* before. We can barely even *cook* for ourselves. We've survived for years on takeaway meals and pre-packaged dinners. If we didn't live in a city with take-out restaurants on every corner, we'd starve! Remember when we threw that Thanksgiving party in Tokyo? We had it catered. Seriously, we would have absolutely no idea how to get by in the country. No idea at all.'

CJ just smiled. 'We can learn.'

The entire thing was such an obviously stupid idea that I refused to even go see the place. CJ, however, can be very stubborn. He had been smitten by a piece of land, and he was not going to let it go easily. Over the next week, he brought up his beloved 'lifestyle block' approximately every 10 minutes. Eventually, more to shut him up than anything else, I agreed to go with him to visit Martinborough.

'Okay, okay. I'll look at your precious property,' I said. 'But that's all. And I won't like it. Guaranteed.'

STARING OUT THE CAR WINDOW, I saw the rows and rows of grapevines that surround the tiny village of Martinborough. Their perfect lines flickered as we zipped past. When we entered the village itself, I looked out at the quaint wooden buildings of the veranda-lined main street. Martinborough is laid out like a Union Jack, with angled streets coming off a central town square. The square itself is grassy and filled with trees and a few park benches. Around its edges you can see the beautiful wooden balconies of the Martinborough Hotel, the historic post office that has become a restaurant, and the Winemaker Services building where local winemakers bottle their wines.

An Irishman named John Martin founded Martinborough in 1879, and he named the streets after the places he'd visited in his travels. As we drove around, I liked seeing the odd intersections — the corner of Naples and Panama, and the place where Strasbourg meets Ohio. It was as though the entire world came together in a random order here. John Martin, it seemed to me that day, had the spirit of a nomad. And he'd come here to establish a small town to call his own. He'd come here to settle down.

On a good day Martinborough has only 1300 residents; but with the arrival of the vineyards in the early 1980s, this forgotten little village transformed itself into a weekend destination for Wellingtonians, and with Martinborough's reputation for fine weather it can become very busy indeed. On the main street, CJ and I saw people ambling in and out of cafés, small shops, and the Martinborough Wine Centre. There was a slow, lazy weekend feeling in the air. Mud-spattered rural utes were parked next to the sleek sportscars of visiting weekenders. (For those of us from the Northern Hemisphere who think they speak English, it's always astonishing that a word that looks like 'ute' is actually pronounced 'yoot'. Back then, I still called a ute a pick-up truck, but not any more. Now, to me, it is definitely a 'ute'.) As we drove on and left the village behind, we passed one boutique vineyard after another, and then some olive groves.

Martinborough's claim to fame is pinot noir. Very few places in the world have the combination of soil and climate necessary to cultivate this grape, which many winemakers consider a kind of 'holy grail'. In the late 1970s, a government report from a wine-loving soil scientist indicated that Martinborough had similar growing conditions to Burgundy, the renowned French wine-producing region famous for its pinot noir. A core group of dedicated but inexperienced winemakers started planting vines, and it wasn't long before their wines were winning international acclaim. Although pinot noir is Martinborough's specialty, other grapes do well here too, including chardonnay and sauvignon blanc, and aromatic whites such as riesling and pinot gris.

In time, the wineries began spreading out from Martinborough, and there are now more than 50 vineyards in the region. Not long after the grapes arrived, the olive groves started popping up. The first olive grove was planted in 1991, with only 60 trees. Now the region has 70,000 olive trees, producing 15 per cent of New Zealand's total olive oil harvest.

As we drove past vineyards that day, they were completely lost on me. I was not a wine drinker, having always preferred beer. But just a couple of months earlier I'd been diagnosed with coeliac disease, a disorder of the small intestine. It meant I could no longer eat gluten, which is everywhere — in wheat, barley, rye and oats. So beer was off my list. Not only was I having to completely change my relationship with food, I realised I probably needed to learn a little bit about wine.

CJ and I came to a curve in the road and we entered a tiny river valley. Then, at long last, CJ turned the car up the driveway of the property he had been rattling on about for days on end.

The house had been empty for some time, but as we pulled in it almost seemed as though it had been waiting for us. It had put on its best clematis and trumpet vines just to greet us, and it was absolutely charming. Even I could see that.

It's a long, one-storey, wooden building, painted a soft, creamy yellow. The roof is corrugated iron, like so many New Zealand homes, and is a deep, rich green. When I first arrived in New Zealand, I thought the tin roofs made the houses look like garden sheds, but in my two years in Wellington I had already grown to appreciate their simple, practical and unpretentious appeal. Perhaps I was already going native.

CJ and I got out of the car, and we walked past the goldfish pond and up onto the long deck that spans the front of the house. Then we stood under the wisteria-covered pergola and looked out at the view.

In front of us there were clusters of lavender, leading out to grassy paddocks. In the middle distance a line of massive, dark green macrocarpa trees framed a view of the large bottom paddock and some willow trees. CJ told me that beyond the willows there was a trout stream. Across the river we could see a horizon of green hills sprinkled with tiny white dots — sheep — and topped with two noble pine trees side by side. In the middle of all of this, right at the heart of everything — between the top paddock and the tall macrocarpas — stood an absolutely gorgeous olive grove of nearly 500 trees. CJ was right. This was paradise.

We were early, and the real-estate agent hadn't arrived yet, so we walked around the house and peeked in the windows.

'A lot of bedrooms,' I said.

'Three guest bedrooms,' CJ said. 'Plus ours. They used to run it as a B&B. We could do that too. If we wanted.'

Back at the front of the house, I looked through a pair of French doors into the main living space. I saw terracotta floor tiles and a high wooden ceiling.

CJ nudged me. 'Doesn't that high ceiling remind you of a Japanese farmhouse?'

I nodded. 'Yes. It looks nice. Very homey.'

We looked around a bit and took everything in: the fruit trees, the raised vegetable beds overtaken with weeds, the neglected greenhouse, the old and abandoned chicken coop. Off to one side was a big hay shed. Then CJ pulled at my hand. 'You have to come see the olive grove up close.'

We stepped off the front deck, walked down alongside a huge hedge of fragrant rosemary, opened a small gate, and walked over a small wooden footbridge into the main paddock. Then we headed towards the grove.

The air was warm. The sky was perfectly blue. Along both sides of the wide paddocks were rows of poplar trees, which marked the boundary of the property and provided a shelterbelt. I realised the property was one great rectangle, with the house at the top and the river at the bottom, the olive grove in between. We continued down a slight slope and across another small footbridge until we arrived at the olive grove gate, where we paused.

Underneath the olive trees, sheep were grazing. It looked almost biblical. A light breeze was moving the branches, turning up the grey-green undersides of the leaves to the sun so that the entire grove seemed to ripple with silver.

I don't know the historic or religious reasons that the olive branch is associated with peace. I only know that standing there at the gate, looking at that olive grove up close on that very first day, I felt peace. And I was somehow overwhelmed with a deep fondness for those trees, a longing to care for them, be a part of them.

Honestly, it really did feel a bit like falling in love. I know that sounds absurd, but that's how I felt. I don't know if love at first sight is possible with people (my feelings for CJ have always been more like a bud sprouting than a bomb exploding), but I know now that love at first sight is perfectly possible with trees.

I opened the gate and stepped inside.

Chapter 2

Conquering the road that scared me

It may seem unlikely that a bunch of silly trees made me change my mind about CJ's obviously stupid idea, but it did. Imagine this: the one you love stands you in front of overwhelming beauty and says, 'Let's take care of this. Let's make this ours. Let's live in paradise.'

CJ had fallen in love with that piece of land and I had fallen in love with those beautiful trees and there was no way at that point that either of us could say no.

YET WE WERE NOT ENTIRELY IMPRACTICAL. There remained two hurdles to pass before we could realistically consider moving out to the middle of nowhere. The first was the train commute.

We knew we wouldn't be able to afford to quit our day jobs, especially not with the mortgage for the property. We would have to commute back into the city for work. We knew some people did this. So we found accommodation in Martinborough midweek in order to actually experience the commute, just to see how bad it was.

For two nights we stayed in a refurbished old villa. When I first arrived in New Zealand I expected a 'villa' to look something like an Italian mansion with a courtyard, but I had quickly grown to love the quaint, Kiwi wood-clad bungalows. This villa had a gorgeous garden and was adjacent to some vineyards.

Right away we learned that nights in the country are different. They are pitch black and intensely quiet, as though the darkness itself were a physical substance muffling sound, like fog. That first night we slept more soundly than we had in years.

So we were doubly surprised to be woken in the early hours of the morning by a low humming sound. It came out of the darkness from every direction. Then came such a loud, vibrating whir that it seemed a UFO was hovering directly over the house. In my half-sleep, I was certain we'd been targeted for alien abduction.

Only later did we learn that the initial low hum was from the giant fans standing in the vineyards, blowing to keep the frost off the vines. Although it was the beginning of spring, the night had been incredibly cold. The loud vibration that followed was a helicopter, flying low over the vines in order to fight the frost with wind. Spring frosts can cause serious damage to the tender shoots of the vines, and can spell disaster for the winemakers of Martinborough. After learning what those noises were, CJ and I were grateful that the property we were considering buying wasn't adjacent to any vineyards.

The commute itself was not a problem. It's a 20-minute drive to Featherston and then an hour-long train ride from there. The train tracks go through a tunnel under the Rimutaka Ranges rather than over them. You can work or read or sleep, or listen to podcasts. Many Kiwis are horrified to think of anybody travelling for over an hour to work. But CJ and I had grown used to long commutes in Chicago and Tokyo. The key difference was that in those cities you'd travel for an hour to get home from work and still be in the middle of urban sprawl. Here that same commute would take us from the central city to the heart of paradise. Not a bad deal, we thought.

So now only one hurdle remained. One thing stood between me and living in paradise with all those beautiful olive trees: the horrible Rimutaka Hill Road itself.

I could avoid the daily drive to work by taking the train, but there would undoubtedly be times I'd need to drive into Wellington. My friends were there. The theatres and art museums were there. The city was there. I didn't want to feel trapped out in the back of beyond. I'd lose my mind. At any point, I might need a quick escape from all that fresh air.

It was obvious. If we were going to live in Martinborough, I had to conquer that awful road. I had to face the blind turns, the high winds, and the sheer drop-offs that threatened to swallow me whole. I had to drive that road myself.

THE NEXT WEEKEND, THERE I WAS, sitting behind the wheel of our little Nissan Pulsar, driving toward the Rimutakas from the Wellington side. CJ sat in the passenger seat as official navigator and voice of reason.

A misty rain was falling as I drove into the foothills. When we came to the sign that announces whether or not the road is closed that day, it was with great disappointment that I saw the road was perfectly open.

The first incline is steep, and that's where our little Nissan always begins to struggle. I floored it, but the car was barely putting along. There's a passing lane there, and the more powerful cars overtook us. Then suddenly the side of the road disappeared to my left, and the drop-offs and hairpin turns began.

Here is my frank confession. When it comes to a mountain road, I'm a hopeless nana behind the wheel. You wouldn't know it to talk to me. I seem confident. I'm a reasonably smart and together person. But give me altitude and a steering wheel, and all my childhood fears of high places come rushing back into my throat. I learned to drive on the long, straight, perfectly flat roads of Michigan, not these turny, curvy death traps.

It didn't take long before there was a big red ute directly behind me, riding my tail.

'You're fine,' CJ said. 'Just go at your own pace.' Of the two of us, I'm usually the more calm. But when it matters most CJ can muster up the deepest peace. He's good that way.

In my humble opinion, the locals follow too close on the Rimutaka Hill Road. Of course they grew up with it, know it well. They always want to go fast. But tailgating doesn't make a nana go faster. It just makes that nana all the more nervous. That's when accidents happen.

Soon that big red ute was joined by a sedan directly behind it, and then another car showed up behind that. I felt like the leader of Dim-witted Nana's Slow Parade. I wanted to go faster, but I was afraid. I was approaching the worst part of the road — a part so bad that it has a special name of its own.

Up ahead was 'Muldoon's Corner'.

This lovely little hairpin of horror was named after former New Zealand prime minister Robert Muldoon because it is 'tight and to the right'. Muldoon was also finance minister, and he was known for his extremely tight budgets.

In place of a shoulder at Muldoon's Corner, there was a steep drop-off into nothingness. What's more, the road there was so narrow that large trucks had to cross the centre line in order to make the sharp turn. If two trucks approached in opposite directions, one actually had to back up for the other to pass. Those reversing trucks, combined with the sheer drop-off, the fence made of toothpicks and dental floss, the extreme blind turn — oh, and did I mention the high winds? — made Muldoon's Corner especially dangerous for everyone.

Local politicians had advocated for improvements to Muldoon's Corner for years. Finally, in 2009, the government announced they were moving forward on a $20 million upgrade on the Rimutaka Hill Road, taking the bend out of that corner. But that was three years away, and it was no help to me back then. On that day I was approaching Muldoon's Corner in all its unstraightened and terrifying glory. I prayed for no oncoming trucks.

In fact, as far as I was concerned, coming across trucks at *any* point on the Rimutaka Hill Road was terrible. One time a trailer truck transporting cereal tipped over up there, spilling cornflakes everywhere and closing the road for six hours. The local paper called it a 'cereal cliffhanger'.

Even before I'd made it all the way to Muldoon's Corner, I laid eyes on my worst fear. Suddenly there it was, barrelling towards me: a huge truck.

But this truck wasn't carrying cereal. It was some kind of tanker, and it clearly contained something flammable. What more could the gods throw at me? Earthquakes? Thunderstorms? A plague of locusts to cover my windscreen?

'You're okay,' CJ said, sitting in the passenger seat beside me. He must have felt me cringe.

I didn't care what he said. The truck was obviously far too wide to stay on its side of the road. Any idiot could see we were about to die in a great, all-consuming fireball. Just a few feet away on my left was yet another treacherous drop-off into the bush. I was most definitely NOT okay.

I watched the centre line. My heart beat violently. My mouth went dry.

Turning around at that point was not an option. There was no place to pull over. Getting CJ to take the wheel would have been impossible.

Looking back now, I suppose I could have allowed my fear to define me. I could have — even before getting on that stupid road — allowed my fear to make my decision. I could have said, 'I'm never living in paradise because I cannot drive the road to get there, and I will not try.'

But somehow I never even considered that. I'd fallen in love with those olive trees, with that beautiful property, and there was absolutely no way I was going to let a little life-threatening road stop me.

On I went — carefully, slowly, watching the truck ahead of me, aware of the abyss beside me, the cars close behind me. But I continued to drive.

And you know what? The truck passed me by. It did not explode into a fireball beside me. It did not cause me to careen down the bank and into the tangled bush.

In fact, as it went by I realised the truck wasn't carrying flammable liquid at all. It was a milk truck. Milk! I laughed at myself. If it had collided with a cereal truck, we would have had breakfast enough to feed all of Wellington.

Then, out of nowhere, a passing lane opened up, and all the cars that had been accumulating behind me up to that point finally zoomed past. So when it came time to actually go around Muldoon's Corner, I was no longer so nervous about holding people up. That does not mean I was not terrified.

WHEN I FINALLY MADE IT down off that mountain and was cradled in the Wairarapa valley, I felt huge relief. A light rain was still falling. I thought the worst part of the drive was over, but I was wrong. Turning off the main road at Featherston, we headed towards Martinborough.

About five minutes beyond Featherston, we came to the small S-shaped bridge that spans the Tauherenikau River. Technically the bridge itself is straight and the road curves just before and after it. To this day I don't know exactly what happened as I crossed that bridge, I only know that it all went wrong.

When I saw the sign for the reduced speed limit around those curves, I slowed down. And when I came out of the last curve, I lost control of the car.

I hadn't driven on ice since living in Michigan over a decade before, and although there was no ice on the road that spring day, immediately I recognised the feeling. There was no longer any relationship between the direction I turned the wheel and the direction of the car.

I suppose it could have been 'black ice' on the bridge — a thin sheet of frost without the white colour to betray its presence. Or perhaps the light misty rain had brought all traces of oil and petrol to the surface of the road, making it slick. One friend told me that boy racers sometimes pour diesel on the road to make their tyres spin and smoke. But I can't imagine they'd do that on a narrow bridge. Who knows? Maybe.

It doesn't really matter. What matters is that when I hit the brakes it was like pushing on a sponge, and when I turned the wheel the car did not respond.

I began pumping the brakes, as I'd learned to do on Michigan ice. I quickly checked the rear-view mirror to make sure nobody was coming up behind me. A green station wagon was coming around the corner off the bridge, some distance back, and it was doing fishtails. The bridge was definitely slick.

It was then that our little Nissan Pulsar started spinning. We were suddenly travelling sideways down the road, straddling both lanes. If somebody had been in the oncoming lane at that moment, it would have been awful.

I managed to turn the nose of the car back towards the road. A blue van slowed down in front of us. It was in the oncoming lane but at a safe distance. The driver pulled to the side of the road, watching us, out of our way.

All of a sudden the nose of the Nissan spun in the other direction, and we then began sliding off the road. I continued pumping the brakes furiously as we headed towards a fence. On the other side, cattle were grazing in a green paddock.

In front of us, a large, thick fence post stuck up out of the ground like a tree trunk. We were headed directly towards it.

I watched, helpless, unable to steer, still pumping the brakes, as we went into a small ditch, up the other side and then — lightly, ever so lightly — kissed that fence post with the nose of the car.

The station wagon behind me had come to a stop. The road was empty. The driver of the blue van was still watching.

I asked CJ if he was okay.

'I'm fine,' he said. You?'

'Fine.'

Stunned, I backed up, saw there was no damage to the fence at all, and began to drive on. As we passed the blue van, I gave a thumbs-up. The guy in the driver's seat was staring at the nose of our car.

I pulled to the side of the road to look. There, in middle of the front grill, was a large V-shaped dent. It was bad enough to look terrible, but so not bad as to have damaged the engine. We were lucky. We were both okay. The car, although a bit squished, drove fine.

'Do you want me to drive the rest of the way?' CJ asked.

'Hell no,' I said.

I was not going to quit then. I'd made it over the Rimutaka Hill Road, dealt with tailgaters, drop-offs, oncoming trucks of rare flammable milk, and finally a booby-trapped bridge. I was going to drive all the way to those damn olive trees and that beautiful property if it was the last thing I did.

I got back in the car and drove. The roads were easy from there, and the way was calm. When we finally arrived at the property, which I was by then determined we were going to buy, I practically jumped out of the car and kissed the ground.

I felt like I was home.

Chapter 3

Meeting the neighbours

A group of six of our city friends helped us move out to the country. It was November, two months after I'd first fallen in love with that olive grove. The day was absolutely gorgeous, and it felt like a party.

Nobody wanted to drive a rented truck over the treacherous Rimutaka Hill Road, so CJ and I hired movers to tackle our big things like the bed, sofa, washer and dryer. The rest of our stuff we piled into everyone's cars and drove over the hill together, convoy style. I let CJ drive.

OUR CITY FRIENDS were all people we'd met since arriving in New Zealand two years before. They were an odd mix, perhaps, but went together well — Kiwis and Brits, straight and gay, Quakers and not religious at all. To them we were the gay Americans from Tokyo, city boys through and through. What were we doing, they wondered, moving out to eight hectares in the country?

When we pulled up the driveway, it was their first time seeing our new place. We stepped out of our cars and everyone took in the property — the long, low house overlooking the olive grove, the two-bay hay shed, the raised vegetable beds overtaken with weeds, the old and abandoned chicken coop.

The hills on the other side of the Huangarua River were green from the spring rains. The two noble pine trees stood together on top of the crest in the distance, surrounded by small white dots of sheep. A lone hawk circled over the olive grove. Immediately our friends understood why we were moving here.

CJ and I, however, both noticed that something amazing had happened since we'd last seen the place. The grass had grown. All eight hectares of it. In the five large paddocks, in the olive grove, and all around the house. When we originally viewed the property, the sheep grazing on it had made it look like a golf course. Not only were the animals gone now, but there had also been a good deal of rain. The place looked like it had been invaded by Radioactive Grass from Mars. It was chest high. If you fell down in it, you'd be lost forever. And we didn't even own a lawnmower.

After unloading the cars and bringing everything inside, everyone strolled down to the river together. We sat on the river bank and talked. The willows swayed and the water sparkled. Eventually, slowly, we wandered through the long grass back up to the house.

There was still a lot to do — boxes to unpack, furniture to move — but it didn't matter. This property has a way of making you relax. It has a mind of its own and it soothes you, calms you, even as you do the chores necessary to take care of it.

We talked about dinner. We were going to cook our first meal in the house together, the eight of us. Everyone was staying the night.

But then there was a knock on the door.

One of the key concerns CJ and I had about moving to the country was how the rural neighbours would respond to a gay couple living down the road. We'd even asked the real-estate agent about it when we were considering buying the property.

'Oh, people here are pretty good,' the agent told us. 'I'm an ex-dairy farmer, and even I've come a long way.' He laughed and nodded.

CJ and I answered the door together on that first day. There stood a man about five and a half foot tall, with a white beard and wire-framed glasses. He looked like Santa Claus in a tattered baseball cap. His eyes were bright and full of kindness. His clothes were rugged and thick. There was a patch of mud on his leg. It looked as though he'd just come in from the fields.

He introduced himself as our neighbour John, and said that he was having a 'barbie'.

I knew he wasn't talking about playing with dolls. I had already learned that 'barbie' in Kiwiland means barbecue. I love how everything here is shortened: sandwiches are 'sammies', presents become 'prezzies', relatives are 'rellies', and chickens are 'chooks'. Words that are plain and dull become things you feel affection for.

John said, 'I heard you were moving in today. I thought you might like to join us.'

How did a total stranger know when we were moving in?

This was my first lesson in how quickly news travels in a village. We later learned that the real-estate agent had told John our moving date. People talk. Everyone in the neighbourhood already knew about the gay Americans.

CJ and I thanked John for the invitation, but we explained we couldn't join him since we had six house guests with us.

'No worries,' John said, smiling broadly. 'Your friends are welcome too. I do my own home kills. I'll just pull more meat out of the freezer.'

Home kills? It sounded creepy. Suddenly I pictured this man wrestling a cow to the ground, slitting its throat, and chopping it up into pieces with a bloody axe.

'No, that's okay,' I said, not wanting to impose.

'Of course you'll come,' John said. 'All the neighbours will be there.'

I suggested that we just join them for a drink before dinner.

'That's great. Come by around six.' John told us where his house was down the road. Then off he went.

That evening we all walked down the road towards John's house, bottles of wine in hand. We'd already made plans for what we'd make for dinner when we got back home. The city friends were going to help with the cooking; there was no way CJ and I could have prepared dinner for eight without help.

As we walked along the gravel shoulder, we passed paddocks where some cattle and sheep grazed. I would learn later that those were John's animals. I was looking at another night's potential dinner.

I've never been so closely connected to my food source as I have been since living out here. I haven't got used to meeting my dinner when it's still breathing, seeing next month's juicy meat grazing at the roadside as I wander by, and seeing it stare back at me. It's a little disturbing.

John greeted us at the door. 'Oh, good! You showed up for dinner.'

'Just for drinks,' I reminded him.

He shook his head in a friendly way. 'I already pulled the meat out of the freezer. I have to cook it now. Come in!'

It looked like we were staying for dinner.

John put us at ease right away. He made sure that we all had a glass of wine in our hands and that we knew where the 'nibbles' were. Hors d'oeuvres are almost never called hors d'oeuvres here.

As John had promised, all the neighbours were there. We met Bronwyn, John's wife. We also met Bronwyn, Jim's wife. They do not share a wife. There are two Bronwyns.

John and Bronwyn and Jim and Bronwyn are our nearest neighbours. While John and Bronwyn live on the opposite side of the road and down a ways, Jim and Bronwyn live in the red house whose roof we can see beyond our hay shed.

Later on, CJ and I would begin differentiating between the two Bronwyns by referring to John's wife as 'Aussie Bronwyn', since she's originally from a farm a couple hours outside Sydney, and Jim's wife as 'Kiwi Bronwyn'. The distinction still comes in handy when, for example, one of us says 'Bronwyn called,' or 'Bronwyn stopped by.'

'Aussie or Kiwi?' the other will ask. It does the trick.

IN TALKING TO OUR NEIGHBOURS that night, we learned just how closely everyone was connected to the land. John and Bronwyn have cattle, pigs, chickens, an enormous vegetable garden, an olive grove, an orchard with nut and fruit trees, and, in their backyard, the classic Kiwi lemon tree.

Our friend Debbie says, 'Every Kiwi house should have a cabbage tree in the front and a lemon tree out the back.'

Jim and Bronwyn run cattle and have a hazelnut orchard of around 1000 trees. Other neighbours have similar set-ups. Murray, who lives further down the road with his wife, Suzanne, drives a tractor for a living. He cuts hay and harvests wheat. Olwen and David, a retired couple who live in Martinborough village, have an extensive garden with an orchard full of fruit trees and several large peacocks wandering around their yard.

The country neighbours were incredibly nice to the city friends. You would have thought all eight of us had moved in. Everyone talked and laughed, and John stood over the barbecue, cooking the beef and lamb that until recently had grazed in his paddocks just beyond the deck.

At one point Aussie Bronwyn came by with a tray of crackers topped with cream cheese, smoked salmon and dill. I asked her if they were rice crackers. I'd spent a year being incredibly sick before finding out I had coeliac disease, so I took my gluten-free diet seriously.

'Yes, they are,' Aussie Bronwyn smiled. There was something vaguely bird-like about her small, angular features and her gently spiky, tousled brown hair. She wore a skirt with large red flowers on it and a red top with a large cowl neck. She looked like a gypsy in fiery, colourful clothes.

'That's great,' I said, reaching for a cracker. 'I'm gluten-free.' I'd already learned how much of a hassle it could be to break this news to your dinner host — especially in a situation like this, when the meal was somewhat impromptu. I expected Aussie Bronwyn to look grave and concerned that she had a difficult guest.

Instead she smiled and said, 'Oh, thank goodness. It's always tiring being the only one. I'll show you what you can eat when we sit down to dinner.'

I breathed a sigh of relief. I was in good hands. In time I would learn that Aussie Bronwyn suffers from fibromyalgia. Avoiding gluten lessens her chronic joint stiffness and fatigue.

LATER IN THE EVENING I was talking to Suzanne from down the road, and she said, 'I understand you don't have a tractor.'

How did she know we didn't have a tractor?

'You'll need one,' she continued. She was immaculately dressed from head to toe, and she had the faultless posture of a ballerina. Her red, shoulder-length hair was perfectly in place. She didn't look like a woman from the country at all, not even when she stood next to her much more simply dressed and somewhat scruffy farmer husband, Murray. After that night, CJ and I began affectionately referring to Suzanne as the 'Glamour Farm Wife'.

'You need a tractor to keep the grass down in your paddocks,' Suzanne told me. 'Unless you're going to run cattle. They'll keep the grass down for you. But you can't run cattle in the olive grove. They'll destroy the trees. Animals eat to their height, and the cattle are just too tall. Some people graze sheep in their groves, but others say even sheep can damage the trees.'

Clearly, in addition to being glamorous Suzanne was also deeply practical.

But run cattle? Graze sheep? It was all CJ and I could do to learn how to care for those 500 olive trees — about which we knew absolutely nothing at that moment.

'Priscilla had a trailer mower,' Suzanne said. Priscilla was the woman we'd bought the house from. 'She mowed the olive grove herself.'

The fact was that just after we'd finished the paperwork to purchase our property, CJ and I had received an email from the real-estate agent asking if we'd like to buy Priscilla's tractor. In our city-boy minds, a used tractor would break down and require mechanical know-how that we didn't have. We wanted a new tractor, but we were already broke from the mortgage. We planned to wait a few years before investing in equipment. Besides, we weren't planning to sow any crops, or till the ground. Isn't that all you need a tractor for?

So we'd sent an email back to the agent confidently telling him that we did not yet need a tractor.

That single act, more than any other thing we've done in our stumbling transition from city boys to olive growers, demonstrates how utterly clueless CJ and I were about what we were getting ourselves into. It was only that evening, talking to the immaculately dressed Suzanne, that I finally understood we needed a tractor to mow the olive grove.

I thought of all the long grass in our paddocks, and in the olive grove. 'So, what happens if we don't keep the grass down?' I asked Suzanne. It was just a field, I figured. Let the grass grow.

She looked horrified. 'Well, fire hazard for one. When the grass goes dry in the summer, it'll be a risk to us all. And you'll lose your paddocks to the bush. They won't be any use.'

Oh. Got it. Must. Keep. Grass. Down.

I realised that if our neighbours were going to have a problem with us, it wasn't because we were gay. It was because we didn't have a tractor.

So it was that the importance of keeping the grass down became the first lesson of many that the rural Kiwi neighbours would teach the gay American city boys.

God bless those neighbours. Without them we would have never survived out here as long as we have. We owe them so much.

We had an incredible dinner — deliciously tender lamb chops, fresh garden vegetables, and good stories told around the outdoor table as the sky turned lavender and the sun began to set. There was a meat I didn't recognise, rectangular strips that were tender and fatty on one side and crunchy on the other.

'What's this?' I asked John.

'You like that? It's grilled pork belly from our pigs.'

CJ interrupted. 'Oh my God, it's delicious!' He couldn't get enough of it.

'Pork belly?' I said.

'Sure,' John answered. 'It's what they make bacon from.'

CJ mumbled through a piece of pork belly in his mouth. 'No wonder I love it.'

John was more than happy to share how he'd prepared it.

When the last of the light was gone, when all the grilled pork belly and lamb chops were devoured, and when the last story wound down to a final close, CJ and I thanked our neighbours and walked home in the dark with our city friends. Aussie Bronwyn had lent us 'torches' — a word which always makes my American brain think of flaming sticks rather than battery-operated lights. Halfway home we stepped off the road and clicked the torches off.

Up above us there were thousands and thousands of stars. You don't see stars like that in the suburbs of Detroit, or in Chicago, or in Tokyo. My old friend the moon was out, too. It was unbelievably bright, and it wasn't even full.

I have always loved the moon. When I was growing up in suburban Michigan, I used to sneak out of my bedroom window at night and sit on the roof, just to gaze at it.

Now I looked up at the moon that marked our first night in our new house. It was just past full, what they call a 'waning gibbous' moon. I looked around me at my friends in the dark, and at John and Bronwyn's house across the paddocks behind us, their porch light still on. With every cell of my being I felt that I was in a good place, and I knew I was going to like it here.

John's Pork Belly Crackling on the Barbie

If you love bacon as much as CJ does, you'll love this pork belly.

Ingredients

slab of pork belly
extra virgin olive oil
rock salt

Preparation

Heat the barbie until it's good and hot (about 170 °C). This recipe works best on a smooth, cast-iron hotplate with the barbie lid closed.

Lay out the pork belly slab, skin side up. Score the skin in long strips. Drizzle both sides with olive oil and sprinkle with rock salt.

Place the slab skin side down on the hotplate and close the lid.

Check from time to time. When the skin starts to bubble, turn the slab over on the hotplate.

When the slab is cooked through, lay it skin-side down on the open grill, keeping the lid open, to increase the crackling of the skin.

Remove from the barbie and allow the meat to sit for a couple of minutes. Following the scored lines, cut the meat into strips and serve.

Chapter 4

Attack of the energy-draining suckers

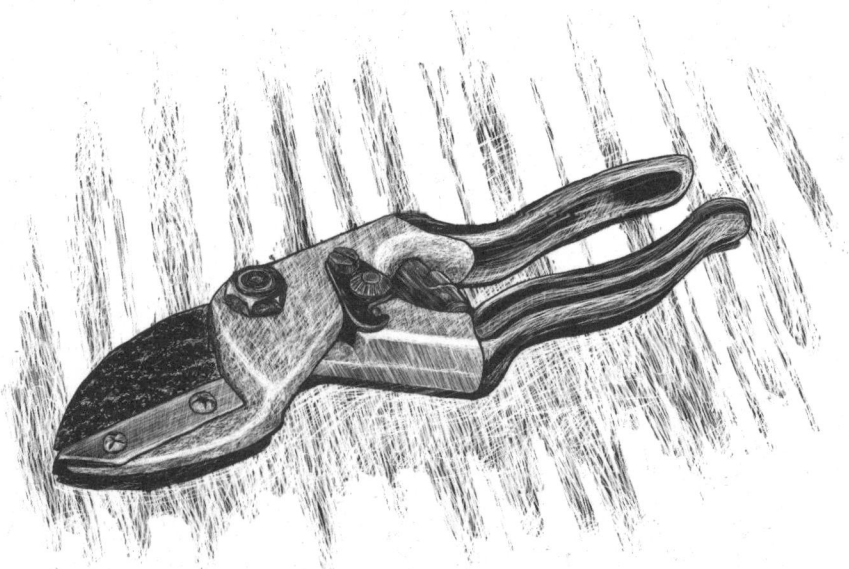

In those first few weeks our grass continued to grow — in the paddocks, in the olive grove, and in the yard all around the house. Thankfully, people far and wide took pity on us. A good friend from Wellington gave us an old hand-me-down lawnmower so we could take care of the yard. And our neighbour John, armed with the knowledge of his own olive grove, came by to perform what can only be described as an olive grower's emergency intervention.

'YOU'VE GOT TO MOW that olive grove,' he said, looking out from our front deck. He sighed and rubbed his thick white beard. 'You did know you'd have to mow it before you bought this place, right?'

CJ said, 'Oh yeah. Sure. Everyone knows you have to mow an olive grove.'

'Mmm. Of course,' I said, nodding diligently.

John shook his head. 'My mower's too small for that high grass. But you can hire a contractor to come in and mow it. After that you're welcome to borrow my tractor and mower to keep on top of it. The rest of the paddocks you can leave for now. It's the olive grove that matters most.'

I appreciated the advice. I would learn in time that John and Aussie Bronwyn were helping not only CJ and me but countless other people in and around the area. They are pillars of this little community of ours, and some of the most generous, considerate people I have ever met. John freely lends out his equipment and tools, is always there to answer questions, and volunteers his time through the Martinborough Lions Club. Aussie Bronwyn volunteers at the local library and bakes for Lioness Club fundraisers. Having them as neighbours is truly like having a pair of guardian angels just down the road, and I'm deeply grateful.

John helped us to arrange getting a contractor in. A couple of weeks later a gruff man showed up with an enormous tractor. The man negotiated the turns and rows of the olive grove with ease, and in a few hours he was finished mowing — up and down the rows one way and then back and forth the other. Finally the grass was even and low again, albeit with 500 rather significant exceptions. At the base of each tree, where the mower couldn't reach, there was a square of tall, unruly grass.

John stopped by to see how the contractor's work had gone, and CJ and I walked down to the grove with him. The trees were thick and green all around us.

'Look how great the grove looks,' CJ said.

John scowled and shook his head. 'Well, you're not done yet.'

I said, 'We can just leave that long grass under the trees, can't we?'

The truth was that CJ and I had always seen the olive grove simply as a kind of hobby. It would give us oil for ourselves and our friends. We could send some to family back in the States. If the grove did well, perhaps we could sell the extra olives to one of the commercial groves in the area. But more than anything, the olive grove was just going to be fun. That's what we thought, anyway.

John looked around at that poor, neglected grove and laughed. Most of the trees were 10 years old then, but they hadn't been properly pruned or sprayed in over three years. While CJ and I thought they looked fine, John assured us that they were in need of some serious attention.

'Your work hasn't even *begun*,' John said. 'For starters you have to cut down every bit of that long grass. While you're at it, you also have to get rid of each and every sucker in this place.'

'Suckers?' CJ said.

I looked around. The only suckers I could see were CJ and me, who had been foolish enough to buy an olive grove without knowing a single thing about olive trees.

'Um, which suckers do you mean?' I asked, afraid John might point accusingly at us.

'These ones,' he said, and he reached down and grabbed a lush, supple olive branch that was growing out of the trunk of a nearby tree.

I looked closely. It looked like just any new branch. 'What's wrong with that?' I asked.

'Suckers don't bear fruit,' John said.

'Fruit?' I said.

John looked at me. 'Yes, olives are a fruit.' Then he looked back at the tree. 'But the suckers don't bear fruit. They just drain the tree. It should be putting its energy up into the taller branches, where the fruit is, not this rubbish down at the trunk. Olive trees just want to revert into bushes. So you have to cut the suckers out.'

Everywhere I looked there were more and more olive trees, each with a patch of long grass underneath. Looking closely, I could now see that each tree had at least 15 to 20 massive suckers coming up out of its trunk. No doubt those dastardly parasites were draining the life out of our olive trees even as we spoke.

I felt a kind of vertigo overtake me. I looked at CJ and he looked back at me. It was clear he was thinking the same thing.

This was a huge mistake. We should never have moved out here to the country. We should have just slapped an olive tree seedling in a pot back in our city apartment and called it a day. Then we could have done something useful like go out and see a movie, instead of being stuck here with an overwhelming amount of work to do.

'You'll need a line trimmer and a pair of secateurs,' John said.

CJ and I had no absolutely no idea what John was talking about. Line trimmer? Secateurs? When we tried to get clarity as to what these mysterious objects might be, our fragile Urban American to Rural Kiwi verbal communication quickly disintegrated into absolute gibberish. In the end John had to resort to sound effects and gestures.

It was his loud 'Bzzzz!' and 'Snip-snip!' that did the trick.

'Oh!' CJ yelled, looking at me. 'He means a weed whacker and a pair of pruners!'

I turned to John and said, 'Why didn't you just say so?'

ONE WEEK LATER CJ and I stood in front of the olive grove, armed and ready. I had our new, heavy-duty, petrol-powered line trimmer clasped into the chest strap I was wearing, with goggles to protect my eyes from flying debris, ear protectors to save my hearing from the noise of the trimmer, and a brand-new pair of gumboots. ('Gumboot' was another new word for me. Back in suburban Detroit, I would have probably called these things 'rubber rain boots'.) CJ had on a wide-brimmed hat to protect himself from the intense sun, and new gumboots that rather embarrassingly matched mine. In front of him he held out a brand-new pair of secateurs which flashed in the sun. We were like two new recruits in front of our first real battlefield.

'We're gonna git you suckers!' CJ yelled. Then we marched directly toward that army of olive trees.

I whipped through the grass under each tree with military dedication and focus. My mad obsession to cut down every single blade of grass was tempered only by my abject terror at the thought of getting too close to the tree and ring-barking the trunk, which John had sagely warned me about. If you cut the bark all the way around the base of a tree, it will die. Given how little CJ and I knew about what we were doing, it wasn't outside of the realm of possibility that we could end up killing every single one of our 500 trees. So I had to be careful.

To our surprise, when I was done moving around the first tree with the line trimmer, the grass just remained floating in mid-air. It was so long it was actually tangled in the branches above. CJ got down on his hands and knees and pulled fistfuls of grass out of the tree by hand. Then he began carefully snipping away all of those heinous, energy-draining suckers.

After an hour, we were both exhausted, dripping with sweat and covered with scratches and bits of dirt and grass. I became convinced the suckers were draining our energy as well as that of the trees.

'I'm tired,' CJ said.

'So am I.'

Then we looked back at our work, and realised with absolute horror that in the past 60 minutes of back-breaking toil we had finished only three trees. We still had 497 to go. At that rate we would be there for another 165 hours.

I wanted to cry. CJ, however, found the courage to be strong. I was already mumbling incoherently about surrender, but he just took the line trimmer from me, along with the goggles and hearing protectors, powered up the engine, and got back to work. I followed behind with the secateurs.

And so began the Grass and Sucker Project. Weekend after weekend we went through that olive grove row by row by row. We charted our progress on a little hand-drawn map, and every evening we counted trees.

We didn't do all the work alone. We bribed city friends with weekend invitations and offers of nice meals that they'd help us cook. In return, we basically subjected them to prison labour. Nobody was spared. Even friends who travelled all the way from the States just to spend quality time with us were heartlessly put to work.

It would take the entire summer to finish. In the end there was not a blade of long grass or a sucker to be found. Since it didn't rain all summer, the grass didn't really grow at all, which relieved us more than you can imagine.

When CJ and I were feeling very proud and relieved to finally be sucker-free, John came by again to inspect our work.

'Look how great the grove looks,' CJ said.

John scowled and shook his head. 'Well, you're not done yet.'

'Huh?' CJ said. 'But we did everything you said.'

John looked around. 'Good. Now you can start pruning.'

'Isn't that what we've been doing?' I asked.

John is a man who is always quick to laugh, and he laughed then. 'Not at all,' he said. 'You've just been cutting out the suckers! Now you have to get up into the tree and start making cuts to major branches. This is when the real work starts!'

It was all I could do to stop myself from running to the edge of the olive grove and throwing myself down the well.

But CJ took a deep breath and calmly turned to John. 'What do we need to prune the trees?'

'All you really need is a good pruning saw,' John said.

CJ looked at me and smiled. 'Well, Jared. Look at the bright side. At least we know what that is.'

Chapter 5

The day the water stopped

When CJ and I were about midway through the long Grass and Sucker Project, CJ's city friend Fiona came to visit. We had mostly unpacked. We didn't have enough furniture to fill all the rooms yet, but we did have one guest bed and we were for the most part comfortably settled in.

FIONA IS LIKE A GRACEFUL, EXOTIC BIRD you feel compelled to pamper and adore, and CJ had promised her a relaxing country weekend far away from her stressful professional life in Wellington. I was happy about her arrival, because by then I myself needed a relaxing country weekend. I'd been wondering where I could go to find one.

So you can imagine how troubling it was when, just hours after Fiona's arrival on Friday evening, our water suddenly stopped running.

I was in the kitchen preparing to cook pasta for dinner — a meal I thought I just might be able to prepare on my own. Surprisingly, we had been managing to get by without a steady stream of takeaway restaurants within walking distance. We were actually learning how to cook. Now I took out two large pots, one for gluten-free pasta for me, and one for wheat pasta for CJ and Fiona. But when I turned on the kitchen tap to fill the pots, nothing came out. I checked the sink in the guest bathroom and found the same thing there.

Out on the deck I made the announcement.

'There's no water.'

CJ and Fiona looked at me blankly.

'What do you mean?' CJ said.

'When I turn on the tap, there's no water.'

CJ looked horrified. We'd just had a new pump installed a few days before.

Fiona, always dignified, managed to hold her composure. She was wearing dramatic, flowing sleeves, a spiralling silver necklace, and beautiful baubles on her wrists and fingers. Her short, jet-black hair is graced with a white shock in front, and she has the knack of wearing make-up in such a way that you never notice it at all. You just notice how gorgeous she is.

She does not, in short, look like a woman who enjoys 'roughing it'.

We have no emergency water tank. When our well is out, that means no drinking water, no cooking water, no flushing toilets, and no showers in the morning. Zip. Zilch. Zero.

Although I was sure Fiona could endure dehydration and starvation with charm and style, I was less certain about her ability to withstand an entire weekend without basic sanitation and bathing facilities. I could already imagine her speeding back over the Rimutaka Hill Road to the safety of the municipal water systems of Wellington, raving about the filth and squalor of the country.

CJ looked at me with desperation in his eyes. 'Well, can we fix it?'

If you knew us, you'd understand that this is pretty much the equivalent of expecting a pair of small, dim-witted puppies to dismantle a nuclear bomb. CJ and I are hopeless at fixing household things, much less wells. We're city boys, after all.

I looked over at CJ and then at Fiona. She hadn't yet expressed the slightest concern over the situation, but there was a nervous twitch developing under her right eye.

By then, of course, it was dark. Although it was a bit late on a Friday night, I quickly resigned myself to the fact that CJ and I are useless, and I did what any city boy stranded in the country without water would do. I called the neighbours.

Here is my advice. If you buy a house in the country, make sure you buy one that is next door to a Welsh mechanical engineer with a DIY fetish and the generous soul of a mad, tool-loving saint. That's our neighbour Jim, husband to Kiwi Bronwyn. He has helped CJ and me more times than I can count. Without him, we would have been found dead in a corner long ago.

'I'll meet you at your well at eight tomorrow morning,' he said. 'Bring a spanner.' I'd been in New Zealand long enough to know that what he really meant to say was 'Bring a wrench.'

We shut the power off to the well and went out for dinner.

THE NEXT MORNING CJ was overwhelmed with the thought of having to work on the well, so he did the only sensible thing. He sped off with Fiona in her Peugeot to have breakfast in the village. I met Jim down by the well on my own.

Jim was wearing the overalls he always works in — with spots of dirt and grease all over, and the sleeves cut off because it gets hot in Martinborough in the summer. I was in clean shorts and a T-shirt, looking more prepared to visit Disneyland than to do manual labour.

'Where's your spanner?' he asked. His salt-and-pepper hair is buzzed short and thin on the top. He has a small, stocky build and a wicked sense of humour.

I proudly pulled out my wrench. It came as part of a burgundy toolbox set I bought when I wanted to hang pictures in our first Wellington apartment.

Jim laughed loudly. 'You call that a spanner?' Then he laughed some more, harder this time. Apparently my wrench was very funny.

Finally Jim held up a silver thing he'd had at his side. 'THIS, my young man, is a spanner!'

It was the same shape as mine, but it was absolutely the single most enormous wrench I have ever seen in my entire life. It was as long as his arm, I kid you not. He growled and held it up in the air in what looked like a Conan the Barbarian sword pose. I trembled.

After I hid my apartment-grade wrench in shame, we quickly got to work on the well. I have never been good with mechanical things. I remember working on cars with my dad back in Michigan — changing the oil, replacing brakes — and I never could get my head around what we were doing. It's as if the moment someone opens the bonnet of a car, my brain is abducted by aliens.

Turns out the same thing happens when someone opens up a well.

Everything was in order, but the guys who'd worked on the well hadn't fastened the pipes securely enough to accommodate the power of the new pump. A round, black turny thing holding two bits of plastic pipe together had come undone.

Jim showed me how to cut off the tattered end of the plastic pipe, wrap some non-sticky white tape around it (which makes a seal for the turny thing to screw into) and screw it all back together securely. We did some other stuff, too, but who knows what it was. By that point my brain was floating in formaldehyde on its way to the outer reaches of the galaxy.

All I know is this: Jim worked with me on our well for most of the morning. We did stuff. We made it better. Jim moved back and forth between being patient with me and gently poking fun at me for not knowing anything. He was methodical and precise. He gave me a list of maintenance things to do, which I said I would do right away. I'm going to do them soon. I swear.

When we were finished that morning he crossed our paddocks to return to his house. I watched him go, carrying his enormous spanner, and I felt incredibly grateful.

By the time Fiona and CJ pulled up into the driveway — laughing and carrying on and looking very cosmopolitan in a kind of Eurotrash, unshowered way — life was back to normal. The well was perfect, and there was water every time we turned on the tap.

Fiona ran immediately to the shower. The Mad Welshman had saved the day.

Chapter 6

Moonlit walk through the olive grove

One night that first summer CJ and I shut off the lights in the main room, ready to go to bed, and suddenly we were surrounded by bright, silver-blue light. It was flooding in everywhere — through the large bay windows and the square panes of glass in the French doors, spilling across the terracotta floor and slipping up onto the edges of the furniture. I pressed my nose to the glass and saw an entire blue world outside. But I couldn't see the moon.

'LET'S GO FOR A WALK,' I said. 'Let's go see the moon.'

CJ smiled. 'You're crazy. It's late. I'm going to bed.'

I left him climbing into bed as I stepped out the back door and into the night. The sky was clear and everything was quiet and still. The gum trees in the backyard cast shadows everywhere. I walked across the backyard to the side of the house and looked up. There in the sky was the biggest, fullest, brightest moon I had ever seen— my first full moon in Martinborough.

Just a few days before, CJ and I had dug out the old, weedy vegetable beds and planted our very first garden. Now the moonlight soaked into the dark, rich compost we'd laid in, illuminating the seedlings of lettuce and silverbeet, cabbage and broccoli. In the greenhouse I could just make out the shadows of tiny tomato plants interspersed with basil.

I walked around to the front deck. We had bought four Cape Cod chairs for the deck, and I'd painted them white. They looked almost phosphorescent in the moonlight, as though they were lit from within. Thick lines from the pergola above them criss-crossed dark shadows all around. At one end of the deck, the climbing rose and the wisteria hid our new outdoor dining table in darkness, and the entire space looked like a safe, shadowy cave underneath all the stars.

I went down alongside the rosemary hedge, away from the house. Out in front of me the moonlight turned the paddocks turquoise and edged the tips of the trees in silver. I headed across the moonlit grass to the olive grove, opened the gate, and stepped inside.

The trees seemed to soak up the moonlight with a voracious, dream-like intensity. Moonshadows gathered at the base of every tree like dark, round puddles. The big macrocarpa trees at the bottom of the grove had become looming silhouettes against the bright night sky.

I wandered diagonally through the grove and went out the far gate, strolling under the shadows of the macrocarpas and continuing on until I had reached the very centre of the large bottom paddock. I was surrounded by nothing but long, silvery grass and total silence. The stars and the moon hung motionless over my head. I stood there for a long time. Then quietly, slowly, I slipped back through that magical blue moonlight, up to the house, in through the back door, and into bed.

CJ was already fast asleep.

Chapter 7

Invaded by woolly monsters

It was a hot December day when we picked up long sticks and walked down to the bottom paddock together. The sun was beating down fiercely. We were about to chase some sheep off our property, and if one thing was certain it was that we had absolutely no idea what we were doing.

CJ LOOKED OVER AT ME. 'How hard can chasing sheep be? They're just sheep.'

I nodded. 'They're fat and slow and stupid. Right?'

'Sure,' he said, not sounding too certain.

A few weeks earlier we'd seen four sheep down at the river. The spring rains had long since ended and the river was shallow and slow. The sheep were drinking on the far bank. One had a black face and the rest were all white. Their wool was thick and clumpy, as though they hadn't been cared for in a while. But they looked peaceful there by the water's edge.

As soon as they saw us, they ran. I had never understood before that sheep *really are* sheepish. The three all-white sheep disappeared immediately, but the black-faced one stopped and looked back at us for a moment. Then he turned and ran through the undergrowth, clonking through the branches and snapping twigs, until he was gone.

Later we saw them again, this time on our side of the river, which by then was only ankle-deep in spots. They were foraging for whatever they could find. I was sure they looked hungry, although truth be told I had no idea what a hungry sheep looked like.

When they saw us they bolted again, the black-faced one once more looking back at us a moment longer, before running off to join the others.

I stopped by John's one day to ask him what we should do about those sheep. He keeps sheep. He knows things.

'There's nothing you can do,' he said.

'Shouldn't we try to tell somebody?'

'Sheep go missing all the time.' He shrugged and looked off at the hills. 'There are farms all along that river. They could be from anywhere.'

That would have been the end of it, I suppose, if they hadn't found their way onto our property.

That summer our fenceline closest to the river was a bit the worse for wear. Here and there, river silt from a flood years before had half-buried the posts. You could hop right over the fence. So could sheep. We found the four vagrants smack dab in the middle of our bottom paddock one day, grazing happily under the mammoth white poplars as though they owned the place. They must have been happy to find all that long grass. After their days of wandering, this was the land of plenty.

At that point I called our neighbour Duane. He and his wife Sharon share our western boundary. They'd come over to introduce themselves a couple of weeks before, and I knew that Duane ran sheep.

'Are you missing four sheep?' I asked him. 'Including a black-faced one?'

'No,' he said. 'I saw them down in your paddock. They're not our sheep.' His voice was steady and slow.

'What should we do about them?' I asked. 'They're in our bottom paddock.'

'Well, you could keep them.'

This is how a farmer thinks; city boys do not see flea-bitten sheep in the bottom paddock as an opportunity.

The fact was that CJ and I had neither the time nor the know-how to care for those sheep, and our fences needed work before we could keep stock anyway. We still didn't even know how to take care of our olive grove, although I'd been reading furiously about olive trees and olive oil production. At least trees can't hop fences and run away.

'We can't keep them,' I said to Duane.

'Well, you'll have to get them out of your paddock then.'

'How?'

'Just chase them. Easy as.'

'Where will they go?'

Duane laughed. 'Who cares? As long as they're not in your paddock.'

I pictured those four sheep out foraging again, looking for grass, wandering around with nobody to care for them. But I felt like we had no choice. We clearly had to get rid of them.

SO WHEN CJ AND I ARRIVED in the bottom paddock on that hot December day, each carrying our carefully selected stick, we were determined to expel the interlopers. We saw them near the bottom fence. Our goal was to drive them over towards the section of fence that was the worst, so they'd jump over it and leave our property. *Easy as.*

I looked at CJ. 'You ready?' I asked.

'Yep. Let's go.'

We started walking towards the sheep, spreading out a bit and holding our long sticks out to the side. CJ started making noises. 'Whoop! Eh! Uh!' He must have seen somebody do that on TV.

I followed his lead, making noises of my own. 'Yoop! Hay! Yah!'

The sheep started running immediately. We ran after them, like fools.

I have since watched farmers herding sheep. Real farmers; not wanabees like us. First of all, real farmers have dogs that help, and there's a special whistle they have that tells the dogs what to do. If for some reason they don't have a dog with them, they certainly never resort to running after their sheep. Instead, real farmers walk in a measured and calculated way, arms out, and the sheep go magically where the farmers want. That didn't happen for us.

The sheep ran towards the bottom corner of the paddock, where the fence was high. Okay. Now we just had to get them to move along the bottom fence and jump out at the low spot.

These sheep, however, were independent thinkers. They eyed the situation quickly. Their little sheep-brains churned. I suspect they realised right away that they were dealing with a couple of extraordinarily stupid humans. Suddenly they turned together and ran directly towards us. I couldn't believe my eyes. Those mangy monsters were charging us! Had they turned aggressive? They must be rabid!

Then I understood. CJ and I had spread out too far, and we'd left them an opening as wide as the Cook Strait. The moment our rookie brains figured out what those scheming, devious sheep were doing, CJ and I started running towards each other as fast as we could.

It was like a bad slow-motion movie. Sheep running towards gap. City boys running to close gap. Who will get there first? You might have guessed it wasn't us. That day I learned a brand-new country lesson: sheep run fast. Really fast.

They not only slipped effortlessly between us, but they continued running all the way to the far side of the paddock — the exact opposite side from where we wanted them to be.

The black one looked back. I swear I heard him laughing. Or maybe what I heard was our neighbour Duane, hiding out in the trees somewhere, watching his new neighbours running around after four mangy sheep.

'Okay, stay close,' CJ said.

'Hold your stick up high,' I said.

Then we charged. We ran right at them, heads down and whooping and hollering as though our lives depended on it. The sheep simply turned left and headed across the top of the paddock. They went nowhere near the bottom fence.

I DON'T KNOW HOW LONG we chased those sheep around that paddock. Suffice it to say it was a long time. We chased them up, down, across, and back again. It's a big paddock. We were soon dripping with sweat under the hot December sun.

I couldn't help thinking that the sheep were being, well, *strategic*. In my overheated delirium, I began wondering if they'd escaped from some nearby secret genetic modification lab. Obviously that was why we couldn't herd them. These sheep had the body of sheep, the speed of cheetahs, and the tactical intelligence of Russian chess champions.

Then, just when CJ and I were both ready to collapse, a wonderful thing happened — not so much because we'd planned it well, but because the Four Woolly Monsters of Martinborough apparently decided they'd had enough of toying with the stupid humans. They ran to the low section of fence at the bottom of the paddock and jumped gracefully over, one at a time, heading back towards the river. At a cluster of willows on the other side, the black-faced one turned back and, somewhat reliably, looked at us again. He was clearly the ringleader. Then he, too, disappeared, right behind the others. We never saw them again.

I have always wondered what would have happened if we had kept them. They could have grazed in that bottom paddock as long as they liked. What harm would it have done?

I like to think that some kind, generous farmer downriver took them in, gave them a lush green paddock to graze in, and shore off the heavy wool that must have been so hot in the middle of summer. In return they could have given him a few pointers on his chess game, or perhaps built him a rocket ship.

Sometimes, as CJ and I stroll along the river bank, we find animal bones — complex things that look like vertebrae, jaws that still have teeth. I always think of the Four Woolly Monsters of Martinborough, and I hope it isn't them.

Chapter 8

Giant beings in the bottom paddock

A s the summer grew drier and drier, the unbelievably long grass in our paddocks turned brittle and brown. CJ and I were concerned about the fire hazard the grass posed, but we weren't too sure what to do.

ALL AROUND US, EVERYTHING was changing colour. The green hills across the river faded, and they began to look like the backs of chestnut-coloured horses. Our paddocks grew drier and more dangerous every day. Then Duane called.

'Would you like to sell your standing hay?' he asked.

I didn't really know what that meant.

Duane was having contractors come to his property to cut his hay. His paddocks and ours share several gates, and he wanted to know if we'd like to have our hay cut at the same time as his. He'd arrange everything. The contractors would pay us.

'They'll pay us?' I asked. Surely Duane had it wrong. As a boy in suburban Michigan, I had made extra money by mowing lawns. So I knew the people with the long grass were the ones who paid.

'They'll sell your hay on to farmers,' Duane said. 'They'll buy all of it. Unless you want to keep some for yourselves.'

'Um, I don't think we'll need any,' I said. We had no livestock and I was unable to think of even the remotest possible reason why we would want hay.

I thanked Duane and said we'd love to sell our hay.

It solved our problem, and we were going to get paid. Once again, what would we do without our neighbours?

About three weeks went by, and the long grass in our paddocks was still there. I called Duane.

'Did they forget about us?' I asked.

'No, not at all,' Duane said. 'The hay's just not ready yet.'

He explained that timing for a hay harvest is crucial. Hay cut too early means less hay per acre and a high moisture content, which can lead to rot. But hay cut too late means it's worthless on the market because it's less nutritious for livestock. There's just a tiny window of a couple of weeks when the hay is right for harvesting.

Eventually we looked out one day and saw tractors in our bottom paddock. They were huge, green John Deere things, and they cut the paddocks flat, leaving behind sweeping arcs of long grass in the corners where they couldn't go. They left the cut hay lying in the field. It wasn't in bales.

I didn't know it then, but you have to let the hay dry before you bale it. After a couple more days they came by and turned the hay with a kind of rotary rake — like a giant red blender — which is towed on the back of a tractor. If it rains while the hay is drying in the paddocks then it ruins everything, because the hay will rot when it's put into bales. This is where the phrase 'make hay while the sun shines' comes from.

Then, one evening CJ and I came home from work and saw something new out in the bottom paddock. We stood at the edge of the deck and looked out, across the olive grove, through the gap in the macrocarpas. There were strange, round structures down there.

CJ yelled out, 'Our hay!'

We put on our gumboots and went down to inspect.

If you've never stood in a paddock with enormous, round hay bales, then I highly recommend it. They are wonderful things.

CJ and I stood there for a while just looking at them, then walked around them and observing them, taking them in. They were like sculpture. They had that kind of presence, that kind of power.

Each was almost as tall as us: a great blanket of hay rolled up tightly and wrapped in a kind of mesh that held everything all together. Most were lying on their sides, like giant wheels from some missing Trojan Horse made of hay.

Some of the bales were wrapped in enormous sheets of white plastic and were standing on end. These, I found out later, are called 'baleage'. Baleage makes a kind of preserved feed, which ferments inside the wrap. It's similar to silage, but made without the silo.

All of a sudden, as CJ and I were walking around the hay bales, somehow, in spite of the fact that we were both in our early forties, we transformed into boys. We began running and jumping up on the bales. We hid behind them. We chased each other around them. We tried rolling them in the flat paddock, but even though they were round, their weight made them unmovable. We laughed the entire time.

Over the next few weeks, those giant beings lived there in our bottom paddock. I went down to visit them many times. I looked at them in the early morning light, in the noonday sun, at twilight. The shadows gathered around them differently.

WHEN THE JANUARY FULL MOON CAME, I went down to see them in the moonlight. The unwrapped bales blended in with the grass. They seemed to be crouching there, waiting for me. But the white wrapped bales were positively luminescent, like giant beacons spread out in front of my eyes, reflecting the moonlight. I jumped up on one glowing bale and watched the stars above me turn, then I looked down at my moonshadow across the grass, tilting away towards the trees.

Later, our friend Donna came to visit from the States. She loved the hay bales as much as CJ and I. We have a series of very embarrassing photos of the three of us doing disco dances on the bales, and riding them like rodeo cowboys.

What is it about hay bales? Countless paintings, poems and essays have been made about them. So much art has been inspired by hay that there's even an online 'Hay in Art' database on the Internet.

It was late February when the contractors came, unannounced at the end of summer, and took away our hay. Even though I knew a cheque was coming to us in the mail, even though I knew our hay was going to a good farmer who needed it to feed his cattle or his sheep, I couldn't help feeling something was wrong. Somebody had broken in to my own private sculpture garden, and they had stolen everything.

Chapter 9

The U.N. Committee on Home Decorating

We were at John and Aussie Bronwyn's for dinner with the rest of the neighbours when CJ first announced our intentions. 'We're going to tear down the wall'.

The room fell silent. Forks froze in mid-air. Mouths full of food had stopped chewing. We didn't yet understand that our house came with an advisory committee.

'WHICH WALL, EXACTLY?' Kiwi Bronwyn said, looking somewhat concerned. She typically has an intense, focused nature about her, and when she gets her eyes on a problem, they're like laser beams.

Everyone was staring at CJ.

'The brick wall between the dining room and the lounge,' he said. We had already grown used to calling our living room a 'lounge' as Kiwis do.

Jim the Mad Welshman spoke up next. As always, he was looking at the situation with the perspective of a mechanical engineer. 'Whoa. That brick pillar's load-bearing. You can't take that out.'

'Listen to him,' Kiwi Bronwyn said. 'He knows about these things.'

CJ shook his head. 'We're leaving the pillar. Just the wall.'

The brick wall we were talking about was a funny thing. It didn't reach all the way up to the high wooden ceiling. It rose only about seven feet, then stopped — a great barrier in the middle of an otherwise large, open room.

Suddenly the sound of somebody clearing their throat came from the head of the table. It was the Great Matriarch of Martinborough, Olwen. She's also Welsh, and she's married to David, a kind-hearted Englishman who used to be in the Queen's Guard. They were in their late seventies. They migrated to New Zealand as newly-weds so many years ago that they actually came by ship.

'How far down are you taking the wall?' Olwen said. 'Are you removing it completely?'

She was watching CJ closely.

I have to say that Olwen is like the most wonderful grandmother you could ever have. She makes these incredible things called Welsh cakes. CJ and I both love them. When she found out I can't eat gluten, she started making batches of Welsh cakes gluten-free, just for me. She also has very strong opinions about nearly everything, and she's not too shy to tell you what she thinks.

CJ was actually fidgeting in his seat. 'Um, well . . . I'm thinking that, maybe, half of it will come down all the way, to make a walkway. The other half will be about seven bricks high.'

In front of our eyes, the pleasant dinner party transformed into something like a United Nations hearing. The Kiwis, Welsh, English and Aussies were discussing the fate of the foolhardy Americans as though we were no longer in the room. I listened with great interest, wondering if we would be allowed to take down our wall.

'It provides thermal massing, so the room will be warmer when winter comes,' John said.

'And the room might feel a bit drafty with it gone,' Suzanne added. She was wearing a deep green, flowing blouse that looked as though it had come straight from a New York fashion house.

'That wall's good,' Suzanne's husband Murray said, and he picked a piece of hay from his no-nonsense flannel shirt. Murray is a good Kiwi bloke. He does not ramble on.

'But it's true you can't see the fire from the dining room table,' Kiwi Bronwyn added, her laser-like mind analysing the problem from every angle. 'And that's a real shame.'

'As long as they leave the pillar, it's okay,' Jim said. 'I don't want their house to fall down. That place is built on a concrete slab, so there's enough thermal massing there.'

The fact is that at that point our neighbours had probably spent more time in our house than we had. For years and years they'd enjoyed dinners in our dining room, back when the property belonged to Priscilla. They'd enjoyed countless glasses of wine on our front deck, and they'd occasionally stored things in our hay shed. Even the goldfish in our pond had originally come from Olwen and David's place. In some ways, this property belonged more to them than to us.

Then Aussie Bronwyn spoke up. 'Oh, the boys could paint that blasted wall purple if they wanted. It's their wall.'

I smiled to myself. I suspected there was a part of Aussie Bronwyn's heart that belonged to the gypsies, and she actually might think painting the wall purple was a good idea.

'But they don't know what they're doing,' John said. 'They'll be so cold in winter!'

'We're used to colder winters than Martinborough gets,' I said, but nobody seemed interested in my opinion on the matter.

'Well,' Olwen announced, and the room fell quiet again. It seemed she was about to deliver a verdict. 'I think it's just fine to take down the wall. In fact, I think it's a very good idea.'

And that seemed to settle it.

Having obtained permission from the Committee, two weeks later CJ and a local builder named Fred took sledgehammers to the wall when I was at work. It created so much dust that it took nearly another two weeks of cleaning before we'd seen the last of the grit.

One by one, the neighbours stopped by to see the result. They stood on one side of the room and then the other. They looked up at the large, wooden ceiling that arches over the main living space. Slowly, they each nodded and gave their approval.

CJ and I breathed sighs of relief.

THEN PRISCILLA CALLED.

'I hear you took down the wall,' she said.

Priscilla had stopped by with Suzanne shortly after we'd moved in. It was an incredibly nice visit. CJ and I had shown them the paint job we'd done in the bedroom and the bathroom, and how we'd planted the garden beds. Priscilla gave us her books on how to care for an olive grove, along with a small map that indicated the specific variety of every olive tree in the grove. It felt like the passing of a torch.

Once upon a time, Priscilla poured a lot of love into this property, and it's safe to say that it's a beautiful place because of the work she did. She's very resourceful and determined in the way many New Zealand women are. She planted that olive grove with her own hands, had the garage converted into our three guest rooms, and had the separate, free-standing garage built. She even laid the terracotta tiles in the main living space herself, when the tiler cancelled on her.

'Um, yes,' I said over the phone to her now. 'We took the wall down. Well, really, CJ did. The whole thing was his idea.' If anyone was going to get in trouble for tearing down that wall, it wasn't going to be me.

'I'm just down from the Hawke's Bay for the day,' she said. 'I'm visiting Olwen. Do you mind if I stop by to see?'

'Um, sure,' I said, somewhat nervous. When I hung up and told CJ that Priscilla was on the way, he immediately started vacuuming.

Priscilla came with Olwen. Fortunately Olwen had already seen the final result, so we weren't nervous about that. But this was Priscilla's house!

Er, I mean, it was our house.

When Priscilla stepped in the front door, her face lit up with a warm smile. 'You've transformed the room. I always hated that wall.'

For some reason, having Priscilla's approval meant a lot to us. CJ and I had become another set of caretakers in the line of people who have loved this place. We were becoming part of the genealogy of the house, like another level in the family tree.

Priscilla and Olwen sat down with CJ and me for a cup of celebratory, wall-be-gone tea. That was when CJ announced his Evil Plan.

'I want to paint the ceiling white,' he said.

Priscilla nearly choked on her biscuit. She suddenly looked like a mother who'd discovered that the people adopting her precious baby were actually axe-wielding, homicidal maniacs.

'Oh, no,' she said. 'You can't do that.'

Olwen looked up at the warm wood grain. 'No. Absolutely not. You'll ruin it. Cover all that gorgeous wood? You must be mad.'

'Don't worry,' I said. 'I'm not going to let CJ paint the ceiling. I like the wood.'

'Oh, thank goodness,' Priscilla said.

'But it's too dark,' CJ said, pleading with his most charming smile.

'Don't you dare, you cheeky boy,' Olwen said. 'You listen to Jared. He's clearly the sensible one.'

Since that day CJ has taken his case to the local Committee

several times. I'm happy to say that the entire valley is against him. When he brings it up with me, as he continually does, I explain that he has a simple choice. Either he can paint the ceiling white, or he can continue to live with me.

He just smiles and says, 'Hmm. That's not an easy choice.'

But I'm not too worried. Recently I discovered an even bigger threat. Now I just say, 'If you painted the ceiling white, Olwen would be so upset that she'd no longer bake us Welsh cakes.'

That pretty much stops CJ in his tracks.

Olwen's Welsh Cakes

Just like your Welsh grandmother used to make. If you don't have a Welsh grandmother, I suggest you adopt one immediately.

Ingredients

220 g gluten-free flour (Bakels Gluten Free Health Flour works well,
   as does Orgran Gluten Free All Purpose Plain Flour. For a wheat
   version, replace with the same quantity of wheat flour.)
1 teaspoon baking powder
55 g sugar
110 g cold butter
110 g currants
1 egg
milk
caster sugar

Preparation

In a medium-sized mixing bowl, sift together the flour, baking
powder and sugar. Grate the butter and use your fingers to rub it in,
until the flour mix is the consistency of breadcrumbs.

Mix in the currants, and beat in the egg and milk until the mixture
forms a dough.

On a floured surface, roll out the dough to about 6 mm thick. (If
cooking gluten-free, be sure to dust the surface with gluten-free flour.)

Use a cookie cutter — or the rim of a tumbler or teacup — to cut the
dough into rounds about 7 cm across.

Cook the rounds in a hot, lightly buttered, cast-iron frying pan until
golden brown, like pikelets. Flip and cook the other side.

Put some caster sugar on a plate, then place the Welsh cakes on
the plate as you cook them, making sure both sides of the cakes get
dusted in sugar.

MAKES ABOUT 2 DOZEN WELSH CAKES

Chapter 10

Stacking wood for winter

As that first summer came to a close, the mornings grew cold. We woke to white-grey mists hanging in the paddocks and a new chill in the air. I suddenly understood how the claret ash by the fish pond got its name when its leaves started turning a spectacular shade of . . . well, claret. Winter would soon be on us whether we were ready or not, so we began stacking wood. We were like two bears, hunkering down at the first signs of autumn.

SINCE OUR HOUSE IS HEATED with a woodburner, we've come to associate a nicely stacked woodpile with security and comfort. John once told me, 'Wood makes you warm three times. Once when you cut it, once when you stack it, and once when you burn it.'

We had seven cubic metres of wood delivered. A young farmer in an All Blacks T-shirt dumped it off his truck in a heap out in the top paddock, next to the hay shed. The pigeons living in the hay shed rafters went crazy at the noise, bursting into flight as though they'd heard a shotgun blast.

While I understood that winter in Martinborough would be

nowhere near as cold as the winters I'd grown up with in Michigan and Minnesota, I hadn't yet experienced a Martinborough winter myself. Soon I would learn that, even though there's no snow in the Martinborough basin, the mornings can be frosty, and you can see snow up on the ranges. Yet winter throughout the entire lower North Island of New Zealand feels to me more like one long, wet autumn with a few days of balmy spring thrown in. The warm midwinter days always take me by surprise. There's actually a special phrase for them in Māori — he rā mokopuna, which literally means 'a grandchild day'. I've been told that these warm days in winter are referred to as grandchildren because they're so precious.

During that first Martinborough winter CJ and I were happy to discover that, while we usually needed a fire in the evenings and again first thing in the morning, by noon it was often warm enough that we were opening the doors and windows and eating lunch out on the deck. It's not a bad winter life at all. We were also happy to discover that our house stayed warm even without the 'thermal massing' from the ugly brick wall that we had removed.

The wood the young farmer delivered that autumn was supposed to be pine, but we lucked out because afterwards we learned it was macrocarpa. John told us. We didn't know the difference. John said, 'Macrocarpa is better firewood because it burns slower than pine.' Who knew? These are the things that city boys learn when they move to the country.

Much of the wood was too thick to fit in our woodburner. So I went out and bought a proper hand-held log-splitter, which is not the same as an axe. The head of a log-splitter is heavier, and it has a large square surface on the back for hitting with a wooden mallet. Again, I would have never learned the difference between a log-splitter and an axe in my old life.

CJ and I split the big pieces, and then we worked together to stack all the wood. We loaded our red wheelbarrow full and wheeled it into the hay shed. The pigeons watched from the rafters, again becoming unsettled with every clunk of wood landing on the pile. A few flew away, their wings flapping loudly above our heads. They're used to having it quiet out there in the hay shed.

I COULD GO ON FOR DAYS about how much I love our shed. It's just corrugated grey tin, a large rectangle with a slightly sloping roof. It doesn't look like a thing most people would find worthy of love. One side is open, with two large fence gates across the opening to keep animals out.

Inside the hay shed you'll find all kinds of junk. Fantastic things. Mysterious things. Metal pieces of some lost machine. A broken picnic table top, round with a hole in the middle for an umbrella. Across the ground there are remnants of another season's hay. If you stand inside the hay shed and look out, you have the most magnificent view of the olive grove and the hills beyond.

Once we'd pushed each wheelbarrow full of wood into that beloved hay shed, we moved quickly. There was a lot of wood. We lifted and stacked and turned to lift again, lining the wood up against the back wall where it's most dry. Then we wheeled the empty wheelbarrow back out again, under the watchful gaze of the remaining pigeons, and went over to the wood heap to repeat the whole procedure. The work had a rhythm, and a tempo, like music — punctuated by cooing and flapping from the rafters.

The neat pile slowly grew taller and longer, until it became just taller than my five foot 10 frame, and as long as two of me lying down. It took a long time, but we didn't mind. As I said, it's satisfying.

We worked that day almost until it was time to start dinner. Finally our wood was stacked and ready for the winter. We both paused and looked at what we'd done. It was at that moment that I realised wood makes you warm a lot more than three times. It's almost infinite. Because just standing there that day, looking at that woodpile, and again every day I looked at it after that, I felt warm. Again and again and again.

Chapter 11

Angry locals demand carrot cake

'**W**hy won't you share it?' I asked CJ. We were standing in the kitchen, looking at a carrot cake recipe written on the back of a long white envelope. 'Because it's too special,' he answered.

'BUT ALL THE NEIGHBOURS are asking for it.'

'Too bad,' CJ said. 'If we share this recipe then everyone will make it, and it won't be special any more. Besides, it's the only cake we know how to make! And we can't serve store-bought ever again. The locals will shoot us.'

It was true. The first time we'd invited our local friend Amber over for morning tea, she actually reprimanded us for not baking. 'We don't serve store-bought out here in the country,' she said. It took us a moment before we realised she wasn't joking.

The recipe on the back of the long white envelope CJ and I were looking at wasn't just any carrot cake recipe. It was an unbelievably rich, two-layer carrot cake — moist to the point of impossibility, graced with just the right touch of cinnamon, and covered in snowdrifts of heavenly cream cheese icing.

Like all good recipes, it has a story.

Years ago, when CJ and I were in our twenties and first dating in Chicago, CJ's friend Dave made this amazing carrot cake all the time. It was Dave's mother's recipe from back in Iowa.

Every time CJ's circle of friends gathered together — at Thanksgiving, Christmas, Easter, and summer dinners — Dave brought his carrot cake. Years later, when CJ and I moved to Japan, CJ asked Dave for the recipe. Without hesitation Dave wrote it down, from memory, on the back of an envelope.

Not long after that, Dave died suddenly of a heart attack. He was only 50 years old.

CJ and I wandered the globe together for years — from Yamagata to Tokyo to Wellington. Our worldly goods were scattered to the wind, and Dave's carrot cake recipe became lost in the sands of time. It was gone.

Then, after we moved out to Martinborough and learned that our neighbours here view store-bought baked goods with a level of disdain normally reserved for large toxic waste dumps, I asked my mom to send me an old, barely used cookbook that I'd stashed away in her Michigan basement.

When the cookbook arrived, out fell the long white envelope. It was like something out of a time machine.

'Dave's carrot cake recipe!' I yelled out to CJ.

CJ almost started crying — half out of love for Dave, and half, I'm sure, out of eagerness to sink his teeth into that cake again.

'We're saved!' he said. 'It's so easy to make, even we can do it!'

Since I have to stick to a gluten-free diet, I experimented with converting the recipe. To my delight, I discovered that the carrots keep the cake so moist that this cake is just as amazing even when gluten-free.

I immediately started baking a gluten-free version of Dave's Carrot Cake like there was no tomorrow. For morning teas, for dinners, for barbecues. Everyone absolutely loved it.

But then things got out of hand. The more people who tasted it, the more people there were who urgently, even desperately, wanted the recipe. When I said no, people insisted. It was exhausting. They hounded me. They tugged at my sleeves like addicts begging for crack.

'Pleease,' they said. 'Pleease give us the recipe.'

I tried reasoning with CJ. 'Come on,' I said. 'Just let me share it with people. Dave would have shared it. After all, he shared it with you.'

'Nope,' CJ said. 'Not sharing.'

It was around then that our neighbours started ganging up on me. When our neighbour Kiwi Bronwyn inevitably asked for the carrot cake recipe, she was a bit surprised when I explained that I couldn't give it to her. But she let it go.

Shortly after that, however, I asked our neighbour across the road, Aussie Bronwyn, for one of her recipes.

'I'm sorry,' Aussie Bronwyn said with a wry smile. 'I understand you won't give Kiwi Bronwyn your carrot cake recipe. When you give her that recipe, I'll give you mine.'

I couldn't believe it. I'd been blacklisted. 'That's not fair!' I whined. 'It's CJ's fault! Punish him!'

Aussie Bronwyn was unmoved.

A FEW WEEKS LATER, our friend Amber invited us over for dinner. I said we'd bring carrot cake for dessert. 'Okay,' she said. 'As long as it's not store-bought.'

The night of the dinner everyone at Amber's raved about the cake.

'You've come a long way, boys,' Amber said.

The next day I received a surprise email. It was from a friend of Amber's, another woman named Bronwyn. This Bronwyn is a musician. She plays double bass in the New Zealand Symphony Orchestra.

It turns out that Musician Bronwyn had stopped by Amber's for morning tea, and Amber had served some of the leftover carrot cake. You guessed it: Musician Bronwyn wanted the recipe. Respectful of CJ's Recipe Gag Rule, I of course explained I couldn't share it. The next time I saw Amber, she told me how upset Musician Bronwyn had been with me.

'This has got to stop,' I told CJ. 'It's completely out of control. I'm being bullied by a band of belligerent Bronwyns!'

Still, CJ refused to share the recipe.

Then, at long last, something pushed him over the edge.

For a bit of cultural education, CJ and I went to an A & P Show, and we happened to see chef and TV presenter Al Brown do a cooking demonstration.

Up on stage, Al started talking about giving away recipes. 'I don't understand why people are so miserly when it comes to recipes,' he said. 'Why don't people give them away? Recipes are like love letters from people you care about. They're meant to be shared.'

I nudged CJ in the side so hard that he nearly fell off his chair.

When Al's cooking demonstration was over, CJ said, 'Okay, okay. Share the damn recipe. I give in.'

Finally. I wasted no time in sharing Dave's carrot cake recipe with everyone who had ever asked for it. It wasn't a moment too soon. Any longer and I'm afraid CJ and I would have ended up with an angry mob of carrot cake loving locals at our door, yelling and brandishing pitchforks.

Dave's Carrot Cake

If you make this cake you need to be prepared to share the recipe, otherwise things might get ugly.

Ingredients

Cake

2 cups gluten-free baking mix (Healtheries Simple Wheat & Gluten
   Free Baking Mix works well. For a wheat version, replace with the
   same quantity of wheat flour.)
2 cups sugar
2 teaspoons cinnamon
2 teaspoons baking soda
2 teaspoons baking powder
1 teaspoon salt
1½ cups cooking oil, preferably canola
4 eggs
3 cups finely grated carrot
1 cup chopped walnuts (optional)

Icing

250 g cream cheese
110 g butter
2 teaspoons vanilla essence
450 g icing sugar

Preparation

Heat oven to 175 °C.
   Sift the dry ingredients together in a large mixing bowl.
   Add the oil, stirring constantly.
   Add the remaining ingredients and mix well.
   Turn the mixture into two round springform pans. Bake for
45 minutes.
   To make the icing, mix the cream cheese, butter and the vanilla
essence, beat until light and fluffy, and then stir in the icing sugar.

Chapter 12

Inspecting the olive trees

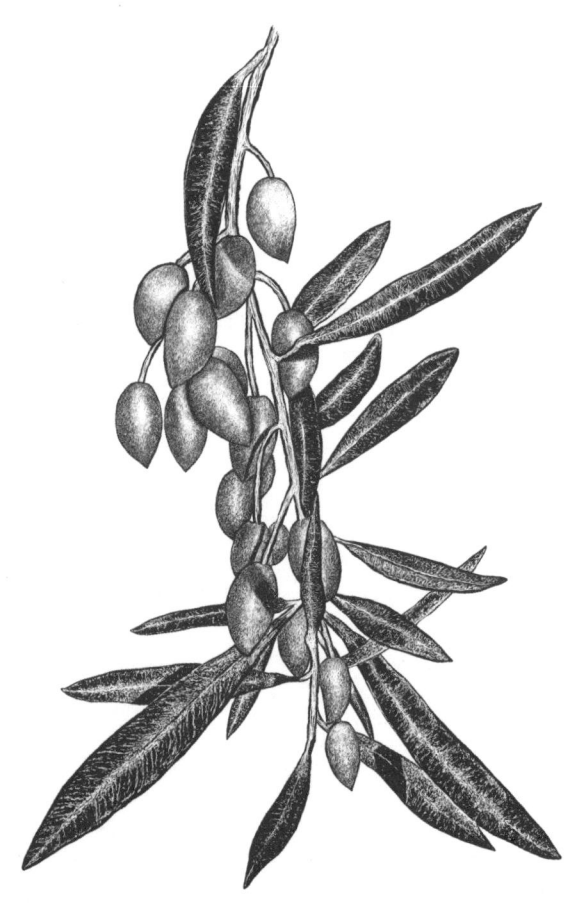

At the end of April I went for a walk through the olive grove to see how the olives were doing. Down by the river the willows had turned golden, but there in the grove the olive leaves were the still the same dependable silvery green. The harvest was just over a month away, and I wanted to check the fruit.

THE AUTUMN LIGHT was sloping through the sky, and the olive trees were literally soaking up every bit of sun they could, casting long shadows across the brittle, still-brown grass. The light was so beautiful across the grass that, for a moment, I forgot why I was in the grove. Eventually I turned back to the trees. I walked down their rows, reached out and touched the branches, looked at the olives.

I had learned a few things about olives over the summer. I'd read books and talked to John and other growers in the area who were happy to share what they knew about these incredible trees. I'd spent countless hours with CJ in the grove cutting out the evil suckers and weed-whacking the thigh-high grass around each and every tree. I'd also studied the little map Priscilla had given us of our grove. It showed rows of letters: M, B, F, L, and N. It was like a secret code, and it had revealed everything.

When we moved in, all 500 of those trees were just olive trees to me, and they pretty much looked the same. But by that first autumn, I already knew that this was as silly as thinking all Asians look the same, or all white folk. People only say that when they haven't actually looked, when they haven't taken the time.

Walking through the low-angled light that day, I saw every single one of our different cultivars, or varieties of olive tree. Here were the Manzanillo. There were the Barnea. On this side of the grove were the Frantoio and Leccino. On that side were the Nabali. They were all different.

The Barnea are an Israeli variety. The trees are long and tall, and their olives are oblong and have little points at the end. Although I hadn't yet tasted the oil from our own trees, by then I'd tasted other Barnea from other growers. Barnea oil is deliciously buttery.

Manzanillo trees are shorter and rounder than Barnea. They're from Spain. The olives are fat, and they ripen sooner than the others. I used to think that green olives and black olives were different types altogether, but in fact all olives turn from green to black as they ripen. Manzanillo olives in particular have a good pit-to-fruit ratio, which makes them good for pickling. So good, in fact, that they're used worldwide by the pizza industry. But Manzanillo can be pressed as well, and the oil has a subtle taste of green bananas. It's not unusual to find that Martinborough's award-winning extra virgin olive oils contain some blend with Manzanillo.

The Frantoio and Leccino are Tuscan varieties. Strolling through the grove that day, I knew these were the youngest of our trees, at six years old as opposed to 10. Their oil has a grassy taste that finishes with a peppery bang. The trees and olives look very similar, but people who know can tell them apart in one very easy way: at harvest time the Frantoio always ripen later.

And then there's our Nabali. Already I'd begun thinking of them as our problem children. They're a Palestinian cultivar, and I find them the most beautiful of all olive trees. They have knobby forked trunks and especially dark green leaves. But as I walked through the grove that sunny April day, our Nabali had absolutely no fruit.

I'd called Priscilla a few weeks before about the Nabali. It turned out they hadn't fruited for her either. She'd planned to pull them out one year, but then that year they actually bore fruit. So, she decided to leave them. They hadn't fruited since. Obviously they were clever. They understood when Priscilla was about to give them the axe, and they'd offered up fruit to save their necks. So when I walked through that section of the grove I said loudly, 'I'm going to rip out all these Nabali if they don't fruit!' But my fear tactics didn't work. There was still no fruit. I began to consider pulling them out for real.

I stood back and looked at the grove as a whole. Not even the Manzanillo had started to turn black yet. The old-fashioned, nonscientific way to assess an olive crop is that one-third of the olives should be black, one-third green, and one-third 'straw', or halfway between the two. There are other ways, of course. If CJ and I wanted, we could send periodic samples off to an infra-red analysis testing facility in Auckland. This would tell us the exact oil and moisture content over the ripening period in order to determine the optimum time to harvest. But we came to the country because we wanted to live simply. The old-fashioned way would work just fine for us.

THE GROVE AROUND ME that day was not bursting with fruit. After all, it had been neglected for years; until recently it had been wildly overgrown with grass, and CJ and I hadn't yet pruned it properly or started a spraying regime. The Barnea had very few olives. The Nabali, of course, had none. The Manzanillo had a bit here and there. Only the Frantoio and Leccino were doing well. They were young and strong and hardy, and I had already begun to like them best of all. Nevertheless, the fruit that we did have throughout the grove was absolutely beautiful, and more precious for its rarity. Each olive was like a tiny miracle to my eyes, and I couldn't wait to harvest everything we could.

But olives alone do not a harvest make. CJ and I had no harvesting equipment whatsoever, unless you counted the two tiny, yellow plastic harvest rakes that we'd found in the garage. I'd never actually *seen* an olive harvest at that point, but I understood that you were supposed to somehow run those yellow rakes through the branches to get the olives off. Other than that, I was unclear on the details.

John had told me that he had a couple of harvest rakes we could borrow, one small net, and a couple of buckets. But it wouldn't be enough. We needed more equipment, and of course we needed people to do the labour.

I left the grove and shut the gate behind me. There was time for the fruit to ripen. I'd been told that the olive harvest in Martinborough starts around the beginning of June. All of May stood between here and there. The olives would be fine.

When I got back up to the house and told CJ what I'd found, he said, 'We just can't harvest this year.'

'Of course we can,' I said.

'We're not ready. It's too much.' He was almost whining. 'We can't do it.' The look in his eyes said, *I am overwhelmed at the thought of it.*

Luckily for us, since we moved to the country only one of us at a time has ever been reduced to a snivelling idiot. We take turns doing that. When one is completely overwhelmed and incapable of coping with rural life, the other is excited and ready to go. God help us if we ever both cracked at once.

'I'm not letting those olives down there go to waste,' I said. 'We're harvesting.'

CJ stared at me like a deer caught in the headlights. 'How? With what? We don't have enough equipment. Even if we could get the city friends to help, we don't even really know how to do it yet.'

He was right, of course.

'I don't care,' I said. 'I'll figure it out. Leave it to me.'

We hadn't made it this far just to let the local birds eat our ripened fruit. I loved those olive trees. Somehow, some way, in just over one month, we were going to have an olive harvest.

Chapter 13

A tractor named Sunshine

The late autumn rains came in the middle of May, and as a result CJ and I found ourselves standing in John's hay shed. It was a little earlier in the morning than we would have liked to be out on a Saturday, but we had important business. We were there to be introduced to a small orange tractor.

'I BOUGHT THE TRACTOR you should have bought,' John said. 'Priscilla sold it to me when you said no.'

Suddenly CJ and I realised we were standing face to face with the very tractor that we had so confidently spurned almost nine months before. The rains meant the grass in our olive grove was now turning green and growing again. Soon it would be out of control, and that struck fear in our hearts. If it got too long before the harvest, we wouldn't be able to lay down all the many harvest nets that we didn't yet have and didn't yet fully understand how to use. We couldn't have that now, could we?

John placed his hand on the ripped black vinyl of the tractor seat. 'It's a Kubota three-cylinder diesel. Must be 20 years old. Rough as guts, but does the job.'

To me, John's tractor has always looked like a story-book tractor, as though it was designed by a child with a thick orange crayon. It's boxy and simple. The writing on the levers and knobs is in Japanese, which, since our years in Japan, fills me with a kind of nostalgia. On the main control panel a picture of a rabbit and a turtle indicates speed.

On the front there's a small chrome bull's head between the

headlamps and below that, across the front grill, there's a shiny nameplate that proudly spells out the word *Sunshine*.

Of course, John would never refer to his tractor as Sunshine. He's far too much of a no-nonsense Kiwi bloke to do that. In my mind, however, as soon as I saw that nameplate, John's little orange tractor became known simply as Sunshine.

I pointed to a large, red square thing that looked as if it dragged on the ground behind Sunshine.

'What's that for?' I asked.

'That's the PTO mower,' John said.

'The what?'

'The power take-off mower. Runs off the tractor's engine, you see.' John climbed up into the seat. 'I'll show you how to start it.'

There's an odd black hole in Sunshine's dashboard. To start the engine, you put your thumb over the hole and turn the key to the left. You leave your thumb there as the hole heats up. When you can smell your skin burning — and not a second before — you turn the key to the right to start the engine.

'You've got to make sure it gets good and hot,' John said, waving his thumb around to ease the pain. 'Then it starts like a dream.'

Clearly, whoever had designed Sunshine's ignition system was some kind of twisted sadist with a strange fetish for farm implements.

John let the engine run for a while and then turned it off. 'Your turn.'

CJ sat down, singed his thumb as instructed, and the engine started immediately. But when it came to my turn, no matter how diligently I seared my tender flesh, Sunshine simply wouldn't start. This went on for nearly 20 minutes. My thumb was blistered and red, but the engine was silent.

'Well,' CJ said. 'I'll just start it when we mow.'

The mowers of Martinborough come out everywhere at the end of autumn. The people in the village, those with square front lawns and a connection to the town water supply, have water restrictions imposed on them during the driest parts of summer. But most people in the Wairarapa are far too no-nonsense to water their lawns in summer, even if there were no legal restrictions. Everyone knows that water is for agriculture — for growing summer vegetables and watering farmers' crops. So the grass doesn't grow in summer around here. The lawnmowers are put away at the start of summer and aren't brought out again until May.

The first time we mowed our olive grove that autumn, CJ had

to do it. That's because every time I sat on Sunshine, she stalled. Obviously the old crank preferred CJ to me. She had no idea what he was about to do to her. From then on, mowing became CJ's job.

It took CJ almost eight hours to do the entire grove. He drove Sunshine back and forth in one direction and then the other, just as the contractor had done at the start of summer. (Although the contractor had a much larger and more manly tractor.)

Because Sunshine is small, she's a very rough ride. CJ was jostled and tossed as he tried to get as close as possible to the trees, not wanting to have to use our line trimmer to cut back 500 squares of long grass again. All the while he was trying unsuccessfully to dodge olive branches that smacked him in the face like whips.

When he was done mowing that very first time, there were red welts across his cheeks and several small, round burn marks on his thumb, but the grove looked fantastic. At least we knew we wouldn't have long grass for the harvest. The next morning he drove Sunshine back down the road, put-putting slowly all the way, and mowed John's grove just to thank him.

OVER THE COMING WINTER and into the following spring, CJ borrowed Sunshine several times. It never went as smoothly as that first day.

The second time, John had left the red plastic container for the diesel fuel on top of the mower. It was tied on, so CJ left it there. After an hour of mowing, he suddenly heard a loud *bam!* and saw fuel arcing up into the air. Behind him, John's red diesel container lay shredded in pieces on the grass. It had fallen under the mower, where the blades made quick work of it. Luckily, the fuel didn't ignite.

When CJ took Sunshine back that day, he had bought a brand-new diesel container, filled it and the tractor full, mowed John's grove as usual, and then gave John a heartfelt apology.

John just laughed and shook his head. 'You left the diesel container sitting on the mower while you were actually mowing?'

Then he said, 'No worries. This container's better than my old one. It's an improvement.'

The third time CJ borrowed Sunshine, he was sitting comfortably when suddenly the seat gave way underneath him, dropping and tilting to the left. The metal supports had actually broken. When CJ took Sunshine back that time, John laughed even harder. 'Maybe you need to lose some weight!' Then John added, 'No worries. I know a bloke who can weld it for me.'

CJ offered to pay for the repairs but John said, 'Pay? I'm not going to pay. My mate will fix it for free and make it stronger than ever. It'll be an improvement.'

I think CJ took this as a kind of challenge. How much damage could he inflict on Sunshine and have it still qualify as an improvement?

So the fourth time CJ borrowed Sunshine, he took out all the stops, literally. He was driving along in Rabbit speed when suddenly a thick, low olive branch jumped out in front of him. It made full contact with the metal exhaust pipe at the front of the tractor. CJ tried to turn and downshift into Turtle, but it was too late. *Crack!* The exhaust pipe bent backwards and broke in half.

Later CJ drove poor, battered Sunshine back to John's house, exhaust sputtering out of a broken hole. 'I'm so sorry, John,' he said. 'I broke your tractor again. It's bad this time.'

When John saw Sunshine, he nearly fell over from laughing so hard. 'Look what you did! You snapped it like a twig!' It took a while for John to get his laughter under control, but once he did he said, 'Aww, no worries. That exhaust was always too tall anyway. It hit branches in my grove, too. I'll get my welding mate to fix it, make it shorter. It'll—'

'I know,' CJ interrupted. 'It'll be an improvement.'

I knew that if I didn't figure out how to operate Sunshine myself, soon there wouldn't be much left of her to 'improve'. So the next time we borrowed her, I hopped on and tried to start the engine. Sunshine must have changed her mind about me by then, because she started right away. And I hardly had to burn my thumb at all. Clearly she was over CJ.

I mowed the grove on my own that time, and Sunshine didn't stall once. More importantly, I managed to return her to John without any CJ-style improvements whatsoever.

I told John, 'I'll mow the grove from now on.'

John shrugged. 'No worries.'

But I suspect that both he and Sunshine were secretly happy.

Chapter 14

Harvest boot camp

CJ and I were not prepared. The olive harvest was only weeks away, but we still didn't have all the equipment we needed. What's more, although we'd had many conversations with various growers about how to do it, we still had never actually seen this mysterious beast called an *olive harvest*. So I picked up the phone and volunteered to help Helen at Olivo with her harvest. That way I could finally see how to do it with my very own eyes.

OLIVO IS A TOP-NOTCH commercial grove in Martinborough. I had seen Helen's beautifully designed olive oil bottles in all the local shops, and CJ and I had driven by the gorgeous olive grove countless times.

So it was that at the end of May I found myself standing on a cool morning in Helen's grove with her and her harvest team — Mavis, Scott and Bernard (pronounced *BER-nerd* here, not *Ber-NARD* the American way). Mavis was a thin elderly woman. Scott and BERnard were clearly used to physical labour. I, it must be said, was still not.

Scott's ute was parked nearby, and from the back of it we started grabbing great bundles of green netting, stacks of bright orange crates, a heavy air compressor, and two mechanical rakes.

'I ordered those rakes from Italy,' Helen explained to me. 'They are expensive, fragile things, and it's nearly impossible to find replacement parts in New Zealand. If they break during the harvest, my harvest is over.'

Helen assigned roles. Scott and BERnard were on rakes. Mavis and I were on nets. I tried not to be insulted that I'd been matched with Mavis.

'Jared, Mavis is very fast,' Helen said. 'You'll each be on a different side of the tree, and you'll each have your own net. You'll have to do your best to keep up with her.'

I looked over and sized up the old lady. 'Not a problem,' I said. This was going to be a piece of cake. I swaggered over and started laying out the nets under the trees.

Helen explained how we would work. The rakers would rake the branches and knock the olives down onto the nets. Then the rakers would move to the next tree, which already had nets under it. Meanwhile, Mavis and I would lift the edges of our nets under the first tree to gather the olives and unload them into the orange crates. Then we'd spread our empty nets out under the next tree in the row, leapfrog fashion, always one step ahead of the rakers.

We had to be careful not to tread on the olives. As soon as olives are crushed, they start to ferment, and it can affect the taste of the oil.

Scott and BERnard hooked up the mechanical rakes to the air compressor and started work. Each rake has two rake heads on the end of a long pole, and the rake heads sort of clap together, shaking the olives off the branches. It was fascinating to watch them move up and down the trees, quickly flinging olives everywhere. The compressor chugged loudly and the rakes went *clappity-clap*.

Before I knew what was happening, Mavis was gathering her first net full of olives. I'd been so transfixed that I hadn't been paying attention to my net. I watched Mavis to see what I had to do. She folded up the corners and brought all the olives to the centre. Then, in one deft move, she lifted the heavy, olive-laden netting up over the edge of one of the crates and poured the olives in. It looked so easy.

I did everything exactly like she did. I swear. I folded up corners. I gathered olives to the centre. But when I went to pour my olives into the crate, they found a sneaky shortcut and half of them poured out all over the grass. Suddenly Mavis was at my side, demurely picking the olives and putting them into the crate.

'They always wash them at the press,' she said. 'But you have to be careful of that.'

Once we got my olives into the crate, Mavis and I carried our nets down the row and started setting them up under the next set of trees. Within seconds Mavis had her net laid out perfectly. There wasn't a fold or wrinkle to be seen. She may as well have laid out a daybed for the Queen herself, right there on the grass. She'd practically used hospital corners. My net, on the other hand, was an absolute mess. There were a million folds and twists. The extreme peaks and troughs looked like the Rimutakas. The net seemed to be screaming out, 'Roll this way, olives! Over here, onto the grass!'

Once again, there was Mavis. After having done her own work quickly and efficiently, she was helping me out with mine. My ego was having a little bit of trouble with this. She took total control of my net and had it straightened out faster than you could say 'I can do it myself.'

Was I so inept that I couldn't even keep up with an old woman?

Mavis looked at me and very gently said, 'The nets need to be relatively flat.'

'Thank you,' I said, gritting my teeth.

She gave me a warm smile, but I saw through her charming veneer. I started to think of her less as a kind, friendly grandmother and more as the scheming arch-nemesis she plainly was.

I made a vow then and there. I would not continue to be made a fool of by this supposedly saint-like senior citizen. I would become faster than her. I would be better. And I would be chivalrous — oh, so very chivalrous! I would help the poor, old dear when she failed to keep up with me. I would walk up to her just as she was struggling to lift the heavy nets full of olives into the crates, and I would say, 'There, there, little granny. Let me take care of that.'

I WENT BACK TO my work with a renewed energy. I worked hard. It was a cool day in late autumn, but I broke into a terrible sweat. As I wiped my brow and felt my lungs heave, I looked over at Mavis. She was as fresh as a daisy. And wait. She had the nerve to be humming to herself. Humming! With a smile on her face!

No matter what I did, she was always there, helping me. The nerve of some people. And if she wasn't helping me, she was five steps ahead of me. When I was pouring my olives into the crates, she was already laying her empty net out under the next set of trees, hospital corners and all. When I was finally laying out my own net, she was already doing something disgustingly helpful somewhere else. Everyone thought she was so nice and sweet. In the meantime, I was ready to collapse.

At one point, BERnard walked over and nudged me, laughing and saying, 'Mate, the old lady's running circles around you, eh?'

I shrugged. 'I just don't want to make her look bad.'

TO THIS DAY I maintain that whatever 'Mavis' was, she was no old lady. It's more likely that she was some nimble young student from Wairarapa College, perhaps an unusually thin rugby player in drag, wearing a very convincing sweet old lady mask. There is no other possible explanation for why I could not keep up with her that day.

Helen must have seen how tired I was at the end of the day. She offered to pay me the going hourly rate for harvesters.

'Absolutely not,' I said. 'This was my education.'

Knowing how much I love her fennel-infused oil, Helen offered me a bottle and said, 'Well, I hope you'll at least take this.'

She then offered to loan us her equipment for our own harvest.

'Are you sure?' I said.

'Of course! You can borrow my four good nets and as many of my crates as you want. I'm terribly sorry that I can't let you borrow the mechanical rakes, but you can borrow every last hand rake that I have.'

'That's fantastic. Thank you so much.'

'And what about containers for your oil? Do you have enough?'

'Huh?'

'After your olives are pressed, you need containers for the oil.'

I suddenly realised I hadn't thought that part through. 'Can't I just rent them from the press?'

Helen held back a smile. 'For the smaller harvests, you have to take your own. Usually you drop them off when you drop off the olives.'

'Where can I get some?'

'You generally have to order them online. They won't get here in time for your harvest now. Come with me. We'll see what we can do.'

Helen took me to her garage and handed me three containers — two white plastic ones and one larger stainless steel one. 'These are yours,' she said. 'Keep them.'

'No, no. I'll bring them back when we're done.'

'Jared, I have so many of the plastic ones.' She pointed over to a line of them hanging from the ceiling. 'But don't store your oil in the plastic indefinitely. Although it's good food-grade plastic, it can change the taste of the oil if you leave it in too long. And really, the stainless steel one is older and I have new ones I like better. So I don't need it back. It's yours.'

'Seriously? You're just giving me these containers?'

'Thank you for your help today,' she said. 'And good luck with your olive oil.'

That was the moment when I started to think of Helen as the Olive Angel of Olivo. I thanked her several more times before saying goodbye.

When I drove off, Mavis looked up and waved. I was covered in dirt and olive twigs, but Mavis didn't have a smudge on her. She smiled, but I wasn't fooled. Around the edges of that sweet little old lady grin, there was a certain glimmer of victory.

At that point, however, I no longer cared. As I drove away with my new oil containers in the hatchback of our little Nissan Pulsar, I took solace in the fact that, miraculously, CJ and I now had everything we would need for our very own olive harvest.

Chapter 15

The very first harvest

It was a Friday night at the beginning of June — the onset of winter — when the city friends started to arrive. They drove over the Rimutaka Hill Road after work, in the dark, ready to settle in for a three-day weekend full of food, friends, olives, and a lot of hard work.

IT WAS QUEEN'S BIRTHDAY weekend, a colonial throwback holiday which I like very much because it happens to be well timed with the olive harvest. It's a good opportunity to invite the city friends out to help. As always, we would be nowhere without our friends.

There were big hello hugs all round and bags deposited in guest rooms. By then CJ had furnished the entire house on a shoestring budget. He was now known by name in all the best junk shops in the Wairarapa. Only the beds and sofas were new. CJ had polished up some old wooden dressers for the guest bedrooms and transformed some hideously ugly chairs with wonderful new upholstery. He'd also pulled out the old things he'd bought at second-hand markets in Tokyo and placed them around the house next to his Kiwi junk-shop finds. Decorative temple roof tiles looked perfectly at home next to an old wingback chair. Vintage New Zealand pottery from Temuka sat comfortably atop a Japanese chest of drawers from Yamagata.

We'd already listed our place as a B&B with the local tourist information centre, and we'd been having the occasional paying guests on the weekends. It was good meeting guests from around the world and having a little extra cash. Now we experienced another advantage of having those extra bedrooms — housing the harvest gang.

Because CJ and I had just arrived home from work ourselves, that Friday night we fell back into old habits and ordered takeaway for dinner. There is a good Thai restaurant just off the town square called Siam Kitchen, and soon our home was overflowing with talk and laughter and the smell of the best green curry I've ever had. Sitting in the main room under the high wooden ceiling, with a fire burning in the old woodburner, all the excitement and the warmth and those good people gathered around made it feel like Christmas Eve.

We discussed the arrangements for the next day. Everything was set. We'd already borrowed John's ute to pick up the equipment from Helen the Olive Angel of Olivo. Now John's ute was parked in our garage for the night, loaded with yellow hand rakes and orange crates and green nets. Because olives need to be pressed within 24 hours after harvest, I'd already booked us in at the local olive press. Our new hand-me-down olive oil containers were by the door ready to go to the press with the olives. That night we all went to bed early, because we had planned an 8 a.m. start.

City people are not like country people. City people don't spring out of bed at the crack of dawn, ready to tackle hard physical labour. When John knocked on our front door at 8 a.m. sharp, harvest rake in one hand and olive bucket in the other, most of the city friends were still in their pyjamas, mumbling incomprehensibly over steaming cups of coffee.

'Oh,' John said, looking genuinely surprised. 'I thought you'd already be in the grove working.'

CJ backed John's ute out of the garage and drove down to the grove. I walked down with John. The morning light was shining at a low angle from behind the tall macrocarpas, throwing long shadows and patches of light across the olive trees. The grass in the grove was freshly mown. The dew sparkled.

John looked up at the clear, bright sky. 'Good day for an olive harvest.'

Slowly the city friends stumbled down from the house, and it wasn't long before we had the ute unloaded and the nets laid down under the first set of trees. Everyone gathered around and started combing branches with the small yellow hand rakes. Olives began falling at our feet — small thumps against the nets in the still morning quiet.

Even with 10 of us, hand-harvesting with tiny rakes was a slow, fiddly business. We moved as quickly as possible at such an early hour. John, armed with his early morning country constitution, moved the fastest. When the nets were full, we gathered them up the way I'd learned at Helen's, pouring the olives into the crates and stacking the crates at the olive grove gate.

At one point I paused and looked around the grove. I saw people working together in twos and threes, talking as they harvested. John was laughing with one of the city friends. I stood still for a moment — looking out at all those good people there in our olive grove, hearing their quiet morning chatter, seeing CJ as he reached out towards a particularly hard-to-reach branch to get just a few more precious olives — and suddenly, from a place very deep inside of me, there rose an overwhelming sense of gratitude. This was my life. Here. In New Zealand. With an olive grove full of trees and kind-hearted people. It was good.

Eventually I turned and went back to work. The sun rose gradually behind the macrocarpas. The dew burned off the grass. The olives continued to fall.

AT 10:30 JOHN SAID, 'What about morning tea?'

I realised then that I'd forgotten something very, very important.

New Zealanders have not only carried on the British tradition of tea, but it seems to me they've added to it with their own 'down-home' touch. A good Kiwi morning tea is one of the many things about New Zealand that I love.

'I didn't think about morning tea,' I admitted.

John laughed. 'Well, you must have *something* for morning tea.'

I quickly went up to the house, made a pot of coffee and a pot of tea, and rustled up a few packets of 'biscuits' — which have no connection whatsoever to American biscuits but really are *cookies*. We had Tim Tams and a half-empty packet of gluten-free ginger nuts. I brought everything down to the grove in an old cardboard box and we stood in the mid-morning light at the back of John's ute, eating biscuits and holding steaming paper cups in our hands. It was a basic morning tea, but it sufficed. Afterwards, we went back to the olives re-energised.

We ate lunch when the sun was directly overhead. It was a simple meal: pumpkin soup in the crock pot up at the house, loaves of crusty bread around the table.

The afternoon passed quickly, and we finally stopped working for good around 4 p.m. We'd harvested 90 or so trees by then, concentrating on the Frantoio and Leccino because they had the most fruit. Stacked at the edge of the grove were 14 bright orange crates full of purple and green and straw-coloured olives. They looked magical. We piled the crates on the back of John's ute and headed off to the olive press. Everyone wanted to go, so we made a convoy of cars full of eager, enthusiastic harvesters.

The Martinborough olive press is one street away from the town square, behind an ornate metal gate and a beautiful stone wall. A small white sign says *Pressing Engagements* in green letters. We were greeted by Diane, who owns the press. She's a tiny, hard-working woman with a gentle voice. She works furiously throughout May and June, then things go quiet for the olive presses of the Wairarapa valley.

We quickly unloaded the crates off the back of the ute and stacked them on top of a large, flat scale. Then Diane subtracted the weight of the crates. We were stunned to learn that we had a total of 193 kilograms of olives. CJ and I posed for a picture next to our crop, like proud parents.

Diane's press is a noisy green-and-silver beast in the middle of a special climate-controlled room. It was shipped directly from Italy, and the small metal plates on the side are etched in Italian. She invited us into the room and showed us how it works. First it washes the olives and blows out any stray twigs and leaves. Then it crushes the olives — pits and flesh and all — into a paste, which is churned and mixed before being passed into a centrifuge. Finally the paste is spun, and it magically separates according to its different densities. Water goes out one way, the solid sludge goes out another, and the precious oil comes trickling down a stainless steel spout, all by itself.

Diane was still pressing someone else's fruit then and it was in the churning stage, so no oil was coming out at that moment. She said, 'Your oil should be ready tomorrow morning. I'll call you when it's done.'

'Can you call when our oil starts coming out?' I asked.

She smiled. 'Sure.'

Our convoy headed home and I did something for the first time that night. I put a roast lamb in the oven for dinner, poked full of holes and stuffed with rosemary and garlic, then drizzled with store-bought extra virgin olive oil. CJ chopped up potatoes, carrots and kumara into rough pieces and sprinkled them with fresh ground pepper, rock salt, and more olive oil before sliding them into the oven.

'Next time we use olive oil,' he said, 'it'll be our own.'

We had a long, slow meal. John and Aussie Bronwyn joined us. They brought nibbles, and the city friends made several salads. It all turned out perfectly, and everyone said my first roast lamb was delicious. I felt inordinately proud. We sat talking at the table until late into the night and emptied several bottles of beautiful pinot noir from Martinborough Vineyard. Our city friend Anne had brought a gluten-free almond-orange cake for dessert, which was absolute heaven. We ended the meal with fennel tea.

THE NEXT DAY, we were actually playing tag in the olive grove like children when my cellphone rang. It was Diane.

'Your oil has just started coming out of the press now,' she said, her gentle voice competing with the laughter around me in the olive grove.

'The oil is coming!' I yelled out to everyone hiding in the grove. 'The oil is coming!'

We ran up to the house and piled into cars and drove directly to the press.

Suddenly there we were, all of us huddled together at the side of the green-and-silver beast, watching our oil trickling out the silver spout and down into our container. It was a rich, greenish yellow.

'It'll be a couple of hours before it's finished being pressed,' Diane said.

I had brought with me a clear glass jar. I slid it under the spout and watched it slowly fill. But when I pulled it away, I was dismayed. Something was wrong with our oil. It was all murky and cloudy. It looked like *dirty* olive oil.

'Diane, what's wrong?' I said. 'It's not clear.'

She smiled. 'It's fine. That's how olive oil looks straight out of the press. That's why the spouts on your containers are an inch or so above the bottom. You have to leave the container at room temperature for six weeks. The sediment settles and you drain off the clear oil.'

'So it's okay?'

'It's perfect.'

'Can we taste it now?'

'Absolutely. It'll be amazing.'

Standing there holding that clear glass jar full of our just-pressed oil, I remembered what Helen the Olive Angel had said the day I helped her harvest.

'Most supermarket oil is rancid,' she had told me. She was walking me through her grove, pointing out the different trees. 'You don't know where supermarket oil comes from or when it was pressed. It's often five, six years old. Horrible.' She visibly shuddered. The light was streaming through her trees. 'The Italians call freshly pressed oil *olio nuovo* — new oil. They have special festivals for it, and special recipes. They celebrate it. If you've only ever tasted mass-produced supermarket olive oil, I'm sorry to say that you've never really tasted olive oil.'

As I stared at the murky richness of the oil in my hand, I didn't yet know that when our pressing was finished we would have 31 litres of it in total, with an overall yield of 16 per cent, which was good.

But I did know, because I could see very plainly, that the olive oil inside that small jar bore no resemblance at all to the mass-produced supermarket oil I'd known my entire life. This was a different creature entirely. This was the real deal.

IT HAD TAKEN MORE than just the weekend to produce it. It had taken years, and it had taken the work of more people than I could count. It went far beyond CJ and me struggling with the Grass and Sucker Project over the summer. This oil went back to Priscilla, who had planted those olive trees with a husband who had since passed away. It went back to John, who had helped Priscilla plant that grove and had helped her and her husband harvest, just as he'd helped CJ and me.

And it went back to the city friends, gathered around us now. They were passing the glass jar back and forth and oo-ing and ahh-ing at its glowing green contents. This oil went back also to Helen the Olive Angel of Olivo, who had so generously loaned us her equipment. Yes, this small glass jar of olive oil held an entire community. It contained multitudes.

'Let's taste it now,' CJ said, and everyone yelled 'Yes!' Suddenly we were savages, dipping our fingers into the jar and licking the oil off our skin.

When it touched my tongue, it was even stronger than I'd expected. It was more full and rich, and somehow it completely occupied my entire mouth. I tasted grassy opening notes, a mild and fruity middle, then a slow delay before finishing in a strong and peppery bang at the back of my throat. Diane was right. It was amazing.

As the jar went around again in the chaos of everyone reaching and dipping another finger in, CJ and I glanced over at each other for just a quick moment. There was no need to say a thing. We both broke into large, triumphant grins.

The
Seco
Yea

ond

Chapter 16

Old Man Henry and the Chook House Race Wars

By the time spring arrived in our second year, CJ and I had become the somewhat hesitant owners of a geriatric rooster we called Old Man Henry. He was mangy and decrepit. The feathers on his head were just quill stubble. He was half-blind and bow-legged, and he paused strangely after every step.

ON CERTAIN MISTY MORNINGS, when the light was right, he looked as though he'd stepped out of some twisted chicken fancier's version of *Dawn of the Dead*. Yet that unlikely old man was a Nobel Peace Prize winner among poultry. And it was by peacekeeping that he earned his keep.

I had decided over the winter that I wanted hens. Not just any hens. I'd read about a breed called Araucana — an old South American breed that lays pale blue eggs. Blue eggs! How fantastic! I imagined a bowl of farm-fresh, blue eggs on the kitchen counter as I chopped veggies for omelettes on a Sunday morning.

The only place we had for poultry was the old, rotting chook house. It was up near the house, just on the other side of the Granny Smith apple tree. You could see it from our bedroom window. Priscilla used to keep free-range chooks there. She'd mentioned once that the hens used to get up on the deck in front of the bedroom and poop on it.

I was, and still am, a city boy at heart, and didn't think I could handle chickens living that close to me. We moved the chook house out into the top paddock next to the hay shed. The city friends graciously helped us to heave and roll it there one sunny winter weekend when they were out visiting. Afterwards they began calling themselves the 'Communist Egg Collective' and demanding fresh farm eggs from any future chickens in return for their labour.

Next, CJ hired Fred, the local builder who helped take down our wall, to build us a large chicken run. CJ told me they did it together, although I suspected that CJ held nails and pointed while Fred, who is an experienced builder, built us the run.

After all, it was going to house not just *any* chickens. It was not just *any* chicken run. It was a fortress. To stop rats and stoats from burrowing in, Fred sealed off the floor of the chook house with chicken wire, and around the chicken run he buried corrugated aluminium a foot deep into the ground. To make the chook house watertight, he reclad it from top to bottom in new plywood. To stop any hawks from swooping down and carrying off chickens — which has been known to happen — he covered the top and sides of the run with a pergola of massive boards and sturdy chicken wire.

'It's pest-proof!' Fred said proudly when it was done, and then he gave us the bill. I have no doubt that it was the most expensive chicken run in the history of the Wairarapa. We dubbed it the 'Chicken Palace'. When Aussie Bronwyn saw it, however, her free-range sensibilities were offended and she began calling it the 'Chicken Penitentiary'.

It was then that I learned my blue-egg-laying Araucana were hard to find, so I got myself put on a waiting list with a breeder online. It would be weeks and weeks before they'd arrive. But I wanted hens, and I wanted them now. So I hopped in the car and drove to a local, no-nonsense breeder, where I purchased our first two young hens — the sisters we named Henrietta and Ethel.

At that point I had no plans to get a rooster. I didn't want to deal with baby chicks hatching left and right, and I had nightmarish visions of cracking open an egg for breakfast to find a half-formed foetus inside.

Henrietta and Ethel were sizable chooks of a breed called Light Sussex, which are white with a black ring around the neck. They ate voraciously, and very quickly after arriving they grew thick and plump. CJ began calling them 'the Fat English Ladies'.

They lived together in peace for all of two days. Then they turned their backs on sisterly love and started doing what chickens do. They began the Battle for Ultimate Chicken Supremacy.

It was bizarre. In the middle of pecking peacefully, suddenly one would lift her head and run full-speed straight at the other. Then they'd both start squawking, stretching out their necks to full length, and flapping their wings wildly. Imagine two sumo wrestlers in chicken suits, trying to push each other over, and you get the picture.

CJ and I watched all this with great curiosity, wondering which of the Fat English Ladies would win the contest and become Queen of the Whole Wide Coop. Who needs reality TV when you've got chickens?

SHORTLY AFTER THE INFIGHTING started, our two Lavender Araucana were delivered on the 'Pet Bus', which travels up and down the North Island. (I am not making this up.) We named them Natasha and Françoise. They were all-grey, with an upright, noble posture and tufted feathers on their heads. Araucana chickens are much smaller than the Light Sussex, yet what they lack in size they seem to make up for with a kind of haughty demeanour.

The Fat English Ladies did not like the aristocratic South Americans at all.

Suddenly Henrietta and Ethel were brought back together by their common foe. You could almost hear them whispering to each other over by the water dispenser in the corner: 'Truce, sister. United we stand. Divided we fall. Now let's kick their puny South American asses.'

The gloves were on, and the beaks were out. The Great Chook House Race War had begun. The Fat English Ladies used their size to their advantage. They bullied and harassed. They chased. They pecked. Then, in a clever tactical move, they refused to let the invading South Americans eat. Every time the Araucanas tried to get at the chicken feed, the Light Sussex would chase them away. It happened over and over, even when the Light Sussex themselves were not actually eating. Eventually those poor South Americans resigned themselves to taking food by stealth, when the enemy's back was turned.

The Fat English Ladies were winning the war. You could see

them practically high-fiving each other back in their corner, where they had hatched all those wicked plans.

AROUND THIS TIME OUR NEIGHBOUR Suzanne stopped by; our neighbours were still in the habit of checking on the inept city boys from time to time, just to make sure we hadn't killed ourselves falling down our well or trying to chainsaw something. CJ and I took Suzanne out to see the new chicken run and meet the hens. The inspection over, the conversation turned to the topic of how much the birds were fighting.

'You need a rooster,' Suzanne said. Her golden earrings sparkled in the sun and her gumboots glistened with dew.

Several other people had already told me we needed a rooster. I wasn't listening. I was still haunted by visions of half-formed foetuses in my scrambled eggs. Hens still lay eggs without a rooster, but the eggs are thankfully infertile. Nevertheless, several people had told me that roosters calm hens, make them fight less because the rooster is unquestionably the top bird.

'I don't know,' I said to Suzanne. 'It strikes me as somehow sexist to think that hens need a rooster to keep them in line.'

Suzanne looked at me strangely. 'Jared, they're chooks. They're not *human*.'

Oh, yeah. Right. Clearly I was forgetting that.

'I have got just the rooster for you,' she said, and she told us about Henry.

Henry was originally Suzanne's daughter's rooster, and he'd been in the family for years. She couldn't remember his age exactly, but he was old. He'd had hens to keep him company in his younger days, but recently the last hen had died. Of the entire family flock, only Henry remained.

Now he spent all his days alone. Lately he'd begun sleeping right up by the house, just outside the back door. Suzanne would come out and see him there in the morning. She'd been trying to find a home for him for some time, where he could be surrounded by his own kind.

'Nobody wants him,' she said. 'Everyone tells me I should turn him into soup, but I just can't do it. Besides, he'd be as tough as old boots.'

I was touched by Henry's geriatric solitude, but I remained firm. 'I'm sorry. We can't take him. We really don't want baby chicks.'

Suzanne smiled. 'Oh, Henry is far too old to cause you that problem. No worries there.'

That clinched the deal. We agreed to take him on a trial basis. If he became hen-pecked, or if we decided we didn't want him for any reason whatsoever, including miraculous impregnation of our hens, she'd take him back.

In hindsight I think Suzanne must have been incredibly happy to get rid of the Rooster That Wouldn't Die. She went right home that minute and came back with him, along with a bag of his favourite poultry wheat.

When she set Henry down in our chicken run, the old man looked around and blinked. All the hens, suddenly struck shy, stood back and watched. Henry took a couple of unsteady steps. He saw the young ladies eyeing him. And then a miraculous thing happened: Henry started to dance. He held his mangy tail feathers up high, stuck out his wimpy chest, spread out one tattered wing, and did his best 'I'm a sexy rooster' strut.

Henry is half bantam, which means he's small — almost half the size of the Fat English Ladies — and of course he's incredibly feeble, but that didn't matter. He was thrilled to suddenly find himself in the middle of a young harem of his very own. Henry, it turns out, is the poultry equivalent of a dirty old man.

The young ladies continued to watch, and Henry, perhaps feeling a little too confident, continued his dance with a somewhat difficult turn. And fell flat on his face. It broke my heart. The old man was so humiliated, he never attempted that sexy rooster dance again.

WITHIN A COUPLE OF DAYS CJ and I noticed that the hens had stopped fighting. Sure, they had their odd pecks at each other here and there, but for the most part they seemed to co-exist peacefully.

A week passed, and then another. The spring rains came. The chicken battles never happened again. The South Americans no longer had to resort to guerrilla tactics to get food. The Great Chook House Race War was over.

Henry was never hen-pecked. He was too crotchety and aggressive for that. While he may have been slow, at close range he could still pack a serious peck. From time to time he used that peck to remind the hens that 'he still da man' — even if he was impotent and too old to dance.

He did struggle, and some days were clearly more difficult than others. Every so often Henrietta and Ethel would push him out of the way to get at the special treats I brought. Sometimes his tail feathers would drag in the dirt behind him, as though they were just too heavy to hold up anymore. Once I saw him with a clump of mud stuck on the side of his head.

One day he suddenly looked so haggard and so much more decrepit than usual that I was sure he wouldn't make it to the end of the week. But he bounced back.

The average lifespan of a hen is about eight years, although in extreme cases they've been known to live 12 to 15 years. I figured Henry must be at least 108.

He got special care. He was too frail to make it up to the high perches in the chook house to sleep, so I built an especially low senior citizen's perch just for him. I knew that one day I would come out to find Henry dead. But until then, CJ and I were happy to have Henry be our peacemaker. We liked knowing that in his final days, at least the old bird was no longer alone.

Chapter 17

Island
Martinborough

'**T**he sign says the bridge is closed. Should we get closer and see?' the bus driver called out.

THERE WERE SEVEN OR eight Martinborough commuters in the back of the bus. We were on our way home from work, riding the bus from Featherston on a Monday evening. Everyone nodded or called out a hearty 'yes', and we drove on toward the possibly washed-out bridge. CJ, who was sitting next to me, reached over and squeezed my knee.

The residents of Martinborough are used to the Ruamahanga River flooding. It happens at least once a year. When the river is very high, the aging Waihenga Bridge is closed for safety. The piles supporting the bridge are shallow and risk collapsing under the force of raging waters. If the flood's not too bad, the Waihenga Bridge stays open, but State Highway 53 sometimes becomes submerged at a place in the road the locals call Jenkin's Dip. If that happens, there's a little one-lane emergency bridge you can drive over to get past Jenkin's Dip. There's never a dull moment around here, at least not during the spring rains.

As we drove forward, some passengers craned their necks to see what was up ahead. Like CJ and me, most of the people on that bus lived in Martinborough and worked in Wellington. Over time, we'd learned small details about each other. This one owned an olive grove. That one owned a vineyard. Another one lived on a massive farm out past Hinakura, toward the coast.

The camaraderie we shared made it feel more like a school bus than public transport. I had come to feel a real fondness for the group, for the way we happily took up that commute together. Here was a collection of people with one foot in the city and one foot in paradise. (Although even in paradise rivers flood.)

By then, CJ and I knew the commute home well — the 55-minute train ride from Wellington to Featherston, and then the 20-minute bus ride from Featherston to Martinborough. Trains don't go to little, out-of-the-way Martinborough.

Now the bus pulled up to the T in the road that has a panoramic view out over Martinborough's hill-rimmed basin, and the driver chuckled. His name was Graham. In the country you know the bus driver's name.

'You think he'll let us past?' Graham said.

There was a large truck blocking the road down to the village, and a red sign with *Road ahead closed* written across it.

'Tell him we live just down the road!' somebody shouted from the back of the bus, laughing.

Graham rolled down his window. A man in a bright yellow safety vest stood nearby.

'Will she open up soon?' Graham said, nodding in the direction of the bridge.

'Well, if you want to wait,' the man said. 'The river's supposed to peak around nine tonight.'

It was not quite six o'clock then. Only out in the country would waiting in a bus for over three hours while the river dropped be seen as a viable option.

'Hmm,' Graham said, as though he were considering it. 'Need to get these people home. Thanks, mate.' Then he turned the bus in the opposite direction.

ALTHOUGH MARTINBOROUGH WAS JUST five minutes down the road, the river was in the way and we now had an hour's drive ahead of us. We were going further north, out towards Carterton, where the land is a bit higher. You can usually head back into Martinborough on dry land.

'Make yourselves comfortable, people,' Graham said. There were calls on cellphones to tell loved ones we'd be late.

When the rains are really bad, Martinborough can virtually become an island. Even the back way floods. In the middle of the previous winter, there had been such a bad rainstorm that in the morning the bridge out of town was out, the mountain road over the Rimutakas was closed, and the trains were down because one train had actually been derailed by what the Kiwis call a 'slip' (which is an understated way to say 'landslide'). Needless to say, I hadn't made it to work that day.

As Graham drove the bus, I looked out the window at the pastures and hills rolling by. I turned around and chatted with Jim the Mad Welshman, who was sitting behind us. He asked how our well was doing and told us about his latest do-it-yourself project, renovating his kitchen. He needed a hand that weekend carrying in some cupboards, so CJ and I offered to help. We told him about the gardening work we wanted to do, and our plans for putting in another flower bed. It was a nice, neighbourly chat. There are worse ways to pass the time.

We who take the bus never ask each other if we think the commute is worth it. We all know it is — in spite of the spring rains, the road closures, the occasional derailed train. This gives you some indication of how great it is to live out here. It would have to be pretty incredible to make up for all that.

When the bus finally pulled into Martinborough, everyone was relieved. CJ and I got out at the little grey stone church, where we all park our cars in the mornings.

'Thanks, Graham,' I said as I stepped down off the bus behind CJ. I meant it. I appreciated him getting me home safely.

'See you tomorrow, mate,' he said. Then the bus door closed behind us, and Graham drove away.

Chapter 18

A strange morning at the chicken run

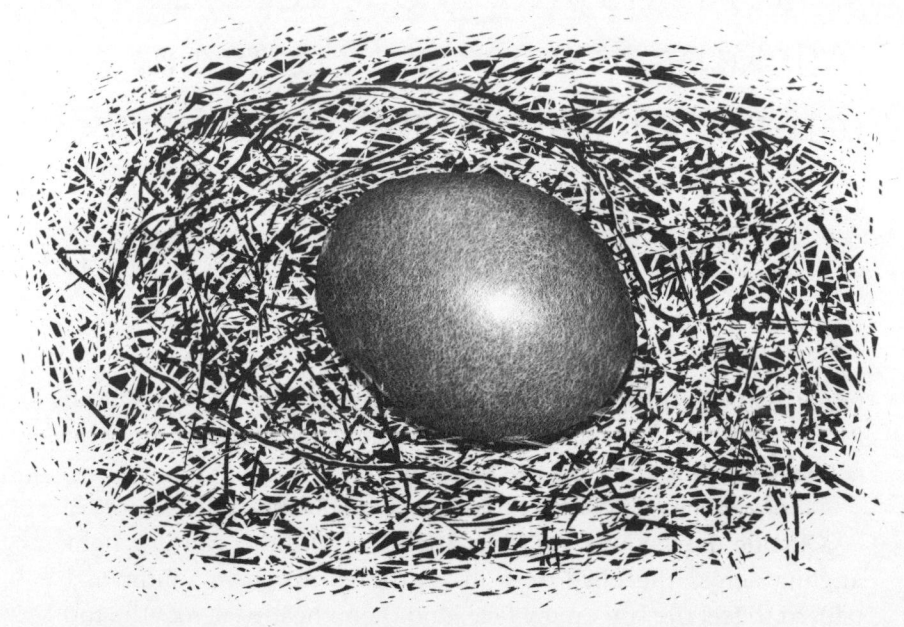

It took a long time before I became used to the routine of having hens. There had been no farm-fresh eggs in my life growing up in suburban Detroit. There were no hens on the back porch overlooking the alley in my Chicago apartment.

On one particular lazy Saturday morning in October, it was already 10.30 a.m. by the time I remembered to feed the chickens. It was as if I'd had a temporary brain blip, and for a moment I forgot I was living on a tiny olive farm in New Zealand.

I RAN TO THE REFRIGERATOR to get a special treat I'd been saving for the chooks. CJ saw me and said, 'You're so late. By they time you get out there, the chickens will be dead.'

I took out a small plastic container. 'Don't be horrible.'

Outside the day was gorgeous and clear, and the morning light angling across the olive trees made the entire grove shimmer. I paused to feel the sun on my face, and then I headed across the top paddock and toward the Chicken Palace. Our hens were still young. For all the entertainment they'd given us, they still hadn't offered us a single egg.

Henrietta began running frantically back and forth as I approached. She always made a fuss when she saw me coming with the red chicken-feed bucket. She was a total glutton and just couldn't wait for the food. Her especially loud clucks that day reprimanded me for being late.

The metal latch on the gate to the chicken run was cool in my hand as I opened the door and stepped inside. When I leaned down, Henrietta came right over. Standing quietly nearby was Henry, along with his young harem ladies, Ethel and Natasha. Suddenly I realised there were only four chickens. One was missing. It was one of the grey Araucanas, little Françoise. Where was she? I called out to her. She didn't come.

Many city folk don't know that flocks of chickens live in an established hierarchy. This is where the phrase 'pecking order' comes from. The rooster is the dominant one, or the village bully depending on how you look at it. As for hens, I learned in Alice Stern's *Poultry and Poultry Keeping* (picked up second-hand at the Martinborough Fair), 'The larger a hen's comb is — i.e. the more "masculine" she is — the more she will be feared by others.' So it's a bit like a lesbian biker bar.

Our poor little Françoise has always been the lowest on the totem pole. She's got a small body and a dainty little comb on top of her feather-tufted Araucana head. Even after the Chook House Race War was over, she would never go near the other chickens while they were eating (except for her sister, Natasha), or she would get pecked.

I called out again. 'Here chook-chook-chook!' But Françoise was still nowhere to be seen. She *had* to be in the chook house. She'd come out as soon as the feeding started. At least that's what I hoped. I opened the small plastic container that held their special treat. The luncheon ham we buy has a beautiful line of fat around the edges. I always trim this off and save it in the fridge until the weekend. The chickens love ham fat as they would a juicy worm, and when the ham fat comes out, the chook house goes mad.

Henrietta stepped even closer. She's the only one courageous enough, or perhaps greedy enough, to eat directly from my hand. Henry saw she was getting ham fat and wobbled over. He's a cantankerous, disagreeable old man. He waited for Henrietta to take the fat from my hand, then he promptly stole it from her mouth.

I started tossing bits out to the other birds, so Henry wouldn't get it all. Feathers fluttered and chickens were running everywhere, racing toward the ham fat that was falling from the sky. But all this commotion still didn't manage to bring little Françoise out of the chook house. Never had one of them not come out of the chook house at feeding time — especially when Saturday-morning ham fat was involved.

I had heard tales of small, sickly chickens being pecked to death. Was Françoise okay? Had the recent cold got the better of her? Or maybe it was my fault. Had my late feeding time sent her into something like a diabetic chicken coma?

I tossed down the rest of the ham fat and the chicken feed and stepped out of the run, heading over to the door to the chook house. I opened it and looked in. After the brightness of the sun it was extremely dark inside, and I squinted. The perch where Françoise has always slept was empty.

I stuck my head further in the doorway and looked at the hay-covered ground. She was nowhere. I looked back out into the chicken run. No, she definitely wasn't there. Finally, I opened the lid to the nesting box, and there she was. But she wasn't moving. Was she dead? Leaning down more closely, I saw that she was actually breathing in short, sharp breaths. It looked like she was in pain. I'd never seen one of our chickens do that, ever.

THE WEEKEND BEFORE I had stood in Aussie Bronwyn's backyard, watching as her multitude of hens milled at her feet. I was there out of frustration. After all that time spent caring for our own chickens I had become annoyed that we still didn't have any eggs. I had called Aussie Bronwyn to ask for advice.

Aussie Bronwyn and John are almost entirely self-sufficient. Theirs is the only house I've ever been to where I've had an amazing high tea with home-made scones made with fresh farm eggs, home-made jam straight from the strawberry patch outside, and home-made cream from the cow out back. (The cow's name is Blossom.)

'Why don't we have any eggs?' I asked Aussie Bronwyn as her chickens ran around at our feet.

'Your chickens are still relatively young,' she said. 'That wet southerly that went through not long ago may have chilled them a bit too much and put them off the lay for a bit longer. You may not get eggs until summer.'

She knows these things. She's lived on farms most of her life. I quietly resigned myself to an eggless spring. But now, as I looked down at Françoise in the nesting box, I figured there were only two possible explanations for the odd behaviour. Either our precious Araucana chook was seriously sick and dying, or she was laying an egg.

I decided to give the poor little girl her privacy and check back in half an hour. Either there would be an egg, or Françoise would be dead. When I returned later, I made CJ come with me just in case. I didn't really know what to do with a dead chicken. But as we walked up to the chook house, I saw little Françoise out in the middle of the run, pecking hungrily at the ground. I lifted the lid to the nesting box. There, in front of my eyes, was the most amazing egg I have ever seen.

'An egg!' I yelled. It was like a tiny miracle, and I was thrilled. But there was something wrong. It wasn't blue. It was green!

I didn't care. After all, it was a miracle, and it was beautiful just the same. It was the most amazing shade of pale, chalky green. I was so proud of little Françoise. She might be the smallest of our chooks, and at the bottom of the pecking order, but she was the first to give us an egg. 'Thank you, Françoise,' I said.

CJ reached down and touched the egg. 'Eeew!' he said. 'It's warm! It came out of her body.' He pointed accusingly at Françoise.

'Duh,' I said. 'Did you think eggs came from a box in the grocery store?'

CJ didn't answer. He just scrunched up his nose and stepped back. Somehow the reality of being faced with a warm, farm-fresh egg was too much for him. He has eaten eggs his entire life, and he loves meat and dairy more than most people. But suddenly he was acting like a newly converted vegetarian who'd just seen the abattoir.

'I'm not eating that,' he said, and then made loud retching sounds.

I laughed. 'You're crazy.'

'You eat it,' he said. 'Not me.'

And that was it for CJ. For the next two weeks, Françoise gave us six more eggs, about one every other day. CJ didn't touch a single one.

Trouble in the olive grove

Spring in the olive grove. The peace I felt the first time I saw those trees is still there, every time I look at them. There's no problem that a stroll through the olive grove won't make better.

Left — One of the Fat English Ladies slipping into the chook house.

Below — Fresh eggs from our chooks: light brown from the Fat English Ladies, pale blue from the aristocratic South Americans, and dark brown from the surly Barnevelder Sisters.

Above — Old Man Henry alone. The poor old bird had trouble keeping up with the sprightly young ladies. He was sometimes left behind.

Right — Ethel on the left and her two adopted daughters, the Barnevelder Sisters, on the right. Ethel was a very protective mother when those girls were chicks.

The beautiful Martinborough basin is a giant, hill-encircled bowl with a dot of a village in the middle. It's home to boutique vineyards and olive groves, and beef, dairy, and sheep farms.

Standing at the town square and looking towards the Martinborough Wine Centre, which is the red building. The Wine Centre was the very first store to carry our Moon over Martinborough olive oil.

Native grasses in front of the house and the wisteria-covered pergola over the front deck. In summer that deck becomes another room. We live out there.

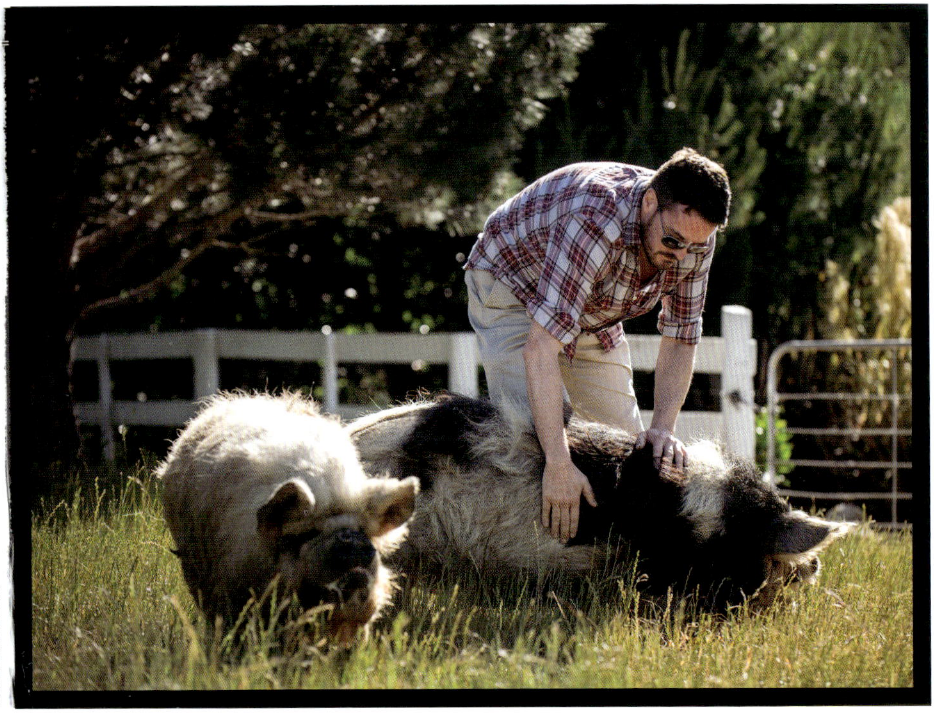

MIKE HEYDON

MIKE HEYDON

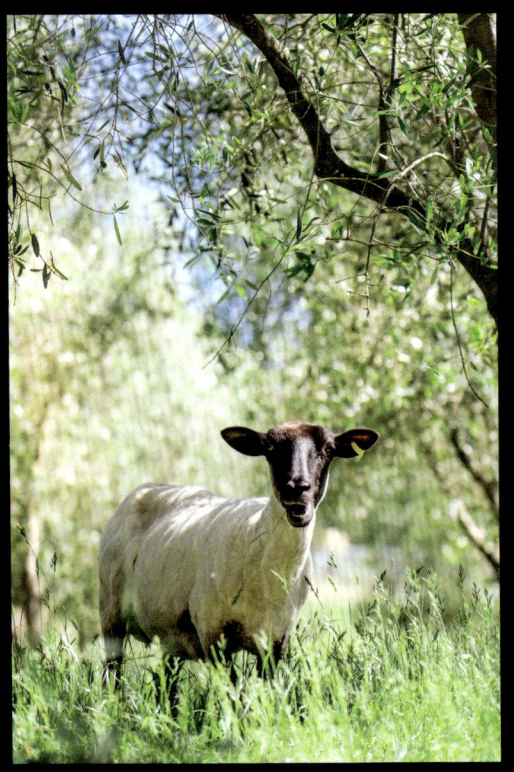

Above — Here I am patting Dougal the Dim-witted Eunuch. His sultry sister, Mrs D, is on the left. Although I was reluctant to have kunekune pigs as pets, I've grown incredibly fond of them.

Left — Instead of using nasty chemicals to keep the grass down around the base of the olive trees (a common practice in commercial groves), we use sheep. This is Bonnie, twin sister to Clyde.

A

fter our first olive harvest, we made a mistake. We relaxed. It's important to know that if you ever move to the country, you should never, ever relax.

IT WASN'T LONG BEFORE all 500 of our olive trees were once again covered with those nasty, energy-draining suckers. On top of that, although CJ had mowed the grove twice during the winter (and made his famous 'improvements' to Sunshine), we were again looking at 500 squares of long, unruly grass at the base of each tree, where Sunshine couldn't reach.

This time we knew what to do. We pulled out the line trimmer and the secateurs and started up Grass and Sucker Project, Round Two. By then we'd heard that most commercial groves spray the herbicide Roundup under their trees to kill the grass and make maintenance easer. But CJ and I didn't like the idea of spraying a toxic chemical beneath our trees. So, as before, we used the line trimmer on the grass that grew under the branches. And we wielded the secateurs on the tender green suckers that grew up from the trunks.

We'd never quite got around to doing the proper pruning John told us we needed to do the last time we'd cleared the grove of grass and suckers. We'd been reading books about pruning, and I'd even taken the bold step of attending a pruning demonstration sponsored by the Wairarapa chapter of Olives New Zealand. But neither CJ nor I had yet found time to lift a saw to even one neglected tree.

They say that if an olive tree is pruned correctly, a bird should be able to fly through it. You need to open up the interior of the tree to air and sunlight, in order to encourage olive growth. Our trees were so dense that a bird would have had more chance of flying through a brick wall.

CJ and I both found the Grass and Sucker Project easier the second time. Either we'd become used to living in a constant state of exhaustion, or we didn't get as tired. I'm not sure which. Regardless, what had taken us all summer to do our first year now took only four solid weekends of intense work. It was November, late spring, and the sun around the olive trees was warm and comforting. The grove felt like a magical, sheltered place — part hedge maze, part grassy meadow, and part tree-lined reserve. Yet as CJ and I moved from tree to tree eradicating the long grass and evil suckers, I began to realise that something wasn't quite right in the olive grove.

By that time I knew a handful of other olive growers in Martinborough, and every time I bumped into one — crossing the town square or picking up a bottle of pinot at the Wine Centre — I heard stories about how prolific the flower buds were in every single grove in Martinborough that year. That is, every grove except one. Ours. Our trees had no flower buds at all.

Olive trees are wind pollinated, and in Martinborough the olive blossoms start forming in November and open up into small white flowers in early December. John had told me that when the blossoms started opening we needed about 10 good dry days with moderate wind in order to get a good fruit set. If there was too much wind or too little, or if it rained, then we wouldn't get the pollination we needed, which meant we wouldn't get the olives we wanted. But even the best weather couldn't pollinate a tree if there were no flowers.

When I mentioned the lack of flower buds on our trees to CJ, he said, 'Maybe our grove just blooms later than other groves.'

'Hmm. Maybe,' I said. I decided to wait and see, but each time I looked at our budless wonders I felt a strange, sinking dread.

Shortly after we'd finished Round Two of the Grass and Sucker Project, I left CJ at home alone for an entire Saturday afternoon. This is never a good idea. When I got home that day he was walking up to the house from the olive grove, pruning saw in hand.

'I started pruning the grove,' he said.

'Oh. Really?' I knew that CJ had only skimmed the pruning books, and he certainly hadn't attended the demonstration I'd gone to, so suffice it to say that I wasn't entirely convinced he knew what he was doing. Add to this the disturbing fact that over the past year I'd seen a fair amount of what CJ had called 'pruning' in our garden. Over and over again I'd seen him — diligently and with much passion — turning beautiful shrubs, rose bushes and entire trees into pathetic, withered stumps.

'Um, how many trees did you, ah, "prune",' I asked him, looking out at the grove. I was relieved to see that the trees were still there.

CJ seemed to mistake the worried look on my face for excitement. 'Isn't it great?' he said. 'I did one whole row. Let me show you.'

We immediately walked down to the olive grove together. As we approached the gate, I could see no obvious damage. Maybe it was okay.

'My row's in the middle,' CJ said proudly. 'Over here.'

We wandered over to CJ's row, and my heart sank. Where there once had stood a regal row of lush, green olive trees, there now stood a long, thin line of post-apocalyptic toothpicks.

I tried not to look shocked. 'Well, ah, don't you think you pruned them a little hard?'

'No. I did what the book says. I opened them up.'

'CJ, you didn't open them up. You practically chopped them down.'

'What do you mean? They're still standing.'

I had read about the dangers of pruning an olive tree too hard. Doing so shocks the tree and sends it into a juvenile growth state, which means the tree ends up putting all of its energy into growing new branches, at the expense of growing olives. I explained this to CJ. 'I think these trees may go into shock,' I said.

CJ's face went from pride to concern. 'You think I screwed it up?'

I felt terrible, but I said, 'Yeah. I really think so.'

'Oh.'

I tried to lift his spirits. 'Well, at least it's only one row.'

CJ stopped pruning the grove altogether after that, which made me feel even worse.

I continued to watch for flower buds — in CJ's row as well as all the other, unharmed rows — but week after week it was the same story. There were absolutely no flower buds. I couldn't believe it. I wanted to be able to control those trees, to strangle their trunks until they screamed for mercy and started coughing up buds. My sinking dread turned into terrible despair. Were our trees sick?

IN ORDER TO FIND OUT whether something was wrong, that December I took a walk through our grove with Simon Duchamp, another local olive grower. Simon is probably in his late fifties. He's tall and tanned, and keeps in shape by doing most the work in his grove himself. I'm convinced that in another life he was some sort of broad-minded aristocrat — as comfortable in the opera house as he would be working in the fields with the peasants.

It was a hot day and the sky was bright. I reached out and pulled down a branch to show Simon.

'See?' I said. 'Nothing. No buds. No flowers. Nothing.'

Simon frowned and looked down his nose at the disobliging branch. 'Hmm.' Then he glanced up at the shelterbelt trees. 'Where's the prevailing wind?'

I pointed toward a gap in the hills off to one side of our property. 'Over there. South-westerly.'

He turned and walked on, carefully inspecting branches as he went. He hmm-ed and humphed and frowned again and again.

Finally he turned towards me and said, 'I don't know.'

'Huh?' I said.

'Clearly something's not right,' Simon explained. 'But I don't know what.'

I felt a tightening in my chest. If this regal and industrious, olive-growing New Zealander was stumped by what was going on in our grove, it had to be bad.

'Why don't you come by and see my grove tomorrow?' he said. And I did.

The next day I spent about half an hour with Simon. Strolling down the rows of his grove, I couldn't believe how perfect everything looked. His trees were tall and healthy looking, just like him. But it was the flowers that amazed me. There were so many of them — tiny and already opening and creamy white. The entire grove seemed to be obscured by their softly glowing haze.

I noticed that there was no grass growing directly under Simon's trees. He did what many olive growers do. He sprayed Roundup or some other vegetation killer under his trees in long, perfect lines. That way he didn't have to struggle with a line trimmer, as CJ and I had been doing, and he only had to mow in one direction. It looked neat and tidy.

'See,' he said, pulling down a branch and showing me an abundance of flowers. 'This is what your grove should look like. You should have a lot of flowers by now.'

I felt woefully inadequate. There was no softly glowing haze around me.

'Thanks, Simon,' I said.

He rubbed his tanned forehead and ran his fingers through his salt-and-pepper hair. 'I don't know what to tell you, Jared. But something's not right in your grove.'

By the time I left that day, my brain was spinning into a hysterical frenzy of doubt and fear. I imagined all sorts of new and horrible diseases that our grove surely must have. Terminal bud encephalopathy. Cataclysmic biotoxic deflowerment. Our trees would probably never bear fruit again. And the disease would no doubt spread. We were ground zero. The Ministry of Agriculture and Forestry, as it was called back then, would be knocking on our door soon, demanding that we quarantine our grove and burn the entire thing to the ground.

I may have a highly active imagination, but I knew one thing for certain: something was wrong with our trees.

Chapter 20

Chicken blood on my boot

Aussie Bronwyn and I stood outside the Chicken Palace on a warm sunny day. In one hand she held a long pole with a round net on the end, and in the other hand she held a jar of Vaseline. She was limping a little from a recent knee surgery, and I felt bad asking her to walk across the top paddock to our chickens.

'I'M FINE. I'M FINE,' she said, throwing back her shoulders. 'Now, let's get those chooks!' She smiled broadly, as though ready for a battle of epic proportions. Little did I know what an epic battle it would eventually turn out to be.

A few weeks earlier CJ had noticed that something was wrong with one of our chickens. 'Eww,' he said, his voice full of his new-found aversion for the birds. 'Look at that one's legs. They're gross.'

It was Natasha, one of our two Araucana. Françoise, the other Araucana, was strutting around on legs that were smooth and black, but Natasha's legs were bumpy, thick and grey.

'That's just how Natasha's legs look,' I said, apparently forgetting for a moment that I knew absolutely nothing about chickens.

CJ shook his head. 'You should call Aussie Bronwyn. She'll know if it's okay.'

I refused. There was nothing wrong with our chooks. No way. Over the next week I began paying special attention to Natasha. She didn't seem sickly at all, but I had to admit that her legs did look weird. Was something growing on them? Was this normal for a chicken?

Although I still wasn't really worried enough to call Aussie Bronwyn, I decided to do some Internet research just in case. After a couple of searches, I found a reference to 'scaly leg mites', complete with disgusting pictures. The chicken legs in those pictures, I had to admit, looked a bit like Natasha's.

When I told CJ about it, he absolutely beamed. 'See, I told you,' he said. 'I could sense that something was wrong. I'm a chicken whisperer.' Then he adopted some sort of bad Eastern European accent and added, 'Do not underestimate my powers.'

With nothing but Google and a phoney chicken whisperer to turn to, I decided it was finally time to bring in the big guns. I picked up the phone and called Aussie Bronwyn. By then I had come to think of Aussie Bronwyn as something like a High Priestess in the Church of Chicken Wisdom. She wouldn't let me down.

'In all my years,' she said, 'I've not come across scaly leg mites. But I'm happy to come by and take a look. I might learn something.'

'So, your chickens have never had scaly leg mites?' I asked her.

'No. Never. I've never even seen it before.'

I was dumbfounded. There I was with my first flock of hens ever, and I was having to deal with something that not even the neighbourhood Poultry Priestess knew about. It hardly seemed fair. I began to feel that the gods were against CJ and me. Not only were our olive trees dying, but now our chickens were, well, *infested*.

I told Aussie Bronwyn what I'd learned online about scaly leg mites. They're tiny parasites that get under the scales in chicken legs. They cause the scales to become discoloured and bumpy, and are irritating and painful to the chicken. If left untreated they can spread to the entire flock, and can cause the host chickens to go lame. Once they're lame they starve. An infestation is also difficult to get rid of once it enters a flock.

'Ah, yes,' Bronwyn said. 'Aren't you supposed to treat it with fat?'

I told her that the websites I'd read said you should cover the legs of the chickens with petroleum jelly. It suffocates the mites and they die.

'Of course, you'll have to catch them first,' she said.

'I've never done that before.'

'Oh, that's easy.'

THIS WAS HOW I ENDED UP in the preposterous situation of relying on my retired, limping neighbour to save my chickens from a microscopic parasite.

I opened the gate to the chicken run and put out my hand to help Aussie Bronwyn step over the corrugated metal, rat-proof threshold. She paused for a moment, using the pole on the net as a cane. She was wearing farm clothes: purple track pants and an old sweatshirt. I stepped in behind her. CJ stood outside and watched.

Immediately something spectacular happened. One moment Bronwyn was standing right next to me saying, 'It's that one, isn't it?' and the next moment she was gone. There was an incredible blur of purple and flapping wings and loud squawks. Frenzied chickens darted everywhere.

When the dust and feathers settled, Bronwyn was squatting down on the far side of the chicken run, holding the net down over Natasha, her hand gently on the bird's back. She didn't seem to be pinning the chicken down so much as calming it through her touch. And she was whispering.

'There, there, girl. We're not here to hurt you. It's okay.'

She told me to hold Natasha over the wings as she slowly lifted the net. And suddenly there I was, holding a chicken in my hands. When we had brought them home months before, we just opened the box and they went out, so I'd never actually held one. It seemed amazing that, while I had eaten chicken my entire life, had it roasted and baked and stir-fried, I had never so much as *touched* a live one before.

If you have never had the pleasure of holding a living chicken, I can tell you that they are unbelievably soft and fragile things — like fine china, but with claws. Underneath Natasha's feathers I could feel her tiny heart pounding furiously with fear.

I held on while Bronwyn greased the nasty, bumpy legs. Then she sprinkled flea and mite powder over the feathers. She stroked the bird, working the powder down to the skin. And we were done.

Or so I thought.

When I set down Natasha, Bronwyn said, 'We'll need to treat all of them to stop it spreading.'

I looked around. In the initial flurry of feathers the other four birds had all shot out the chicken run door, which I'd foolishly left open behind me. There were chickens running all over the top paddock.

We then proceeded to run around the top paddock after them. Bronwyn couldn't run very fast, what with her limp and all. CJ and I are able-bodied, but we proved beyond a shadow of a doubt that city boys don't make very good chicken catchers. I couldn't stop laughing long enough to catch anything.

Eventually CJ managed to swoop the net down over Old Man Henry. This isn't really much of an accomplishment, since Henry is so unbelievably decrepit. On several occasions I've seen the worms outrun him. But CJ was proud of having caught Henry, so I didn't mention that.

Bronwyn and I gave Henry the same grease and powder treatment that Natasha had received. By then the remaining three chickens were clearly thinking, 'No way is that happening to me.' They were hiding in the woodpile.

Bronwyn said, 'You might have an easier time of it if you get them back in the Chicken Penitentiary later this evening. You can catch them in there, with the door shut.'

CJ and I invited Bronwyn in for a cup of tea. We chatted together and looked at disgusting chicken leg pictures on the Internet, and then Bronwyn limped off to her car and drove away.

Later that evening, with all the chickens back in the enclosure, I decided it was time to finish the job. CJ had been digging in the garden all day and was in the shower. He was going to make dinner. It was just me out at the chicken run, and three sets of chicken legs that needed to be slathered with Vaseline.

I tried my best to capture those chickens with the same speed and efficiency Aussie Bronwyn had demonstrated. I failed. The chickens went flapping everywhere. I ran in circles after them, penned up inside the chicken run. Fortunately I'd remembered to close the door.

It took forever to catch just one. Finally I caught Ethel, one of the Light Sussex. I held her in one hand and greased her legs and powdered her with the other. It wasn't easy.

I was already exhausted, but I still had two chooks to go. Next I went for Henrietta. She's the only chicken that has ever trusted me enough to eat from my hand, and for that she's become something of a favourite of mine. She's also the dominant hen, and she's by far the most aggressive.

She did not like a net coming down over her at all. She pushed her head against it and struggled vehemently. I tried to place a gentle hand down on her back, as Bronwyn had, but it was like trying to put your hand on the back of a squirming, angry octopus, with wings.

At last I got her in my hands and held her to my chest. That's when I saw that she was bleeding. The comb on top of her head had ripped against the net. Bright red spots of blood were dripping down onto the white feathers of her head. I felt absolutely awful, and cruel, and terribly, terribly inept.

I held her and said I was sorry. I tried to calm her. I don't know how much pain she was in. She seemed stunned. As gently as I could, I greased her legs and powdered her. All the while the blood dripped slowly, very slowly, down her head. When I looked down I saw a drop of her blood on my boot. I was devastated.

I would never make it as a proper farmer. I was born with something like a sensitive artist's heart, not the heart of a no-nonsense agrarian homesteader. I was not built for this. I become too attached, too quickly.

As I was finishing up with the powder on Henrietta, working it down into her feathers as I'd seen Aussie Bronwyn do, Henrietta suddenly flapped her wings, struggled again, and got out of my hands. She stood for a moment on the ground, looking around. It seemed like she would be okay. But I still had one more chicken to go.

It was little Françoise. I liked her too, for her underdog ways. Although she was the smallest of all the hens, at that point she was still the only one who had been providing us with eggs — which had gone from pale green to a nice blue. It took a while for me to catch her. She moved fast, and she kept running behind the others and getting tangled up with them.

When I had her in the net, I got my hands around her and lifted her up, and she let out the most horrible cry I've ever heard a chicken make. It sounded like she had lost a leg. There was a small drop of blood on her beak. Had I hurt her, too? Had I broken her beak? Was I really so bad at this?

I HAVE ALWAYS CONSIDERED myself a Vegetarian Sympathiser. This, I thought, could push me over the edge. I looked at her beak closely. It seemed fine, except for that drop of blood. I greased her legs and powdered her. The blood on her beak didn't drip, didn't flow. I think it must have come from Henrietta, when Françoise was hiding behind her.

Finally I set Françoise down. I stepped out of the chicken run and watched them all for a long time. Henrietta still had fresh blood on her head, but she was walking around and very alert. They all seemed okay.

I cleaned out their bedding, sprinkled the chook house with flea and mite powder, and put in new hay. I wouldn't be able to eat the eggs for a couple days after spreading the powder. CJ still wasn't eating them at all, since he'd discovered the terrible truth about where they come from.

I sighed, knowing that I was going to have to do the Vaseline treatment weekly for an entire month. I was already dreading the next round. But I decided I would make sure I had CJ's help then.

Before I went to bed that night I went back out and checked on all the chooks, but especially Henrietta. The blood on her head was dry, and she was up on her top perch ready for sleep. I left some poultry wheat on the ledge near her, which I used to do when she was little.

She looked afraid as I came near, and she backed away. I wondered if she would ever eat out of my hand again.

Chapter 21

Home for wayward agapanthus

We were officially over-whelmed. We could not handle this property on our own, as well as holding down our full-time jobs. We needed help.

SO WE SIGNED UP as hosts for Help Exchange, or HelpX. It's a volunteer exchange programme in which hosts provide room and board to travellers in exchange for work. Inevitably everyone gets a nice bit of cultural exchange in the process. That spring, our first volunteers came to stay — a Belgian and a Korean.

Right away CJ asked them to do a very special job. 'Dig out these agapanthus, divide them, and plant them in a long row along this line of trees.'

Little did those unsuspecting volunteers know that in doing this work they were contributing to one man's slightly crazed and deeply disturbing obsession. The next day, the Belgian and the Korean began digging.

I never knew what agapanthus were before I moved to New Zealand. They're native to South Africa, and they can't survive the freezing winters in any of the places I've previously called home. They have long, strap-shaped, evergreen leaves and their flowers are big balls of blue or white on top of tall stems. They're incredibly easy to grow. In fact, they have a tendency to spread and sprout up in every nook and cranny imaginable, sometimes actually choking out native species. Because of this, many people in New Zealand consider agapanthus a weed. Not CJ.

In CJ's world, agapanthus are a thing to be revered, treasured and, dare I say it, loved. And I don't mean love as in 'I love choco-late.' For CJ, agapanthus love is a bit more like 'I love my small, helpless child and would cripple and maim anyone who tries to hurt her.'

Except this small child is a plant. And not only is she perfectly capable of surviving a nuclear holocaust with no help from you, but once you bring her into your home she'll start choking all your other darling children and replacing them with freakish alien space pods à la *Invasion of the Body Snatchers*. I've seen what they've done to our hydrangeas.

Some of our friends think I'm joking about CJ's special love of agapanthus. To them I say only this: 'Take a blowtorch to those weeds while CJ is around and see what happens. Go on. I dare you.' So far, nobody's taken me up on that.

Throughout the week that the Belgian and the Korean stayed with us, CJ and I came home from work each evening to find more and more progress had been made on CJ's mad plan. The long line of agapanthus besides the trees was extending farther every day. It was like some kind of botanical death march.

This was not the first time CJ had undertaken a mad agapanthus plan. Once, when we'd gone to visit our friends Ruby and Adam for morning tea, we were having pleasant chit-chat when CJ complimented our Ruby on the agapanthus in front of her house.

Ruby is from Thames, and she's the only person I've ever heard refer lovingly to her family as 'redneck bush pigs'. She's not one to mince words.

'Oh, I hate those damn weeds,' she said to CJ. 'Every year I go running around like a blue-assed fly trying to deadhead their nasty seedpods before they spread. I want to dig them out and burn the whole lot.'

CJ nearly choked on his tea. 'B-b-b-burn them?' His mind was clearly racing. He had to do something. Finally he said, 'Can I have them?'

Ruby shrugged. 'Sure. If you want them.'

CJ set down his tea. 'Can I borrow a shovel?'

'Now?' Ruby said.

So, while we sat there eating biscuits and sipping on gumboot tea (which I'd happily discovered was not made of gumboots at all), CJ ran outside and started digging out agapanthus. He was a man on a mission.

Agapanthus are headstrong, stubborn things, and they grip the ground with clenched fists. But CJ was undaunted. He heaved and hoed, digging with Ruby's shovel and then prying at the roots with a crowbar. Soon he broke into a mighty sweat. We could see him out the window, making a mess of Ruby's front lawn.

I apologised and Ruby said, 'Hell no! It's a huge help. Glad it's him out there busting his boiler and not me.'

Then suddenly CJ stopped digging. We saw him walk back towards the house, and when he stepped inside he looked a bit sheepish. 'Um. Sorry, Ruby. I broke your shovel.'

'Aw, that old piece of horse shit?' Ruby said. 'It's older than the Treaty of Waitangi. No worries! I'll just go and borrow the neighbour's one.'

Soon CJ was back outside digging away again, and the pile of agapanthus at his side was getting larger. Frankly, I wanted no part of this impromptu Agapanthus Rescue Operation, but I felt bad seeing CJ work so hard. I must love him, because I went out and started throwing those horrible weeds into the hatchback of our Nissan Pulsar.

Suddenly I heard a strange *crack* and turned around. CJ had broken his second shovel of the day.

There are times when a laid-back Kiwi attitude is a really good thing. Like when your guests for morning tea start compulsively digging up your lawn and then go breaking the only shovel you have, plus your neighbour's too.

Adam said nothing, but Ruby started laughing hysterically. She screamed at CJ, 'Mate, you're as mad as a cut snake! They're going to lock you up soon!'

CJ stayed behind and used the crowbar to pry roots free while I drove Ruby to the local hardware store, hatchback half full of agapanthus, and bought two brand-new shovels at 50 bucks each. So much for the free agapanthus.

Suffice it to say we stayed longer than expected that day, and when we left Ruby and Adam had large holes in their lawn where once they had had agapanthus. At least they, and their neighbour, had new shovels.

BY THE END OF the week, the Belgian and the Korean had made a very, very long line. CJ was thrilled. Every night he was outside watering the agapanthus as we were setting the table for dinner. I joked with our guests. 'He's out there talking to them. "Are you okay? Do you like your new home?"'

Only after his babies had received their nightly watering could CJ bring himself to come inside the house and sit down at the table for dinner.

As we ate, I felt a little uneasy knowing those agapanthus had multiplied and were now standing in a guard formation alongside the trees in the backyard. In our house, I'm the only one truly in touch with what those demon plants are up to. First it was the hydrangeas. Next, I'm convinced, they're coming for me.

Chapter 22

Uninvited guest in the chook house

It was early one morning in late December when I heard it for the very first time. It was still quite dark, and I was approaching the Chicken Palace with my red bucket of chicken feed and a flashlight· when suddenly a strange, wild flapping noise came from the direction of the enclosure. It was not the sound of a hen.

I SQUINTED INTO THE GLOOM. Although it was getting lighter out every morning, in the half-light I couldn't really make out what it was. But that flapping sound was familiar. It reminded me of what we used to hear at night in the trees during summer vacation in Northern Michigan. Bats.

Was there a bat in our pest-free chicken run?

You never see bats in New Zealand like I used to see in Michigan, although I'd learned that bats are the only native land mammals here, so they do exist.

I shined my flashlight into the chicken house and counted the birds on their perches. Two Fat English Ladies, two aristocratic South Americans, and one geriatric rooster down on his senior citizen's perch. They were all there sleeping peacefully. By then all four hens were giving us one egg a day, and even CJ had started eating them, albeit tentatively. What we couldn't eat I gave to the Communist Egg Collective to thank them for helping us to move the chook house.

Now I set down my bucket and shined the flashlight into the

high-security enclosure. Suddenly, on the other side of the chicken wire, something brown whipped by in a blur. Then it was gone.

Whatever it was, I figured that with my luck it probably had very sharp teeth, carried rabies, and had a penchant for blood. And it was in my chicken run.

I turned the latch and opened the door. *Fwap!* It zipped past again, right near my head. I ducked just in time, and I heard it hit the chicken wire. I was on my guard. This undiscovered, rare species of blood-sucking native New Zealand vampire bat was not going to make a meal out of me. But then the most horrible thing happened. It came right for me, flying towards my chest. Any idiot could see it was going directly for my heart.

Or wait, was it flying toward the flashlight?

I dodged to the left. It swooped past me and clung to the chicken wire to my right. Then I turned the light towards it, and for the first time I saw that ungodly monster in all its terrifying splendour. It was a tiny, brown-grey creature with a short tail and a small (but no doubt deadly powerful) beak.

It was a sparrow.

City people think sparrows are cute and harmless, but country people know the truth. A sparrow is far, far worse than a vampire bat. Not only do sparrows eat an amazing amount of chicken feed, but they and other wild birds carry the Dreaded Infestation: scaly leg mites.

CJ and I had been treating the chickens' legs diligently, once a week, for the past three weeks. We'd learned to do it after dark when the chickens were asleep and placid, so as to avoid trauma to them and us. In fact, Monday night at our house had become known as Scaly Leg Mite Night. (Don't ever let it be said we don't know how to have a good time.) I would hold the bird and CJ would slather their legs with Vaseline. Who would have thought, back when we were a young couple in our mid-twenties, dating and enjoying the night-life of Chicago, that our Monday evenings would eventually be reduced to this?

The good news was that the treatment had already started working. The sick bird, Natasha, had started laying, which was a good sign, and her legs were slowly changing from a bumpy grey to smooth, lately with increasing spots of healthy off-black. Her normal scales were growing back slowly.

Now this sparrow in the Chicken Palace threatened to ruin everything. But how did it get in? This place was supposed to be pest-free! Our chooks could easily become reinfected. After three weeks of dedicated Scaly Leg Mite Nights, I wasn't about to let that happen. I had to get rid of the sparrow.

I turned and looked at that nasty little beast in the dark. It flew around a bit more, clearly confused. It kept flying at my flashlight, perhaps thinking it was some opening to the sky.

I shooed and waved with my one free hand. But the sparrow couldn't see me. It flew back and forth from one end of the run to the other, banging into things, banging into me, never once going towards the open door. I was running around after it, of course. It was flying circles around me. I nearly tripped on the water dispenser several times. If there's one thing more pathetic than a sparrow that's flying around in the dark, it's a city boy who's shooing a sparrow that's flying around in the dark.

I yelled and grunted and howled. But I couldn't get that stupid bird to fly out the door. The chickens in the chook house must have been wondering what all the racket was. Whenever the sparrow landed, I considered trying to catch it, but I didn't want to hurt it. Finally I tried shining the flashlight on the open doorway and shooing the bird in that direction. That did the trick. The sparrow flew out and into the dark paddock.

It was gone. I was triumphant. I was the vanquisher of disease-carrying sparrows.

THE NEXT MORNING, WHEN I came back to the chook house to feed the chickens, I did not find one sparrow. I found three.

Clearly the first sparrow didn't mind being shut up in the chicken run all night, and he'd come back with several of his closest friends to eat our chicken feed and spread disease.

Thus began a ritual. Every morning I chased sparrows out of our pest-free chicken run. Every weekend I inspected the run for any tiny, sparrow-sized openings. I cut chicken wire into small bits and stuffed up every knot-hole and gap I could find. I spent entire afternoons adding staples to the chicken wire enclosing the run. Inevitably I returned the next day to find at least two sparrows in the run, their bellies full of chicken feed and flying around in a panic.

It wasn't long before I found myself considering elaborate stake-outs that involved hiding in the nearby bushes with leaves glued to my head, just to find out how the sparrows kept getting in. I began fantasising about video surveillance cameras. I wanted a 'Sparrow Watch' monitor mounted in the kitchen, right just above the micro-wave, but CJ refused.

I was a man obsessed. I'd become a twisted, sparrow-hating Elmer Fudd. 'I'll get those wascally spawwows!'

The next time the city friends came out to visit, I took them over to the chicken run and asked if they could spot any holes big enough for a sparrow. They laughed. I told them it was a very serious problem. They just looked at me with a deeply concerned, blank stare.

CJ said later, 'Maybe you should just learn how to live with the sparrows.'

'*Live* with them?'

'Yeah, you know, accept it.'

All that evening I mulled over CJ's outlandish suggestion. Perhaps he was right. Maybe it was time to come to terms with it. I should learn to accept the sparrows' enigmatic entry into our chicken run as a part of the mystery of life. I could view it as simply another unexplained phenomenon in the world, like the Loch Ness Monster or the Bermuda Triangle. I could put a sign out front and sell tickets.

In the end, however, I knew I was not wise enough for that. No. I was not spiritually evolved enough to perform the strange and mystical act of Acceptance. I tried. It lasted half an hour. Then I was back out at the chicken run, checking for holes just one last time before heading off to bed.

As I climbed under the covers I made a promise to myself. I would not be defeated by sparrows. I had no idea how, but somehow, come hell or high water, I would win. After all, I was smarter than a bunch of wimpy sparrows.

Wasn't I?

Chapter 23

Yurts and magic underwear

Nothing is normal at our house. Even a simple dinner party comes alive with bizarre and friendly characters. Martinborough's dry, hot summer was already well underway when CJ and I decided to throw a dinner party.

WE HAD A VERY SIMPLE REASON: the neighbourhood was crawling with Americans. Our American, TJ, was setting the table as John and Aussie Bronwyn arrived. Their American, Lillian, was walking in just behind them. These surplus Americans were actually HelpX volunteers. I'd helped John and Aussie Bronwyn set up their profile on the HelpX website; they appreciated meeting new travellers and, of course, having the extra help.

TJ had arrived a couple of days before. He was a courteous, 18-year-old ex-Mormon who grew up on a sheep farm in Wyoming. He was helping us put a fresh coat of white paint on the wooden fence that surrounds our yard and take out an old, cracked slab of concrete near the gravel driveway.

Lillian was a 71-year-old Californian with round glasses and short grey hair. She was helping John and Aussie Bronwyn with cleaning and weeding.

'I have presents for you!' Lillian yelled — or at least that's how her boisterous American voice sounded to me. In fact, she wasn't yelling. This was just her American accent. It had been a long time since I'd been around an American accent that strong, and it actually took me back.

But she charmed me immediately. She was full of enthusiasm and energy. 'Wine and cheese!' she announced, pulling out a bottle of Martinborough pinot noir and some double cream brie. By then I'd grown extremely fond of the local pinot noir, and I never could say no to brie, so I was very happy.

'And a mystery present!' she yelled. She handed me a small, carefully wrapped item. I unwrapped it and inside I found a tiny fork with three prongs whose points made a triangle. It was too big to be an olive fork, and too small for anything else.

'Well, thank you,' I said. 'What is it?'

'Nobody knows!' She threw her hands up in the air. 'Not even me! But it's yours now!'

Next our Kiwi artist friends Leelee and The Wolf arrived. They live closer towards the Martinborough village and have an olive grove of their own. The Wolf is a talented artist and designer, and Leelee is a writer and a counsellor. They both have passionate, playful natures. In some circles, Leelee is known as the Martinborough Pig Whisperer because she has such an uncanny ability to communicate with pigs. She and The Wolf have a pet kunekune pig that sleeps at the foot of their bed.

How lucky I was to have all these fascinating people in my home, ready to share a meal!

We stood around the kitchen island counter that is the heart of this house, and we chatted, drank the local wine, and tasted delicious things. Lillian's cheese. John's honeyed walnuts (honey from his hives and walnuts from their trees). Aussie Bronwyn's amazing gluten-free focaccia (which caused even the gluten eaters to oooh and ahhh).

We dipped the focaccia into the fresh olive oil from our three groves. We tasted the difference. John and Aussie Bronwyn's oil and Leelee and The Wolf's oil are both buttery and fantastically mild, while our Frantoio-Leccino blend is a gorgeous, peppery Tuscan style.

And all of this was just appetisers.

Then we sat down to a dinner that was, in honour of our helpers, an American one — hamburgers on the grill, potato salad, French fries and roast veggies. Throughout the meal, the conversation revolved around two improbable things: yurts and magic underwear.

As soon as we started eating, the conversation turned to Lillian and her home back in California.

'I live on 200 acres,' she said. 'And I live in a yurt!'

Everyone started laughing.

'No, really. I have three yurts. The main yurt, a sauna yurt, and a guest yurt!'

'A guest yurt?' CJ asked.

'Yes. And I've named them all. The guest yurt is "Gurt." The sauna yurt is "Burt." And the main yurt is just "Yurt". Gurt, Burt and Yurt. Those are my yurts!'

The Wolf said, 'Yurt kidding!'

THEN SOMEHOW THE CONVERSATION turned to TJ and his decision to leave the Mormon Church.

The fantastic thing about TJ is that he has the friendly wholesomeness I've come to associate with the Mormons I've met over the years, but since he's an ex-Mormon he has none of the religious dogma, racism or homophobia that I've witnessed in some Mormons. He was an absolute pleasure, and after having him in our house for just a couple of days it felt as if he'd always been there.

'My parents were pretty upset when I left the church,' he said, 'but they got over it. I left before I took my endowments.'

'Really?' Leelee said. 'You mean you never got your magic underwear?' Leelee has some relatives who are Mormon, so she knows about the underwear.

TJ smiled. 'No, I never did.'

I'd heard about the sacred Mormon undergarments before, and I'd always been fascinated. You get them when you become an adult and go through the 'endowment' ceremony. They're supposed to remind you to be good. I'd never had the chance to ask a Real Live Mormon about them. I used to work with a Mormon who was still part of the church, but asking your office co-workers about their underwear isn't really something you do.

'What does the Mormon underwear look like?' Aussie Bronwyn asked.

I imagined something extraordinary. Embroidered silk, perhaps. Or purple chiffon.

'It's just like a little T-shirt and briefs,' TJ said. 'White.'

'Briefs?' I said. 'Not even boxers?'

'Nope. Briefs for men and women.' TJ shrugged, and years of Mormon mystery fizzled and died out in my head.

Dessert was Leelee's pavlova, and it moved our American visitors to bring out their cameras. Pavlova is an important part of Kiwi cuisine and this one was stunning, topped with whipped cream, kiwifruit and pink marshmallows.

'Oh no!' Lillian shouted. 'It looks beautiful, but I'm allergic to kiwis!'

John laughed. 'If she touches a New Zealander, she gets a rash.'

We ate our delicious pavlova (Lillian's minus the kiwifruit) and sipped chamomile tea. Then, when the evening had wound down, when we couldn't eat another bite or laugh another note, we slowly walked out to their cars.

My old friend the moon shone down beautifully as the goodbyes went around. Car tyres crunched on the gravel driveway, and before I knew it everyone was gone. CJ and I walked back into the house together to find the ex-Mormon at the kitchen sink, already doing the dishes.

Clearly he didn't need magic underwear to remind him to be good. He was welcome back any time.

Leelee's Kiwifruit Pavlova

Here are Leelee's four steps to a perfect pavlova. They were inspired by a recipe from an old issue of *Your Home and Garden*.

Ingredients

4 egg whites
pinch of salt
225 g caster sugar
2 teaspoons cornflour
1 teaspoon white vinegar
½ teaspoon vanilla extract
300 ml cream
To decorate: sliced kiwifruit and pink marshmallows

Preparation

Step One

Heat oven to 120 °C.

Place the egg whites and salt in a squeaky clean glass or metal mixing bowl and whisk with an electric beater until very stiff.

Continue whisking while you add sugar, 1 tablespoon at a time.

Whisk for several minutes until you have voluptuous clouds of glossy stiffness.

Step Two

Sprinkle the cornflour, vinegar and vanilla extract over the egg white.

Use a large metal spoon to fold the ingredients together, carefully so as not to deflate the egg whites.

Step Three

Spoon the mixture onto a baking tray lined with baking paper, shaping it into a rounded mound about 20 cm in diameter.

Bake in the middle of the oven for 1 hour, by which time the meringue should be crisp on top. Don't panic if it looks a little sunken.

Turn off the heat, but leave the pavlova in the oven for at least 1 hour, and preferably overnight.

Step Four

Just before serving, carefully peel the baking paper from underneath the pavlova and transfer it to a beautiful serving plate.

Whip the cream and pile on top. Decorate with fruit. Throw a couple of marshmallows on for the fun factor.

Enjoy!

SERVES 6 TO 8

Aussie Bronwyn's Gluten-free Focaccia

This beautifully soft focaccia is heaven when served with a fine extra virgin olive oil.

Dry ingredients

3 cups rice flour

1 cup tapioca flour

1 tablespoon guar gum

2 tablespoons sugar

1½ teaspoons salt

2 teaspoons gluten-free bread-making yeast

Wet ingredients

460 ml tepid water

3 eggs (2 will do if you are short of eggs)

⅓ cup canola or olive oil

1 teaspoon white vinegar

Topping

Selection of:

olives

rock salt

tomato, sliced

salami or bacon

seeds

dried herbs

Preparation

In a large mixing bowl, sift the dry ingredients together.

Stir the wet ingredients into the dry mixture to form a smooth, elastic dough. Place in a warm place to rise until nearly doubled in volume, 1 hour or so.

Beat dough down and let it rise again. Meanwhile, heat the oven to 250 °C.

Spread the dough onto a suitable flat baking tray approximately 22 x 35 cm.

Arrange the olives, salt, slices of tomato, bits of salami or bacon, seeds, herbs, or whatever you like on the surface and bake in the middle of the oven for 10–15 minutes.

You can use a bread maker for the mixing and rising stages if you prefer.

Chapter 24

The triumph of Evil Cow

To us city boys, one farm animal had always seemed the same as another. But during our second summer in Martinborough, CJ and I met a cow that was an absolute standout. She not only made an indelible impression on both of us, but she left CJ with an ongoing remembrance in the form of a dull ache in his side when it rains. We called her Evil Cow.

LOCAL FARMERS SAY CATTLE are smart. One farmer once told me he'd actually seen a cow push another cow into an electric fence just to see if it was on. Before I'd met Evil Cow, I didn't believe that such calculated bovine malevolence was possible. Let's just say that I believe it now.

While we had been mowing the grass in the olive grove with John's tractor Sunshine, the grass in our five large paddocks had grown a lot over the previous winter and spring. Now it was all drying out. It was at least knee-high again — higher in some places.

Jim the Mad Welshman suggested that we lease our paddocks to a stock agent who could run cattle or sheep. After all, he said, there was already a 'cattle race' in the side paddock near the driveway. When we'd moved in I'd wondered what that thing was. To me it was like some kind of modern sculpture — a narrow wooden fenced area with an absurd ramp leading to nowhere. Soon I learned that it was used to load and unload livestock from a truck. Jim said that leasing our paddocks would give us a little money and it would also keep the grass down. We started asking around, and eventually we found Hamish.

Hamish is in his mid-sixties, I'd say. He's got a broad New Zealand accent and a gravelly voice. A man of few words, he's nevertheless friendly in a low-key, Kiwi farmer kind of way. After stopping by to meet us and see the property, he came by with a lease for us to sign. The lease specified the five paddocks and excluded the grove, because CJ and I didn't want livestock doing any damage to the trees.

Our poor olive trees were suffering enough as it was. By then the neighbouring groves had an abundance of olives forming. But for some strange reason, our grove had only two or three olives on each tree. I was more certain than ever that was something seriously wrong with our trees.

After we signed the lease with Hamish, he started fixing up the fences. We paid for materials and he did the labour. Then one day he showed up with what he referred to as 'eight cattlebeast'.

Suddenly there were huge animals in our paddocks, and CJ and I absolutely loved it. They animated the property, made everything come to life. We liked hearing them lowing out in the distance, and watching them from the deck as they grazed on our long grass.

CJ said, 'We have chooks in our chook house and cows in our paddocks. It almost feels like a real farm.'

At first the cows seemed the same as every other Black Angus that we'd seen in the area. But then we noticed that one cow in particular had unusual markings. Her head was entirely white except for two large, black circles around her eyes and a black triangle just above her nose. The effect was a little spooky, because it looked alarmingly like a skull. We commented on the cow's markings to each other, but we didn't think any more of it until one day when CJ and I were walking through the paddocks, right near the cows.

Before I moved to the country, I didn't understand that cows watch people. Whenever a human walks by the paddock they're in, they look up and stare, as if it's the most interesting thing they've ever seen. Cows, it turns out, are curious.

On this day, as we walked past Hamish's eight cows, it became clear that the beast with the skull markings was watching us even more closely than your average cow. She didn't just stare. She positively leered. The other cows quickly grew bored with us and looked away, but this one maintained her cold, steely gaze. She appeared more cognisant than the others, more shrewdly and deviously aware.

'There's something creepy about that cow,' I said. 'Like she's calculating a plan for the annihilation of the entire human race.'

'Nah,' CJ said. 'That's just your imagination.'

After we spent a couple hours in the grove cutting out more suckers (they are terrible, always-returning things), we wandered back up towards the house. There she was again, watching us as intently as before.

That time CJ noticed it, too. 'Okay, you might be right,' he said. 'That's an evil cow.'

AROUND THAT POINT IN time we had several months of no rain. The ground was hard and the grass was brown. Olive trees, however, don't mind a bit of drought, and their leaves were still a bright silver-green.

The cattle were in a dry brown paddock next to the grove. Occasionally we'd catch them looking longingly over at the fence at the olive trees, like children staring at candy behind glass. Then, one day we looked out to see Evil Cow standing in the middle of the olive grove, merrily munching on some branches.

CJ and I still hadn't learned Farming Rule Number One: when you're moving stock, don't run. So, we immediately sprinted down to the grove, opened the gate, and began tearing around — chasing the cow like complete and total idiots. It was the same method we'd applied the summer before, when we banished the Four Woolly Monsters of Martinborough from our bottom paddock.

However, this was not an empty paddock. It was an olive grove with 500 trees, so there are plenty of places for a cow to hide. Nevertheless, we ran around after Evil Cow for about 20 minutes, yelling and screaming the entire time, before she finally took off out the open gate.

Unimpressed by our amateur theatrics, Evil Cow waited all of one day before breaking into the olive grove again. CJ was home alone that time, so he did the Mad Cow Chase on his own. That was when he learned that cows in a panic usually run out of a paddock the same way they broke in. Evil Cow took off at a gallop, straight towards a particular stretch of fence.

Clearly she'd pushed her way in through a gap in the wire there, but now she was running too fast to push her way back out. So instead, she tried to jump the fence. CJ said she leaped up into the air and, when her body was almost entirely on the other side, her hind feet hit the top wire. She spun and fell to the ground on the other side of the fence and then rolled once more. Fortunately she got up unharmed. Then she turned around, leered, and walked slowly away.

From then on you could almost hear her muttering under her breath as she chewed her cud. 'I'll have revenge, stupid humans. You'll be sorry.'

She bided her time patiently, and stayed out of the grove for two whole weeks. Every day the grass turned browner and the ground grew harder with lack of rain. Then, one day, the skies opened up and rain fell fast and hard. It was exactly the opportunity Evil Cow had been waiting for. She knew we hadn't fixed the weak patch of fence.

After it had rained for most of the morning, she pushed her way into the grove. Once inside, she began defiantly chewing on juicy leaves in full view of the house, just below a small, steep slope.

Meanwhile, CJ and I were in the front room. CJ saw her in the grove and yelled. 'Evil Cow's in the grove again!'

His jandals were by the front door, and he quickly slipped them on. If there were an official, modern-day national costume in New Zealand, jandals would definitely be part of it. Americans call them flip-flops, some people call them thongs, but the Kiwis proudly claim the trademark on these rubber sandals. Inspired by footwear in Japan, an Auckland businessman trademarked 'jandals' in 1957, naming them from a combination of the words 'Japanese' and 'sandals'.

So there was CJ wearing his Kiwi jandals, ready to run to the grove.

'Wait,' I said. 'It's muddy. I'll grab our gumboots.'

But CJ just shouted out, 'I'm going now!' He was so mad at that cow.

By the time I had gone to the back door, put on my gumboots, and walked around the house, CJ was already tearing across the top paddock towards the olive grove in his jandals. I looked away for a moment, and the next time I looked back he was gone. He'd disappeared over the edge of the slope.

'CJ?' I called out.

There was no answer. 'CJ?' I started running towards where I'd last seen him.

Then I heard a long, low moan come up from over the edge of the slope. When I got to him he was still lying down, covered in mud. He was holding his side.

'I'm fine. I'm fine.'

'Right,' I said.

The morning's rain had made a layer of slippery mud on top of the hard-as-concrete ground, and CJ had come down hard.

Evil Cow stood in the olive grove, munching and sneering, no doubt chuckling to herself in great satisfaction. Her plan had worked.

I helped CJ back up to the house, though he protested all the way that he was fine and didn't need any help. We left Evil Cow in the grove. She had won.

CJ CONTINUED TO INSIST he was fine until two days later, when he was in so much pain that we had to take him to the emergency room in Masterton. It turned out he'd actually broken a rib clean through and popped it out of the cartilage that holds it in place. Fortunately there was no other damage, and it would just need time to heal.

In the end I made the mistake of telling Jim, the Mad Welshman, what had happened. He laughed and laughed and laughed. For the rest of that summer, every time Jim saw CJ he yelled out, 'Look, it's the winner of the Golden Jandal award!'

Suffice it to say, some things changed around here after that. We stopped chasing cows, or sheep, or even chickens for that matter. Both of us always made sure we were wearing gumboots when doing farm work. And although Evil Cow has long since been sent to the meatworks, CJ still thinks of her every time it rains.

Chapter 25

The ballad of the broody hen

O ne morning, late in the summer, I discovered that overnight one of our chickens had transformed into a growling, rabid beast. She'd taken command of the nesting box, and every time I went near her she let out a threatening growl, puffed herself up, and tried to bite me. It was Ethel, one of the Fat English Ladies.

'ETHEL,' I SAID. 'YOU'RE A CHICKEN, not a dog. Stop that.' But she just growled again. Clearly I had a chicken with an identity crisis on my hands. Then it dawned on me. This was even worse than an identity crisis. This was the day I'd been dreading. We had our first broody chicken on our hands.

Before we got chickens, I didn't fully understand what 'broody' really meant — at least not as far as it pertains to chickens. Basically a broody hen just wants to hatch eggs. She sits on the nest all day, getting up only once a day to eat and do her business. But when a broody hen separates herself from the flock in this way, it can upset the entire chook house. The pecking order can go haywire, and that can bring egg production to a halt. Who knew chicken society was so complex?

Our particular situation was further complicated by the fact that Old Man Henry was too decrepit to do his roosterly duties. Not one of the eggs Ethel was trying to hatch was fertile, and they were never going to produce baby chicks. And to make matters worse, I'd heard that a broody hen could stay broody for over six weeks!

By then we'd grown used to our steady supply of farm-fresh eggs. I'd learned how to make beautiful frittatas and gorgeous quiches with flaky gluten-free crusts. (I use Bakels Gluten Free Pastry Mix.) The vegetables from our garden provided an almost endless variety of fillings. Together, the fresh vegetables and fresh eggs combined so beautifully that even CJ ate them with gusto.

After all this progress, I didn't want to wait six weeks until we had order in the chook house and a steady supply of eggs again. So I did what my second-hand poultry-keeping book told me to do. I put on a pair of gloves, reached in, and picked Ethel up. Her response was astounding. She hissed, clawed, growled, and fought as though her life (or her children's lives) depended on it.

I took her over to the chicken run and set her down. She was crazed. She ran around screaming, squawking and puffing up her feathers. I reached into the nesting box and took every last egg laying there. I must confess I felt a little mean, but I thought that meant things would return to normal. They didn't, of course. The very next day, Ethel was back at it again. She was aggressively guarding the nesting box, trying to hatch some eggs.

Over the following week I took that fanatical bird off her eggs repeatedly. Every single time she went right back. It didn't matter whose eggs she sat on. They could have been iguana eggs, and she wouldn't have cared.

IN THE END, ETHEL proved more tenacious than me. I gave up. I moved her and her unfertile eggs out of the nesting box, put some extra hay on the floor in the corner of the chook house, and left her there. At least then the other hens could get into the nesting box.

Ethel sat there on the floor for two more weeks. If she'd been a meditating Buddhist, she would have already been enlightened. Things didn't go as I'd planned. The other hens actually started laying their eggs in Ethel's nest on the floor when she was up for her daily break. It seemed everyone had forgotten all about the nesting box. To continue to get some eggs, I marked Ethel's older ones with big black X's. That way I could tell when new eggs appeared.

From then on, every morning I had to get past a demented, obsessed chicken in order to get any fresh eggs. And given the state of chaos in the chook house, there weren't even that many new eggs.

Three weeks after my initial confrontation with Ethel, I was sick and tired of the whole thing. So I did what I always do when I don't know what do with our chickens. I called Aussie Bronwyn, the High Priestess of Chicken Wisdom. If anyone could tell me how to stop a hen from being broody, it was she. I quickly found out she knew not one way, but two, to deal with the problem.

'There are two main ways to get a hen off the cluck,' she explained over the phone.

'How?' I asked, dying to know.

'For the first way, you need a bucket, and for the second way you need a trap.'

She explained in detail. Get a large bucket. Fill it with cold water (but not too cold). Pick up the offending chicken — holding her tight and making sure her wings are pinned. Now, very quickly, stick her backside in the bucket.

'Once her backside's wet,' Aussie Bronwyn said, 'she won't want to sit down on any eggs, and she'll forget the whole thing. If she's still broody after that, you can use the trap. But I think it's even more cruel than the first method.'

Get a trap. Something like a cat trap will do, but you can use any old cage. Put the chicken inside. Then hang the trap from a tree. Leave it there overnight. Make sure there is air all around the chicken on all sides. Top, bottom, front and back.

'After a night in the air like that,' she said, 'even the most determined hen will go off the cluck.'

I paused, holding the phone in my hand. I didn't know how to respond. Poor Ethel just wanted to have some babies. The thought of doing either of these things to her broke my heart. I admit it. I'm a complete and total chicken-loving wimp.

Aussie Bronwyn could tell I was reluctant. Out of nowhere, she added a sentence that changed everything. 'As for me, I just hate to let a broody hen go to waste.'

'Huh? What do you mean?'

'You could give her some fertile eggs, so she could hatch them.'

In a recent issue of *New Zealand Lifestyle Block* magazine, I had read an article about Barnevelders, a breed the magazine called 'the friendly chicken'. I wanted some. (I won't dwell on the fact that I used to read *Men's Health* and *GQ*. Since moving to Martinborough

I won't even touch a magazine unless there's a picture of a chicken or an olive on the cover.)

Barnevelders have been bred as layers; 'broodiness' has been bred out of them. Imagine, no broody hens! Also, and perhaps most importantly for me, the article said that Barnevelders were more apt to come rushing up to you, and they didn't mind being picked up.

'Well,' I said to Aussie Bronwyn, 'how do you get fertile eggs?'

'Through the mail, of course.'

Of course. Everybody knows you order fertile eggs through the mail.

'I use Precious Poultry,' she added.

I hung up the phone and contacted them immediately. Three days later a cardboard box containing six fertile Barnevelder eggs arrived on our doorstep. I'd explained to Fiona at Precious Poultry that I wanted to get one or two Barnevelder hens out of all this.

'Then you should order six eggs just to make sure,' Fiona had told me. 'Since it's your hen's first time hatching, she won't have such a high success rate. They sometimes make mistakes and step on the eggs. They get better at hatching with experience.' Who knew?

Fiona also said I had to 'let the yolks settle' for 24 hours before I put them under Ethel. I don't understand how fertile eggs can survive being delivered in the mail, or how an 'unsettled' yolk can settle and still manage to produce a baby chick, but there you have it.

The next day, CJ and I headed out to the chook house with our precious eggs. Inside the cardboard box, each egg was wrapped in tissue. We unwrapped them all very carefully. They were a beautiful dark brown.

CJ picked up Ethel off her nest on the floor of the chook house. She growled and fought as usual. I stole her warm, unfertile eggs, and gave her the fertile ones. They were room temperature but still very cool compared to the others. How could they possibly survive?

When CJ set Ethel down, she didn't seem to care that we'd changed the eggs at all. She went right on sitting. We looked on proudly. 'I hope they hatch,' I said. 'But I don't know what we'll do if they turn out to be boys.'

'Don't worry about that,' CJ answered. 'I know what to do with them if they're boys. We'll get the axe.'

Lately CJ had been talking about raising chickens for meat. He wanted to learn how to kill and clean a chicken. Originally I'd thought we might get to that at some point, but once you start raising animals and discovering their individual personalities, it gets very hard to eat them.

'I hope we don't get any boys,' I said.

Back in the house I counted the days out on the calendar. It takes 21 days to hatch a chick, and I marked delivery day. I felt like a kid at Christmas, and I couldn't wait. Each day for three weeks, I checked Ethel every morning to make sure she was still sitting on those six precious, mail-ordered eggs. When she stepped on one egg and broke it, we were suddenly down to five. And then, around two weeks into the incubation period, our dominant hen Henrietta did something that complicated everything.

Henrietta's mind-set has always been one of gluttony and perpetual jealousy. If one of the other hens finds food, Henrietta suddenly wants it, and she'll muscle in to get it. If another hen is drinking water, Henrietta becomes instantly thirsty and must drink NOW. So it shouldn't have surprised me at all when, after Ethel had been broody for so long, Henrietta finally became broody too.

But I didn't want to take any of the fertile eggs off Ethel. She deserved them, and after five weeks of being broody at that point, I didn't want to risk her not hatching any eggs. So Henrietta got none and remained sitting on unfertilised eggs in the nesting box.

WHEN THE BIG DAY finally arrived, I rushed out first thing in the morning to check on Ethel. There she was, still sitting on her nest, no doubt protecting her new baby chicks. I reached over and picked her up, dodging her pecks left and right. But when I looked down I saw something terribly disappointing: five unhatched eggs. Maybe I'd done something wrong. Maybe all the eggs were duds.

As we climbed into bed that night CJ said, 'Maybe tomorrow.'

'Yes,' I answered. 'Maybe tomorrow.'

The following morning I went out to feed the chickens and, of course, check on Ethel's eggs. They still hadn't hatched. It was Day 22 of incubation, already a day longer than it should take for eggs to hatch. It looked like we had five tiny failures on our hands.

But later that afternoon I noticed Ethel had come out of the chook house. She'd settled outside in a corner of the chicken run. What was she doing out there? Why wasn't she watching her eggs? Had she finally given up? Maybe she intuitively understood there was something wrong with the eggs.

I stepped inside the chook house to check her nest. There were three unhatched eggs, already cold and abandoned, never to hatch. But two eggs were broken and empty! I went into the chicken run and walked slowly over to Ethel. She growled and squawked as I leaned down. I slowly put my hand underneath her, lifting her up just a tiny bit. Beneath all her fluffed white feathers, I saw the most amazing thing ever: four tiny, toothpick-thin chicken legs. And they were moving around.

I immediately ran up to the house to get CJ.

'Two eggs have hatched!' I announced.

CJ jumped up quickly. It's a fantastic thing to see a grown man scramble to get outside and look at newborn baby chicks. When CJ and I got back to the chicken run, the two tiny Barnevelder babes were pecking the ground near Ethel. Old Man Henry was looking down at the chicks proudly, puffing his chest out and clucking something that sounded vaguely like, 'I did that. I did that.' (The poor, deluded bird.)

We watched in awe as Ethel carefully picked up chicken feed and dropped bits in front of the chicks, teaching them to eat. It was the picture of a happy family. The little chicks looked incredibly vulnerable, and I was happy the chicken run was at least rat- and ferret proof, even if the sparrows were continuing to torment me.

It wasn't until later that day that I realised there was a very real and serious danger coming not from outside the chicken run, but from inside. On one of my obsessive trips out to the chook house to check on the chicks I saw that still-broody Henrietta had got out of the nesting box. She was acting all crazy and aggressive in the usual puffed-up, broody hen way. But it was worse than just that. She was actually going after the chicks. Every time they came near her, she would growl and run after them, pecking ferociously and nipping at them over and over. Ethel was trying to intervene, but she was no match for Henrietta's wild state of hormonal psychosis.

It was clear what Henrietta was doing. She may as well have been screaming, 'If I can't have babies, NOBODY will!' I'd heard of aggressive hens and mean roosters killing baby chicks, and that was it. I had to do something fast. If Henrietta's aggression against the chicks was even remotely related to her broodiness, then her broodiness had to end. And it had to end now.

Thinking of Aussie Bronwyn's legendary speed and agility, I paused. Then I pounced. Before I knew it, I was holding Henrietta securely in my hands. Clutching the bird to my chest, I calmed her, shut the chook house door, and began the long walk across the paddock, up to the house. Henrietta became quiet, almost peaceful. She had no idea what was about to happen.

She watched as I walked up to the back porch and picked up the red plastic bucket. And she watched as I went over to the hose, turned on the tap, and began filling the bucket. The water was cold, and I felt terrible. My heart was pounding.

I still have no idea how I managed to fill a bucket with water in one hand while holding a hormonal chicken in the other. I guess this means I'm becoming a country boy. At the time I didn't even think of it. I only knew I was dealing with a crisis, and nothing was going to hurt those baby chicks. Nothing. I understood completely what I had to do, and I didn't hesitate. I lowered Henrietta down toward the bucket, and I dunked her backside in.

She took off like a rocket. Straight up into the air. When she landed, she ran as fast as she could for the safety of some shrubs. The amazing thing is that it did the trick. From that moment on she was a broody hen no more. When I finally allowed Henrietta back into the chicken run, I observed her closely. Ethel was also on high alert, watching out for her babies. Eventually the chicks wandered near Henrietta, and I held my breath. Henrietta looked down at them. Then she simply turned the other way.

AFTER THAT, PEACE WAS once again restored in the chicken house. The little chicks thrived. Ethel was a very good mom to them, and Old Man Henry was a good, albeit somewhat misguided, father.

Every day for the next few weeks I checked on the baby chicks and wondered. Were they boys, or were they girls? Then one day Aussie Bronwyn came by and said, 'Oh, they're definitely girls.'

'How can you tell?' I asked.

'Well, they don't walk like boys.'

Clearly I still had a lot to learn. But at least I could relax, knowing that the baby chicks were girls. They were safe from CJ and the horrors of the axe.

Chapter 26

Meeting the Great White Whale

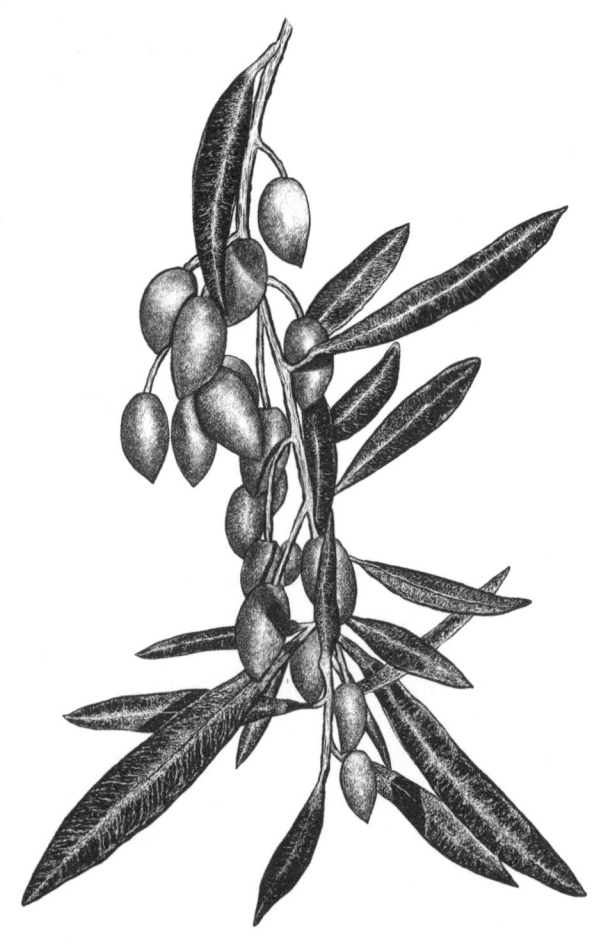

I was in the back seat of Leelee and The Wolf's big black ute, and we were heading down Dry River Road. The three of us wanted to know more about the vineyards and the wines of Martinborough. I was finally going to learn how not to be a wine moron.

AT THE SIGN THAT READ *Murdoch James*, The Wolf turned the ute up a long, ambling driveway. We passed open fields and poplar trees bearing the golden leaves of autumn. A small bridge took us over a bright and sparkling stream. We all had a pleasant, comfortable feeling that we were in for something special.

The Wolf parked and we walked up to the main door. In casual New Zealand fashion, Pepper the elderly Airedale terrier was lying across the threshold to the tasting room.

'Hello,' Roger said, laughing at Pepper. 'Come in.' Roger is the director of Murdoch James and the man we had come to see. Obviously Pepper was a keen watchdog ready to spring to the alert if needed. She lifted her head lazily, blinked at us, and went back to her nap. We stepped over her.

Inside a fire was burning. We met Roger's wife, Jill, and a couple from Auckland who would be joining us on the tour. Jill made sure we all had glasses as Roger put three bottles of white wine into a charming wicker basket. Then we wandered out toward the vines. Cool autumn air surrounded us, and yellows and golds were everywhere. The rows of vines made vertical lines towards a distant hill. As we strolled along Roger told us stories about the vineyard

— about how much work and investment they had to do when they had bought the place years before, about the soil, and about the way the frost rolls off their hills.

As we paused to look at some chardonnay vines, Roger poured us each a taste of chardonnay. Picking had just finished, so the vines had no grapes.

'These vines are 25 years old,' Roger said. 'They've served us well.' He waved his hand. 'Next week we're cutting them out.'

Leelee gasped. 'Why?' she said.

'They have leafroll virus. It slowly kills the vine.' 'There is no treatment, I'm afraid.'

He explained that the virus was spread through pruning and by mealy bugs. 'We have to get them out before it spreads to the other vines.'

'That's a shame,' The Wolf said.

'When we finish taking these out, we'll leave the ground to rest for two or three years,' Roger explained. 'Then we'll replant. In the meantime we've still got 50 acres of healthy, productive vines.' He smiled. 'Just a minor setback.'

The strength and vitality of people who rely on agriculture for a living always astounds me.

Further along we were introduced to rows of hearty pinot gris vines and we sipped their wine, which had hints of sweet peach and pear. Then we tasted the lime flavours of the sauvignon blanc. Along the way we saw 'second set' pinot noir grapes that had ripened after the harvest, and we each tasted a sweet, dark grape.

Having tasted the white wines, we walked back to the winery to see the high-ceilinged processing room. Big vats lined the walls. Old stainless steel vats were working side by side with new, energy-efficient, plastic fermenters. Dominating the centre of the room was a massive white machine with a long cylinder running down its spine. It was like having a giant white whale plonked down in front of you. Everyone was focused on this white behemoth. One man was spraying it with a hose and another was checking some sort of valve. It seemed to me that this machine was the heart and soul of the place.

Back in 1986, when Roger and Jill bought the rundown winery, this mechanical beast lay neglected in the corner. It was an old 'balloon press' dating from around 1960. Rather than sell it for scrap, Roger and Jill had it carefully refurbished. Then they set about using it to press their wine.

Inside the machine there was a long balloon. Winery staff loaded the machine up with destemmed grapes fresh from the fields and then the balloon slowly inflated, gently crushing the grapes against the inside of the cylinder. The slow movement of the balloon prevented the grapeseeds from breaking, which would cause a bitter taste in the wine.

'It's a beauty,' Roger said, touching the side of the machine.

Staff switched on this old 'Moby Dick' and a loud whir came from its belly. Grape juice started trickling out from its spine into a long, narrow trough below. We watched the juice flow so intently that it seemed we were mesmerised.

EVENTUALLY WE STEPPED OVER to a corner of the room, and stood talking among the two-storey-tall stainless steel vats and plastic fermenters. After lifting the lid to one of the fermenters to show us the wine inside, Roger grabbed a basket of red wines, and we went to my favourite room of the day.

We all stepped single file down the stairs into the cellar, and I felt the transition into new kind of space. The noise of Moby Dick faded, and the air became cool and infused with a rich, fertile, earthy smell. Hints of spice and fruit lingered around my nostrils. The light was low, and as my eyes adjusted I saw that the walls were lined with pale brown barrels. Dark wrought-iron gates opened like wings under rough archways.

Roger poured us a taste of the previous year's pinot noir and we drank happily as he told us stories about the wooden barrels, their makers, and the forests in France where the wood comes from.

The last wine we tasted that day was my favourite. It was their Saleyards Syrah, and it had an amazing liquorice bouquet with a background of nutmeg. It was fantastic. When it came time to leave the cellar, I didn't want to go. But the tour was over, and together we left the peace and silence of that place.

Upstairs we thanked Roger and Jill and then stepped over Pepper as we said goodbye. We climbed back into Leelee and The Wolf's big black ute, and drove away. Inside my head there was a cool, quiet space that reminded me of the wine cellar we'd left behind.

Chapter 27

The sweet taste of chicken feed

One day in autumn Hamish took away some of the cows in our paddocks and replaced them with sheep. In any group of animals, I've learned, there are always one or two that stand out. Among these sheep, it was Sweetie. We started calling her that because she really was sweet, even though she did have a bit of a problem.

HAMISH PUT THE REMAINING CATTLE and the new sheep in different paddocks. He asked us about running the sheep in the olive grove, but we were nervous about that because we didn't want them to nibble at the trees. 'Okay, he said. They'll stay in the paddocks.' Then he added, 'One of those sheep is a pet sheep. Belongs to my sister. That one's never going to the butcher.'

At first all the sheep were out in the side paddock with the cattle race, beyond the driveway and a row of gum trees. I didn't see them much. But after a while Hamish moved them into the top paddock where the chicken run is. That's when I got to know them.

Every morning I would cross the paddock carrying my trusty red bucket full of chicken feed. The sheep stared. One had a blue plastic ring in its ear. Another had a large, square head. Being naturally sheepish, they ran away if I came too close. But one sheep never ran. No matter how close I came as I walked by, she would stand her ground and stick her nose out, sniffing the air. After a couple of mornings, she started walking over to greet me.

One day she came so close that I was able to reach out and touch her head. Your average sheep doesn't allow that. This had to be the pet sheep.

She had a dainty face and a large freckle on the side of her nose. She leaned into me, and I rubbed her ears.

'Aww,' I said. 'You're a sweetie.'

Then all of a sudden she thrust her head into the bucket of chicken feed I was holding, and she started eating. For a moment I watched in disbelief. She'd played me like a fool, just to get to my chicken feed. But then I thought that maybe giving chicken feed to a sheep wasn't a good idea. I pulled the bucket away.

I don't know what's in chicken feed that could possibly taste so amazing, but Sweetie loved the stuff. She was very upset when I pulled the bucket away. She wanted more, and she wanted it now. She pushed at the bucket with her snout. She stomped her foot on the ground. She huffed and puffed and, when I walked away, she followed me all the way over to the Chicken Palace. There was plenty of grass in the paddock then, but when she saw me scatter that chicken feed inside the chicken run, I swear she had a hungry, longing look in her eyes.

I went to the garage and checked the chicken feed bag. Written there plainly were the words, NOTICE: Not to be fed to Sheep, Cattle, Deer, Alpacas, Goats, or other ruminant Animals. Oops. That sounded very, very bad. I hoped Sweetie would be okay.

That evening I called John to ask his opinion. He told me about a sheep he'd heard of that died after breaking into someone's chicken feed. My heart sank. Would Sweetie now die a long, slow, horrible death? What would Hamish say? But John told me that he thought Sweetie would be alright as long as she didn't get too much feed. I crossed my fingers and decided to watch Sweetie closely for the next couple days.

Rather than showing any signs of sickness, Sweetie became even more aggressive. She was obsessed with getting more chicken feed. She ran up to the gate when I arrived in the mornings and then followed me around like a desperate chicken feed junkie. She came close and offered her ears for a rub. But I knew her tricks now. She wasn't going to play me.

When I scattered the feed around the chicken run, she went absolutely crazy. She actually started butting her head against the chicken wire and kicking at the corrugated iron. She was not a happy sheep.

'I need my chicken feed!' she seemed to scream.

One morning, while feeding the chickens in a sleepy-eyed blur, I stepped away from the door to the run for just a moment. I left the door wide open. Watching from not too far away was the chicken-feed obsessed Sweetie. She saw her chance and made a run for it.

You could see the absolute delight on her face — her thoughts of leaping into the run and landing in mountains and mountains of chicken feed on the other side. Once there she would gorge herself on her delicious drug of choice like there was no tomorrow. And of course, there wouldn't be. Like a true addict, the thought that her addiction might kill her never entered her mind.

There was only one thing for me to do. I broke into a run, back towards the door. Sweetie was running hard. Fortunately I was closer than she was. I got there first.

I stood in front of the door and breathed a sigh of relief. That is, until I realised that Sweetie wasn't slowing down. She was now running directly towards me, full force ahead. If she couldn't go around me, she was apparently planning to go right through me. I put out my arms and yelled. It seemed we were playing a game of chicken, all because of some chicken feed. At the last possible moment, Sweetie put on the brakes. She slid and stopped just short of ramming into me. Clearly I had a serious problem. I had the world's first self-destructive, chicken-feed addicted ruminant mammal on my hands.

THAT WEEK HAMISH MOVED the sheep to another paddock. I didn't see Sweetie every day then. But I figured it was good for her to be away from the chickens and all that tempting chicken feed. After all, it only served as a constant reminder of the drug she could not have.

After that, every once in a while I'd wander down into the paddocks just to find her. She'd always come running up to me, acting all sweet. I was not fooled by this. I knew what she was doing. She didn't love me. She was still trying to catch me carrying chicken feed.

Chapter 28

The year there was no harvest

When olive harvest season approached, I walked down into our grove and looked at the branches. There had been no miracle over the summer, no divine intervention as we passed through autumn. Our olive trees still had almost no olives at all.

WE DECIDED TO HAVE SOME TESTS done on the grove to try to figure out what was wrong. Someone from the local farm store came out, and they took soil and leaf samples. It took over two weeks to get the results. It was a terrible, long wait.

Then one day we received a large brown envelope from the laboratory. CJ and I stood in the kitchen, staring at the envelope. We were almost afraid to look inside. Finally, CJ picked it up and — very, very slowly — he opened it.

There was a complicated report with graphs and charts that we didn't understand. But then we saw the letter. The trace elements were good, it explained. We could benefit from putting down some lime, but that was all. The bottom line was this: our grove was fine.

It was good to hear, but I still wasn't happy. I wanted to know why the trees hadn't flowered that year. Something had gone amiss. I wanted a complete and comprehensive explanation, and I wasn't going to rest until I had it. That's when I called Andrew-of-the-Olives.

Other growers had told me about him. They said he was a former apple farmer from the Hawke's Bay who'd fallen in love with olive trees. Andrew-of-the-Olives knew everything there was to know about growing olives in New Zealand. He travelled up and down the

North Island pruning olive trees, dispensing advice as a kind of olive consultant, and harvesting olive groves with his Mighty Tree Shaker. He was like a New Zealand Johnny Appleseed, only with olives.

It was a bright sunny day in late May when his truck turned into our driveway. Out climbed a sturdy, smallish man who looked something like a cross between a lumberjack and an elf.

'I'm Andrew,' he said, and shook our hands firmly.

Andrew, CJ and I chatted a bit on the front deck, and then Andrew said, 'So you think there's something wrong with your olive grove? We'll see about that. You two don't know what you're doing, do you?'

From most people, this would be an insult. Andrew-of-the-Olives, however, said this with such an impish, playful grin that CJ and I couldn't help but laugh at him.

CJ said, 'Well it's lucky for you we don't, or you'd be out a customer.'

Andrew laughed loudly. 'Well put.'

We liked him right away.

After showing him the results of our leaf and soil samples, we went for a walk through the grove. The claret ash by the goldfish pond had turned a deep shade of burgundy and was losing its leaves. Olive growers all around us had already started harvesting their olives, and they were having record crops. For us there would be no harvest at all.

'So, why didn't our trees flower this year?' I asked Andrew bluntly. 'Why?' I was a man obsessed. There were so few olives in our grove that you could almost count them on one hand.

Andrew just nodded his head slowly. Then he asked us questions about our grove, about its history, about rain and frosts and this and that. I remembered an unusually late frost that had damaged the wisteria blossoms up at the house that spring.

'It could have been that,' Andrew said. 'A late frost when the buds are just forming on the olive trees could do a lot of damage.'

'So it was that?' CJ said.

'Maybe. Maybe not,' Andrew said. 'It could be just because the grove hasn't been sprayed or pruned properly in years.'

We knew that most people sprayed anti-fungal compounds on their trees to fight things like peacock spot and bacterial blast, but we'd never done that.

Andrew shrugged. 'But to be honest, you'll never really know why.'

I couldn't believe what I was hearing. 'What do you mean?' I said.

This man was an expert. He should know.

Andrew must have seen the disappointment on my face. He leaned in towards me. 'Jared, sometimes you have a good year, sometimes your entire crop fails. Guess what? That's agriculture.' He leaned back and opened his arms and laughed. 'Welcome!'

I took a deep breath, and I laughed with him. CJ laughed, too. Then Andrew added something. 'I'll tell you one thing that's certain. There's nothing wrong with your grove. Your soil's good. The trees are healthy. Whoever planted this grove put in a lot of work, and they did a great job. I wouldn't mind having a grove like this myself.'

I nodded. I had the only answer I was ever going to get. I looked out at the grove and I thought of Priscilla, who had planted those trees. I said a quiet thank you to her in my head. But we had other questions, too — about the Nabali, about the grass and suckers, and of course about pruning.

'The Nabali have never fruited,' I said. 'Except for one year when the previous owner, Priscilla, said they had fruit. She was thinking of pulling them out. So are we. What do you think?'

Andrew walked over to the Nabali. He looked at their branches and leaves. 'How old are they?'

'Ten years,' I said.

Andrew's eyes sparkled. 'They're only babies! There are olive trees in the Middle East that are *thousands* of years old. In the New Zealand climate, Nabali might start fruiting at 20, or 30. We don't know yet. It's early days for New Zealand olives. Just leave them be.'

'What about keeping the grass down under the trees?' CJ asked. 'We know people spray the grass to kill it, but we don't like that.'

'So don't do it.' Andrew said.

'But how are we supposed to keep down the grass?' I asked. 'We've been taking the line trimmer to all 500 trees, to get where the mower won't reach.'

Andrew eyes grew wide. 'You're joking! That would take forever!' Then he pointed to Hamish's sheep grazing on the other side of the fence, out in one of the paddocks. 'You've got a team of lawnmowers right over there.'

CJ said, 'But we heard that they might damage the trees.'

'Not if you do it right,' Andrew said. 'Grazing sheep in olive groves is a centuries-old tradition. You'll need to take the sheep out for just a few weeks in spring, when the sap is running, because they'll chew the bark. You just have to pay attention. But the rest of the year it's fine to graze sheep in here. Not cattle, mind you. Just sheep. And don't let the grass get too low or they'll start eating bark. They'll nibble the leaves of course. They'll eat to their height, but that's fine with sheep.

'Running sheep in a grove means you don't need nasty chemicals to kill the grass around the trees, and you don't need to waste petrol to mow the grass. Their manure also helps to fertilise the soil. But there is one catch. Sheep pellets are just about the size, shape and colour of ripe olives. So you have to be careful.' Andrew smiled.

I thought for a moment about how we had harvested by hand the year before, raking the olives down to the ground on nets. I imagined the hazard. One little sheep poo rolling onto a harvest net and our olive oil would taste like, well, you guessed it.

'So, if you keep sheep in your olive grove,' Andrew continued, 'you have to get them out a couple of months before you harvest. If you're using a tree shaker or what they call umbrella nets for harvest, you've got no worries. The olives never touch the ground. But if you're using harvest mats like you do, you need time for the sheep manure to rot down and disintegrate. As long as you do that, she'll be right. The sheep eat the suckers, too.'

'They eat the grass *and* the suckers?' I asked. It sounded too good to be true. No more Grass and Sucker Projects, ever.

Andrew nodded. 'Yep.'

'One more question,' CJ said. 'I pruned a row a while back, and Jared told me I'd destroyed the trees. I want your opinion.' And he walked Andrew over to his row of post-apocalyptic toothpicks. 'What do you think?'

Andrew shrugged and scratched the brown stubble on his chin. 'Not bad.'

CJ glared at me. 'Hear that, Jared? *Not bad.*'

'What?' I said. 'They're toothpicks!'

Andrew laughed. 'Well, it's obviously the work of an amateur, but really — not bad.'

CJ was gloating. 'Andrew, you don't know the grief I got when I pruned those trees.' He glared at me again. 'Not bad,' he repeated, a bit louder than necessary.

Andrew talked to us about a pruning programme, about taking out a central leader every year so the canopy stays young, about thinning the interior shoots and making cuts to encourage new growth where it was wanted. He went over to a couple of trees and showed us what he would do if he was pruning. 'I'd start on the north side,' he said. 'To let in the most light. Then each year I'd take a different side.'

We told him that by then it had been at least four years since the grove had been properly pruned.

'You need to get on top of it,' Andrew said. 'Let me know if you want me to do it. If I start this year, in three years you'll have a huge crop.'

We wandered back to at the house and thanked Andrew for his time. Then he hopped back into his truck and drove away.

ON QUEEN'S BIRTHDAY WEEKEND, the same early June weekend we'd harvested the olives the year before, CJ and I went for a walk through the grove. It was a cool evening and the sun was low in the sky. A fantail flitted from branch to branch nearby. We talked about how much we'd enjoyed last year's harvest, when the grove had been full of friends and laughter. Now it was empty and quiet.

I turned to CJ and said, 'We need to get the grove in shape for next year,' and he nodded.

We walked on, looking out at those pathetic trees that had no olives. The fantail followed along. It was obvious to both CJ and me that our attempt to work full-time jobs in the city as well as take care of 20 acres and 500 olive trees in the country had been, well, unfruitful. There weren't enough hours in the day to do everything we had to do. The HelpX volunteers were fantastic, but they weren't arborists. We needed professional help. We decided then to hire Andrew-of-the-Olives to prune the grove. We also decided to get a contract sprayer in. We had to take proper care of these trees.

Sometimes bad things happen for good reasons. The fact we had no harvest that year gave us the push we needed to accept the fact that we couldn't do it all ourselves. We walked down to one end of the grove, across to the side, and then began heading back.

'We'll get help,' CJ said. 'And hopefully we'll have a good harvest next year.'

The light around us was beginning to fade. The temperature was dropping. I looked up at the house, at the smoke rising out of our chimney. It would be warm inside. The moon was just starting to rise over the far hills.

'Yes,' I said. 'Let's hope that next year our olive grove will be okay.'

The
Thi
Yea

d

Chapter 29

Your chicken killers are here

When we pulled up Aussie Bronwyn's driveway in our little Nissan Pulsar, CJ and I were both wearing clothes we wouldn't mind getting blood on. There were early spring crocuses blooming in front of the house, and Aussie Bronwyn — the High Priestess of Chicken Wisdom herself — came to the door.

CJ CALLED OUT, 'Your loyal chicken killers are here!'

My stomach turned. Was I really going to do this?

At a dinner party that winter, CJ had said to Aussie Bronwyn, 'If you ever need help killing chickens, let me know.'

In some circles this might be considered an odd thing to say at a dinner party. Not here. I suppose you could say that CJ has a complicated relationship with chickens. He's a lover of a good omelette, and since moving to Martinborough he'd learned how to cook a mean roast chicken, but ever since Françoise laid our first egg, he'd been consistent in his disgust that eggs actually come out of chickens' bums. On the other hand, there he was at a dinner party, offering to chop off a chicken's head off. Go figure.

The fact was that Aussie Bronwyn needed no help killing chickens. She'd grown up watching her mother do it, and learned from her. I once heard her say, 'I can't remember *not* killing chickens.'

But when CJ offered to help, she was courteous. She took a sip of local wine and said, 'That would be lovely. Thank you.' No doubt she saw CJ's offer as an opportunity to teach some fool-headed city boys how to become more self-sufficient.

Now she greeted us at the door with a big smile and quickly led us around the back of the house. When you step through the gate beyond their large goldfish pond, you enter animal territory. Grey and reddish-brown chickens peck the ground. Bright white ducks with yellow beaks waddle by. Blossom the dairy cow looks at you over a fence. On the day CJ and I showed up to kill chickens, only the pigsty was empty, since its occupants had recently been turned into pork chops.

Methuselah — Aussie Bronwyn's geriatric rooster and cousin to our Old Man Henry — hid behind the tractor when he saw us. Clearly he recognised the steely determination in his owner's small frame as something dangerous. You don't get to be Methuselah's age without a highly developed sense of self-preservation.

We planned to kill two roosters that day. CJ was going to do one, and I was going to do the other. Our gracious hostess wasted no time. She went to the shed and got the axe and set it down on an old stump. Then she picked up her trusty chicken net and stepped into the chicken run.

There was a wild flurry of clucks and squawks before Aussie Bronwyn walked out victoriously, carrying a beautiful black-and-white rooster that was nearly as big as she was. She held him by his feet. His head hung down as he twisted and tried to get free.

She explained that he was a seven-month-old Barred Rock. 'This one and his brother are flighty and keep getting over into my garden.' She looked at the rooster. 'I told you. One foot in my garden and it's curtains.'

I laughed nervously and made a mental note to be careful where I walked.

She reached out and handed the rooster to CJ. At that point CJ had already 'helped' her once before — a few weeks earlier when she needed to cull a sick chicken. So he understood what to do. Aussie Bronwyn knows a natural-born chicken killer when she sees one.

We gathered around the wooden stump quickly, shifting positions several times. Aussie Bronwyn held the tip of the rooster's beak to keep the neck stretched out. I don't know how it happened, but somehow I ended up holding the legs of the rooster, and it was going to become headless in a matter of seconds. I didn't know what to do. I wasn't ready. I panicked.

CJ raised the axe into the air.

'Wait! What do I do when it's chopped?' I yelled.

Bronwyn hollered back. 'Drop it and run!'

Down came the axe.

I did not feel life leaving the chicken's body as its head fell to the ground and the blood began to flow. Instead, the two legs began jerking and squirming even more. I did as I was told. I dropped the bird and ran. I nearly ran all the way home.

WHAT HAPPENED NEXT was horrifying, but not in the way I expected. You always hear that headless chickens go running around. Maybe it depends on the chicken. This one didn't run. It did backflips. Two of them. Four feet into the air. Arcs of blood flew out everywhere. Meanwhile its head, lying over on the wooden stump, went into a series of bizarre twitching spasms. It wasn't pretty.

When everything finally stopped moving, CJ and I stood in silence looking at the blood and feathers. Aussie Bronwyn was already in the shed, putting newspapers out on a table to prepare for the plucking and gutting. She is an immensely practical woman.

When she came out, she said, 'It's never pleasant. But it's like the housework. It has to be done.'

She picked up her chicken net and went back into the run. This time she came out carrying a bird that was slightly smaller, another Barred Rock. He was squirming even more than the first one. It was my turn.

For a few years when I was a university student, I gave up red meat on the grounds that I didn't think I was capable of ever killing a cow. I felt I should only eat what I could — at least theoretically — kill myself. Otherwise it seemed hypocritical. I thought then that if push came to shove I could kill a fish, a pig, or a chicken. But not a cow. (They're too big, and have those big brown eyes.)

Now, 20 years on, push had finally come to shove. A kind, retired woman was holding out a rooster for me to kill. Not in theory, but in reality. I looked at the axe, then at the rooster. I literally backed away.

'You do it,' I said to CJ.

'Are you sure?' he asked.

'Yes.'

We did the same as before. I held its feet. CJ swung the axe. Unfortunately, this time the head didn't come off on the first try. The bird made a strange, painful noise — half squawk, half gurgle. CJ chopped it again, and its head finally fell off.

This rooster spared us the backflip show. It just fell over and twitched for a while. Then it stopped moving. But 30 seconds later it got up again and stumbled across the grass. Then it collapsed once and for all.

OUR LESSON WASN'T OVER. Aussie Bronwyn showed us how to put the carcasses into scalding water for a few seconds to make them easy to pluck. She pulled the feathers off one bird while CJ and I did the other. Actually, CJ did most of ours. I was a little grossed out.

Then out came the extra-sharp kitchen knife. If I was squeamish at the plucking, I was positively ill at the gutting. CJ was fine. It seems it's only the egg-out-of-the-bum thing that bothers him. Blood and guts? Not a problem.

Aussie Bronwyn cut a circle around the cloaca, made a long slit at the base of the neck, and pulled out the innards. The intestines came out in long strands.

'You have to be careful not to cut into the bowels,' she said. 'It makes a mess. And if you cut into the gall bladder, it makes the meat bitter.'

She showed us the crop, cut it down the middle and showed us the chicken feed inside. I turned pale and wobbled.

Eventually the two chickens in front of us looked almost like the birds you buy in the grocery store. I felt a strange compulsion to place them in styrofoam trays and seal them in shrink-wrap, just to finish the job.

'You can't cook them right away, or they're really tough,' she said. 'Rigor mortis. You have to wait a couple of days.'

CJ and I dug a hole and buried the innards, the heads, the feet, and the very bloody newspapers. Aussie Bronwyn said that John could bury them when he got home, but we figured we should.

After all, who wants to leave that kind of mess behind at your neighbour's house?

By then ancient Methuselah had come out of his hiding place behind the tractor, and he'd started crowing. He was no doubt screaming, 'I'm alive! I'm alive!'

When the last shovel of dirt was on top of the hole, and Aussie Bronwyn had placed a tyre over it to stop their dog from digging it up, CJ and I joined the High Priestess of Chicken Wisdom inside for a nice cup of tea and freshly made, absolutely amazing scones. What else do you do after a bloody mess like that?

Aussie Bronwyn's Amazing Gluten-free Scones

Aussie Bronwyn says, 'The ingredients should be cold, cold, cold and the oven should be hot, hot, hot.'

Ingredients

2 cups rice flour*
1 cup tapioca flour
1 teaspoon guar gum
6 teaspoons baking powder
½ teaspoon baking soda
¼ cup sugar
75 g very cold butter
1 egg
1¼ cups very cold milk
fruit (such as chopped dates or sultanas), if desired

*For a non-gluten-free version, replace the rice flour, tapioca flour and
  guar gum with 3 cups of wheat flour.

Preparation

Heat the oven to 250 °C.
  Sift all the dry ingredients together.
  Rub in the butter until the mixture resembles fine breadcrumbs.
  Add fruit, if using.
  Beat the egg into the milk and stir into the dry mixture, taking care
not to overmix.
  The mix should be quite moist but hold its shape when patted into
an oblong and cut into 12 scones. You may need a little more milk,
depending on the flour.
  Bake for 10–15 minutes, until the scones are lightly golden and make
a hollow sound when tapped.
  Plain scones are really nice served with whipped cream and
strawberry jam.

MAKES 12 SCONES

Chapter 30

Unruly chickens and the substitute teacher

I was standing at the kitchen sink and looking out the back window when I first saw our chickens sneaking into the backyard. I froze. They were headed straight for The Forbidden Zone.

IT IS A TRUTH universally acknowledged that chickens untended get up to no good. Anyone who keeps chickens knows this. Given the chance, they'll make a beeline for the most freshly planted, unfenced patch of garden and begin wreaking havoc with all the wild abandon of drunken sailors in a bar fight.

We no longer kept our chickens permanently locked up in the chicken run. We had started granting them the occasional shore leave. On weekends I would open the door to the chook house in the afternoon (once the laying was done), so that they could escape into the big wide world. They always put themselves back to bed in the chook house, and CJ or I would go out after dark and shut the door behind them. The six girls were always lined up on the top perch, and Old Man Henry was always down on the senior citizen's perch on his own.

At first the chickens never wandered too far from the chicken run and hay shed, which was fine. But as the weekends passed, they slowly began drifting towards the house. The bottom boards on the white wooden fence around our yard are high enough that the chickens wandered right under them. When the chooks started entering the yard, I sat down in front of them and explained that they could go anywhere they wanted except for the backyard, which — with its unfenced and carefully tended flower beds — was absolutely off limits.

Alas, it seems our birds are headstrong. There they were, as I stood at the kitchen sink that day, marching straight for the beautifully blooming primulas and pansies.

I immediately ran out the back door, screaming and waving my arms as though I was under attack from a swarm of killer bees. The chickens did an about-face and ran away faster than you can say 'dangerous human on the loose'.

From that day forward. I remained vigilant, and to great effect. I soon discovered that running while twirling a tea towel above my head was a particularly effective way to herd chickens. They stopped going anywhere near the backyard.

Then CJ's Uncle Oscar came to visit. He's a 70-something Texan who has lived in New York City for nearly 50 years. He's a retired psychiatrist, a talented pianist and, most of all, a lover of animals. He had visited us in New Zealand several times before, and every time he walked by a paddock full of cows, he would moo to them. Sometimes the cows answered back.

That spring, CJ and I would head off to work in Wellington, leaving Uncle Oscar home alone with the chickens. Here is a rule to live by: Never leave a New Yorker to look after your chickens. Even if he is originally from Texas.

When we got home one evening Uncle Oscar said, 'Oh, the chickens were very funny today. They kept scratching the dirt in the back garden and rolling around.'

'Which garden?' I asked, trying to remain calm.

'The one in the backyard, with all the flowers. I watched them from the kitchen window. They laid on their sides and stuck their legs out in ecstasy. Dirt went everywhere. They were having the best time.' Then Uncle Oscar did an imitation, jutting his hands out at odd angles, rolling his eyes back into his head, and moaning. What can you do when someone you really like travels 10,000 miles to stand in your kitchen and imitate your chickens rolling around in your precious flower garden? I laughed uncontrollably.

I was so used to the chickens steering clear of the backyard that I hadn't thought to tell Uncle Oscar about The Forbidden Zone. When I explained, Uncle Oscar said, 'Oh, I thought they looked like they knew they were doing something bad.' Then he added, 'I feel like the substitute teacher. The unruly children took advantage of me.' I went out to inspect the back flower beds. The chooks had scattered the compost I'd put down as mulch, and they'd tossed some dirt out of the beds, but surprisingly there was no real damage to any of the plants.

I cleaned up the mess and asked Uncle Oscar to leave the chickens in the chicken run the following day.

'But he likes watching them,' CJ said.

Uncle Oscar looked at me with his big blue eyes. 'Please?'

'Okay, you can let them out. But if they go into the back garden, shoo them away.'

'Absolutely,' Uncle Oscar said. 'Bad chickens.' He shook his head.

When CJ and I got home from work on Thursday, Uncle Oscar said, 'Oh, I'm very sorry. They were at it again. I tried to get them to stop, but they just wouldn't listen to me.'

I went out and inspected the damage. This time they'd done something unforgivable. They'd trampled my young delphiniums. Of course, one possibility was to put chicken wire around the flower beds, but who wants to do that? No. I had to lay down the law. 'Sorry, Oscar. Tomorrow we have to leave them in the chicken run. I had them trained. Two days with a substitute teacher, and it's chaos again.'

CJ came to Uncle Oscar's defence immediately, but then I said, 'Who knows, CJ? Tomorrow the chickens might attack your new agapanthus.' The week before, CJ had split and planted even more of his beloved weeds, continuing the long line the Belgian and the Korean had started the year before. The thought of the chickens damaging his precious babies struck terror in CJ's heart. 'Well,' he said, 'I guess we *do* need to lock them up again.'

On the Friday night, Uncle Oscar was mournful. 'Oh, those poor little chickens,' he said. 'Locked up in prison all day. I went by to visit them and take them some wilted lettuce. They looked up at me and said, "Please let us out. We'll be good." I would have done it but I didn't know how to get them back in there before the mean Prison Wardens came home.'

I looked at Uncle Oscar. 'We can let them out this weekend,' I said. 'When I'm here.'

'Oh, they'll be so happy,' Uncle Oscar said.

So that weekend we let them out again. I let Uncle Oscar do the honours, and as they came out of the chook house door he yelled, 'Run, chickens, run! Be free!' All weekend I was on my guard, waiting for those chooks to make a wrong move. But they're not stupid. They must have known the meanest Prison Warden was watching. They never once went near The Forbidden Zone, but then again they never needed to. Every time I turned around there was Uncle Oscar, feeding them bread and crackers.

Chapter 31

Saturday morning fire

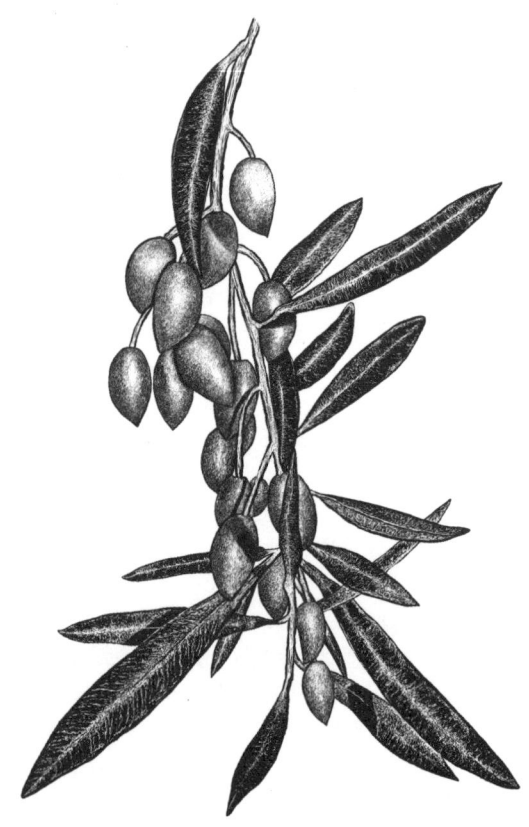

After Uncle Oscar had been here for a couple of weeks, CJ took him away on a little road trip. I woke up alone on a cold Saturday morning with a southerly blowing outside, so I decided to build a fire. I had no idea that my morning would end in a moral dilemma and a nightmare.

BEFORE MOVING TO MARTINBOROUGH, I had never relied on fire to heat my home. Growing up in suburban Detroit, our fireplace was for decoration. Heat came at the touch of a button. But in the past two years I'd grown to like the fact that heating our home in Martinborough involved touching trees — chopping, stacking, piling and lighting.

I first learned how to build a fire when I was in Indian Guides with my Father at the YMCA. We wore feathered headdresses, and instead of merit badges we earned feathers. My dad was chief. My name was Little Squirrel. They changed the programme now, out of respect for American Indians. It's still a father-son thing, but they call it Adventure Guides. (When you think about it, a bunch of white guys dressing up like American Indians is a bit bizarre.)

We were camping somewhere in Minnesota with our 'tribe' when my dad taught me how to build a fire. We weren't supposed to use newspaper to earn the Campfire feather, but he let me.

'The newspaper catches the kindling,' he said. 'And the kindling catches the logs.' He slapped me on the back. 'You cannot take a match to a log and expect it to burn. You have to go in little steps.'

There's a life lesson in there, somewhere.

SO ON THIS MORNING, home alone, I built a fire the way my father taught me. I lit a match and touched it to the newspaper, shut the fireplace door and turned away.

The noise I heard coming from inside the chimney flue was almost immediate. A quick and panicked scratching. There was something in there. And it was alive.

I wondered how I could put the fire out, but the newspaper was burning fast, already catching the kindling. It must have been the fastest-burning fire I've ever built. I suppose my father taught me well.

Then suddenly, there it was. A starling had popped down from the chimney into the firebox, and it was pecking against the glass. It was jumping and twisting, trying to get out, trying to avoid the quickly growing flames.

Instinctively, I reached for the door handle. I had to let it out.

But then I saw that its wing was already on fire. I thought of a burning bird inside the house, setting the curtains and rugs alight.

Should I let it out? What would happen if I did?

Because the starling was already on fire, I pulled my hand away from the door. I watched. A friend later told me that she couldn't have looked on as it happened. Yet somehow, as horrified as I was, I never even thought of turning away. It was like I was there, with the bird. To close my eyes would have been abandonment.

I had my hand over my mouth. My heart was beating fast.

The bird flinched and jumped, clearly in pain. Smoke filled the woodburner, and the bird's beak started opening and closing slowly, trying to pull in air. I have never before seen a bird gasp for breath. As it did, it fell slowly backwards, until it stopped moving.

There are stories of ancient Buddhist monks meditating in front of decomposing human corpses. It sounds gruesome, and it is. It was supposed to focus the monk on the temporary nature of our lives, of all life. I have seen meditation beads made of human bone that serve the same purpose. I have held them in my hand.

Watching the starling die was a little bit like that for me.

When the bird was entirely charred, I opened the door and looked at it. Its legs had burnt up to stumps. The feet were gone. I touched its beak with the wrought-iron fire poker, and the entire beak disintegrated into ash.

Then I pushed the small, black body into the glowing red embers of the fire. I placed some kindling over it and said a small prayer. The bird's hollow bones burned easily. Ten minutes later it was gone.

Chapter 32

What the river taught me

The spring rains slowed at the beginning of November, and I opened the front door one morning and headed outside to go check on the river. I wanted to see what had happened.

I WALKED DOWN ALONG the rosemary hedge and out across the lush green grass of the paddocks. On my way, I cut through the olive grove just to look at the flower buds. There were so many that spring, so many. Every chance I had I wandered through the grove to see them. Andrew-of-the-Olives had come in October to prune, and now CJ's post-apocalyptic toothpick row didn't look that much different from the others — a fact that pleased CJ no end and for several days made him almost unbearable to live with. There was a stack of enormous olive limbs up near the hay shed now, ready to be cut up for firewood. James the Sprayer had also begun coming to our grove, encased in the glass case of his tractor, driving down the rows as a misty spray touched the trees. We had agreed on an organic spraying programme using copper and sulphur as anti-fungals and a seaweed fertiliser. I looked again at the flower buds now, reached out and held a branch. Yes, the trees looked happy. Then I remembered the river. I turned and went out the grove's back gate, headed once again toward the bottom of our property, and to the river.

In the far left corner of the very bottom paddock, there is an old wooden gate. It hangs at an odd angle, and doesn't swing very well. I opened that gate and walked out among the wild fennel, which I'd learned to use in soups, and then I wandered along under a dense cluster of trees. Finally, I could hear the river, just through the trees. It always felt like a small miracle to me that I could go on such an incredible walk without ever leaving home.

I peeked out from between two large trees toward the water. Was the river okay? How had it changed?

I'd fallen in love with this river our very first summer here. Everything about it felt perfect back then. Time seemed to stand still when I was there. I had no idea that the river as I knew it then would eventually disappear.

During that summer, at the end of long afternoons working in the garden or in the olive grove, CJ and I began a small tradition. We'd finish our work and then wander immediately down to the river, sweaty and hot. We'd throw off shirts, boots and socks and fall back into the cool, clear water with a resounding splash. It was mostly shallow, and the water ran slowly. We would drift, watching the branches above us sway in the breeze. Afterward we'd rest on a nearby log, listening to the water bubbling against the rocks, feeling the sun on our skin. One day we found a sandy spot on the otherwise rocky bank, and we dubbed it 'the beach'. It was dappled in willow shade. CJ would pack the most incredible picnic lunches and we'd go down to the beach together, lay out a blanket, and eat and talk and read. Sometimes we'd see a trout fisher just downstream from the beach, his fishing line catching the sun mid-air. Sometimes we'd become drowsy and drift off to sleep, sheltered by the trees. We passed entire afternoons this way. We liked the river just the way it was. We didn't want a thing to change.

As autumn came that first year and the air grew cool, we no longer spent so much time down at the river. We'd still go for walks to see it, but we no longer lounged on its banks. That was when everything began to shift and become unstable. The winter rains came.

Rivers in our part of the Wairarapa don't rise on the day of a heavy rain. They rise the day after, once the waters have had time to work their way down from the mountains and into our part of the valley.

During our first winter in Martinborough it rained so hard that we were at risk of floods. One especially bad night, the rain kept coming and coming. The regional council issued flood warnings. Jim and Kiwi Bronwyn next door moved their cattle out of their bottom paddock, just in case. People have had stock swept away in floods here. A friend of ours tells a story of fishing in a local river years ago, and noticing a terrible smell. There had been floods a few weeks before. When he looked up he saw a cow carcass, rotting in a tree.

We were lucky because on the night of the council flood warnings, the rain finally stopped. The following night the moon came out, and I stood on the deck and looked down past the olive grove toward the bottom paddock, listening. That was the first and only time I've ever heard the river from the house. It was like an angry monster out there in the darkness, roaring beyond the trees.

A couple of days after that, I walked down to the riverside and I was amazed by the change. Gone was our calm trout stream of summer, replaced with a wide and frothing torrent. Debris hung in the trees. New pathways were cut out of the river bank. I couldn't get close, because the water still raged.

When the spring of our second year arrived, the winter rains eased off and the river began shrinking back into itself. CJ and I wandered down to the river bank one warm day. When we tried to find our beach, we realised that our precious spot — where we'd spent so many beautiful days the summer before — was simply gone. The floods had washed it away. It felt like a kind of loss.

We hadn't yet realised that every summer here we would have to rediscover the river, that we'd never have the same river twice. We found a new spot. The river had split in one place, creating a small gravel embankment in the middle. So during our second summer we spent time hanging out on what we called 'the island'. We were surrounded by shallow, sparkling water on all sides. It was a new kind of paradise.

As that second summer continued, the sun began turning the green, grassy hills around us into their annual golden brown. Then one day we discovered something even more spectacular than the island, even more incredible than the previous year's beach. We found our first swimming hole.

Not that far from our island, the winter floods had carved out a deeper spot — not so deep as to go up to your neck, but deep enough. It was hidden in a tangle of tree branches pushed by the flood. CJ and I went down to the river with a pruning saw one afternoon and cleared it out.

We spent a lot of time in that swimming hole that summer. We would watch the light come down through the willow trees along the banks. We would splash and laugh and then climb up to the island nearby to dry off in the sun.

The river gives and the river takes away. Nothing ever stays the same. When the weather turned cool and that summer ended, CJ came back from the river one day with terrible news.

'All the trees are gone,' he said. I immediately went down to see for myself.

In a push for flood control, the regional council had clear-cut a huge section of the river bank. They left behind a barren, muddy wasteland, and they left behind two gigantic mounds of dead tree trunks, like horrible scars.

Again, it was a kind of loss. But worse this time. By then the river had become something like a sacred space for me. Standing there alone that day, looking at the damage, it felt as though somebody had firebombed my church.

I walked down along the desecrated river bank toward where our swimming hole was. I had to see what it was like there. I had to see if the swimming hole was still okay. When I got there, I couldn't believe what I saw. The willows at the edge of the swimming hole were still intact, surrounding the banks on both sides. The council had stopped felling trees before they got there. Thank the gods for that.

CJ called the council about the tree mounds they'd left behind. Not only were they an eyesore, but if we had any floods they could create a dam. The man at the council said they planned to burn those mounds down at the end of winter.

We told ourselves that the river would heal and become beautiful again. It would change, just as it always did. And at least we were less at risk of floods. It was good. We told ourselves that it was good.

Now, in our third year here, as I walked through the olive grove to look at the flower buds and on to the river, I had no idea what I'd find. I wondered what the winter rains had done this time, since so many trees were gone.

I walked forward through a gap in the trees, and I saw that the loose river bank had given way. The tree mounds had been burnt down on the bank, but there were still two ashen mounds. The river itself was wider than ever, and it had split in a new place. The water was still wild with spring rain.

I went down along the river towards where our swimming hole was, and our island. Immediately I saw that the island was gone, entirely washed away, but already I could see that there were several new places for spreading out a picnic blanket and lying down. I looked over toward the swimming hole and, fortunately, it looked like it was still there. But the water was dark and muddy, and I couldn't tell how deep it was. It was too soon to tell if the spot would be any good for swimming this year. We would have to wait for summer to start in earnest, for the hills to turn brown again, for the water to become clear with lack of rain.

I turned around and headed back up to the house, thinking about the upcoming summer, wondering what the river would be like when it completely settled back down into itself.

I looked forward to discovering the river a third time.

Chapter 33

When farm animals escape

Sometimes livestock perform the farm equivalent of a prison break — with one key difference. Instead of breaking out, they break in.

It was the middle of December and the warm summer days were long. The olive blossoms in our grove had just opened, and the weather was good for pollination — dry without too much wind. CJ and I had already started to enjoy the river again, having discovered that our old swimming hole was now even deeper than the year before.

ONE DAY MIDWEEK WE came home from work with plans to enjoy the long summer evening with a relaxing meal on the front deck. But first I headed out to the chook house to collect the day's eggs. That was when I found two cows in the backyard. They were just beyond the laundry line, clearly on the wrong side of the fence. They were like two rough-as-guts convicts staring me down, completely unafraid.

Of course I did what any level-headed city boy would do upon coming face to face with two large cows by the laundry line. I turned around and ran the other way.

I shot along the back of the house and past the kitchen window. CJ was inside pulling steaks out of the fridge for the barbecue.

'Cows in the yard!' I yelled, still running.

CJ told me later he thought I was running in fear. Little did he know that I was doing the most sensible thing imaginable. I was running past the columbine and delphiniums blooming in the flower beds, down along the ever-lengthening line of CJ's agapanthus, so that I could get to the front gate.

We live on a long, empty country road. The speed limit is 100 km/h. It's the kind of road you see in car ads, where a lone luxury vehicle is hurtling through scenic beauty at high speeds. There's a bend in the road just before you get to our place. If a cow were standing in the middle of that road as you came around the corner, you'd have very little time to stop. The results could be deadly, and not just for the cow.

I closed the gate and clasped it tightly. When I got back to the house, CJ was just coming out in his gumboots.

Much to my surprise, our two escaped convicts had not moved an inch. They were exactly where I'd found them, peacefully eating. Then I saw what they'd chosen to have for dinner — the native flax and miniature toetoe that CJ had meticulously planted the weekend before.

CJ saw it too, and he wailed a long and agonising 'Noooo!'

The cows were unmoved. They continued happily munching, clearly very pleased that all those fresh, tasty morsels were so easy to pull out of the ground by the roots. In front of them the garden lay ravaged.

I had misjudged these cows. They were not the jail-breaking prison scum I'd assumed. Why, they weren't thugs at all! These cows were more like bovine versions of Martha Stewart, locked in a minimum-security detention facility and sick of the mediocre food. They were simply desperate for a good meal. In CJ's newly planted native garden they had found an all-you-can-eat luxury buffet. I could almost hear their pleasant tableside chit-chat.

'Oh, this food is so much better than that lowbrow paddock grass on the other side of the fence. Don't you think?'

'Yes, darling. This toetoe is gorgeous! And did you try the native ferns? Simply divine!'

We stepped closer to the cows, and they gazed up at us with a strange look in their eyes. Imagine Martha now sitting in a Michelin Four Star restaurant, looking up at the guard who'd arrived to drag her back to prison.

We city boys had learned a few things since CJ broke a rib trying to move Evil Cow. With the gate to the road shut, there was no longer any need to run. We moved slowly and calmly, just like 'real' farmers would. We both scanned the fenceline, searching for the spot where it had been breached, but we couldn't see how the cows had managed to get in. I began to wonder what use the fence around our yard was. It didn't keep out chickens, and it didn't keep out cows. We might as well be living in the paddocks.

CJ stepped forward, and suddenly one of the two cows went bolting behind some trees — straight for the section of fence nearest to the road. There was the sound of breaking branches and snapping twigs underfoot, and just when I expected to see the cow out on the road, it appeared over in the top paddock. It had pushed through a broken bit of fence. That must have been how they'd got in.

In the meantime, the second cow had turned the other way and ran over towards our Granny Smith apple tree. CJ walked slowly in that direction to keep the cow cornered. I went over to the large gate that leads into the top paddock and opened it. Then we both gradually walked around and blocked the cow's path so that it ran straight out the open gate, just as we'd wanted.

BUT OUR JOB WASN'T finished. I looked at the gaping hole in the fence where the cows had invaded. Hamish had five cows grazing in that top paddock, and there was nothing to stop any of them from immediately re-entering our yard.

We didn't have the materials on hand, or the know-how, to fix the fence so it was clear that we had to move the cows. But we'd never done that before. After all, they were not our cows.

We walked out into the paddock and closed the gate behind us. CJ walked down to the left, toward the boggy pond behind the hay shed where the cows were now trying to hide. I went to the right. We moved slowly, calmly.

CJ drove the cows out and away from the pond, up the far side of the hay shed and towards the middle paddock gate, which I had by then unclasped and left wide open. When the cows tried to bypass the gate and run back into the top paddock, I was there with my arms outstretched to stop them. They finally turned and ran out the open gate, into the middle paddock.

CJ and I arrived back at the gate at the same time, and we swung it shut together.

'We did it,' he said, smiling.

'Yes,' I said. 'You'd almost think we knew what we're doing.'

'Almost,' he said.

We walked together over to the Chicken Palace to pick up the day's eggs.

'I haven't seen any sparrows for months,' I said to CJ, oblivious to the fact that the sparrows were no doubt listening. Then I boasted. 'Guess I finally beat them.'

CJ just shook his head. Then we headed back to the house together, laughing about the cows and talking about what we were going to have with the steaks for dinner.

Chapter 34

Silver monster in the chicken run

A few days later, I was walking blissfully across the top paddock towards the Chicken Palace, noticing how our little valley was flooded with golden light, when I came face to face with the most spine-tingling, nightmarish vision you could possibly imagine.

AN ENTIRE SWARM of sparrows in the chicken run. I had never seen so many of the little devils in one place.

I fell to my knees and howled in anguish. 'Damn you, evil spawn of Sataaan!'

Clearly the sparrows had heard my boast, so they'd came back with a vengeance. In spite of my ongoing and fervent efforts, I had not managed to plug up every possible sparrow-sized entry into the chicken run. There had to be at least 200 of the infected creatures in there. Maybe thousands. They were flapping around, smashing into the chicken wire, and chirping wildly.

'We're in! We're in!' they screamed.

After beating my fists on the ground for several minutes, I stood up, brushed myself off, and marched into the house to call Aussie Bronwyn.

'You should get a Grandpa's Feeder,' she said. 'I love mine.'

There was a time when I would have questioned the sanity of anyone who professed love for a poultry feeder. Obviously I had been in the country too long, because it seemed like a perfectly reasonable thing to say.

'What's a Grandpa's Feeder?' I asked.

She explained that once upon a time a New Zealand farmer got tired of rats, mice and sparrows eating his chicken feed, so he built this contraption. There's a step on the front of the feeder. When the chickens step on it, a lid opens to expose the food. When the chickens step away, the lid closes. Simple. The pests don't weigh as much as the chickens, so they can't open the lid to get the food.

'Since I got my Grandpa's Feeder,' Aussie Bronwyn said, 'the sparrows don't bother my chooks anymore. I don't know where the sparrows went, but they're gone.'

'They're all over at our place,' I said.

I immediately jumped online and spent a whopping $250 on the largest Grandpa's Feeder available. The day it arrived, I placed it proudly in the chicken run. It was beautiful and shiny and new. It was going to solve all of my problems.

'Ha!' I announced to the sparrows watching malevolently from the trees. 'Soon I will be rid of you for good!'

But I still had one thing to do. I had to train our chickens how to use the feeder. Yes, train. Let me draw your attention to the fact that there is no such thing as a Chicken Circus. You never see chickens jumping through hoops and doing cute little tricks, now do you? There is a reason for that.

According to the instructions, there were three training stages. For the first week you use the bolts included to lock the step down and keep the feeder lid in the open position. The chickens can get used to the feeder that way. For the second week you reposition the bolts so the step and feeder lid are in the halfway position. The chickens get used to a slight movement in the mechanism. Finally, you remove the training bolts and you're done. Your clever chickens have learned to use the feeder, showing absolutely no fear when the mechanism moves. Your blissfully pest-free life begins.

I set up the feeder for the first stage, stepped out of the run, and watched. The two Fat English Ladies walked nervously towards the feeder and eyed it carefully. It almost seemed as though they were whispering to each other.

'Good heavens, Henrietta! What do you think that dreadful thing is?'

'Stop, Ethel! It's a death trap! Don't eat that food! You'll get your head chopped off!'

They retreated to the other side of the run and began scratching in the dirt for bugs. From over in the trees, I could hear the evil, maniacal laughter of sparrows.

During the next two weeks, I followed instructions to a T. Since there can't be any other food during training, I ripped out the greens I'd planted in the middle of the run. I tried enticing the chickens toward the feeder with special treats. But they remained firm.

None of them wanted anything at all to do with the big silver monster that had landed in their run — not the two Fat English Ladies, not Old Man Henry nor the aristocratic Araucanas, and certainly not the two Barnevelder Sisters (who, regrettably, had grown up to be extremely unfriendly and never once approached me for cuddles). The only birds unafraid of the feeder were, you guessed it, the sparrows. Every morning I chased more and more of the vermin out.

In frustration I started over at stage one of the training, and I decided to deliver a bit of a pep talk. 'Look at that nice feeder,' I said to the chickens. 'What lucky chooks you are. I wish I could eat from such a shiny new feeder! Yummy yum!'

Clearly I was losing my mind. Instead of being inspired by my rousing speech, all seven of our chickens looked at me with utter disdain, turned up their beaks, and walked away. No matter what I did, the feeder absolutely terrified them. If I touched it and gently moved the step with my hand, they all shrieked and flapped their wings like it was Armageddon. 'He's starting up the killing machine!'

To show their resentment, they stopped laying eggs. They bullied each other. Then they started losing weight. It was as if they'd organised some sort of fanatical, prison-based hunger strike. They had resolved to die before they ate from that damn feeder.

AFTER MORE THAN SIX WEEKS of this, I was practically pulling out my hair. I'd gone through the training stages multiple times, but with absolutely no success. I finally resigned myself to the fact that we had the World's Most Stupid and Untrainable Chickens. I was ready to give up.

'You can't give up!' CJ said. 'We paid two hundred and fifty bucks for that feeder! After all, Aussie Bronwyn's chickens use their Grandpa's Feeder. Maybe ours just need an example. Why don't we borrow Big Daddy? He'll teach them how to use that feeder.'

'You want to bring Big Daddy over here?' I asked.

CJ was deadly serious. 'Desperate times require desperate measures.'

Big Daddy is one of Aussie Bronwyn's Barred Rock roosters. He is an enormous, swaggering lady's man. If he were human he'd wear a thick gold chain and be excessively proud of his chest hair. I agreed to ask Aussie Bronwyn about it, and she thought it was a great idea. In the end, Big Daddy came over with Favourite Wife, the hen he is with constantly. To spare Old Man Henry the shame of no longer being 'Da Man', and to save him from being killed by Big Daddy, we sent him to Aussie Bronwyn's for a holiday.

Our hens were Virgin Queens. They had known only one rooster their entire lives, and that was the geriatric and impotent Old Man Henry. So when Big Daddy arrived on the scene, they were scared to death.

As soon as Aussie Bronwyn set Big Daddy down in the run, he strutted over to the Grandpa's Feeder, hopped up on the step, and started eating. All six of our hens watched in amazement.

Aussie Bronwyn positively beamed. 'I think your hens will be eating from that feeder in no time. You'll just have to make sure that nobody gets hen-pecked.'

Later that evening I saw Big Daddy 'treading' Favourite Wife. He was standing on top of her and holding the back of her neck with his beak. It wasn't pretty, and I became very worried for our little Virgin Queens.

A week later, our hens were spending most of their time hiding in the chicken coop from Big Daddy. They still weren't eating from the feeder. I think they must have been getting by on bugs.

'Give it time,' Aussie Bronwyn said.

ABOUT THAT TIME I took a week off and went to Northland with my mom and step-dad, who were visiting from the States. I left CJ in charge of the property.

When I got home, he said, 'While you were away, something very bad happened.'

He then told me the story of how he went out to check on the chickens one night and saw a large, gaping hole at the back of Ethel's head. Blood had flowed down her neck and covered her back. He immediately called Aussie Bronwyn, who came right over.

When she saw Ethel, she was even more horrified than CJ. 'Oh, I feel terrible,' she said. 'Did Big Daddy do that?' Then she looked a little more closely. 'Are her brains coming out?'

They watched her carefully and the blood seemed to have stopped. They decided to leave her alone as she was already so upset.

'If she dies, Jared will kill me,' CJ said.

'Either way, John and I will be the pariahs of the neighbourhood,' Aussie Bronwyn said. 'Us and our wife-beating rooster.' She immediately packed up Big Daddy and Favourite Wife and took them home, slinking down the road in shame. Then they brought back Old Man Henry.

When CJ told me this story I glared at him and said, 'It's your fault. You wanted Big Daddy.' Then I immediately went out to check on Ethel. Fortunately she recovered very well, although for several weeks afterwards she seemed a bit twitchy and shy.

I immediately sent our precious $250 feeder over to Aussie Bronwyn's on long-term loan. She had two then, hers and ours. She took delight in telling me how her chickens used them both every day.

After that I returned to my old routine of walking out to our chicken run every morning with my red bucket to feed our chooks, and every time I chased out at least 10 or 20 evil, parasitic sparrows. When I walked back to the house, invariably I could hear those same sparrows laughing at me from the trees.

'Just you wait,' I said, glaring up at them. 'Some day. Just you wait.'

Chapter 35

Storm at Palliser Bay

A summer storm came that January. Rain fell hard all night and into the morning, and it was still falling heavily when we climbed into the trusty little Nissan Pulsar that afternoon. I threw four pairs of gumboots into the back, started the engine, and headed for the coast. I hoped the road wouldn't be washed out.

SITTING NEXT TO ME as I drove was CJ's Aunt Charlie — a retired nurse from Iowa who, at nearly 70, still had a passionate enthusiasm for life and the boundless energy of a 16-year-old. In the back seat were Titou and Gabby, a delightful European couple who were HelpX volunteers and who were staying with us for a couple of weeks. Titou is a wiry Frenchman with a quick smile. Gabby is a petite Polish woman whose traditional Polish potato dumplings are so delicious that they'll make you wish you grew up in Warsaw.

That morning CJ had promised our three guests that he would drive them 74 kilometres down rough, narrow and sometimes non-existent roads to Cape Palliser in the afternoon. On the way they'd stop first at the fishing village of Ngawi, then at the local seal colony, and finally at the Cape Palliser lighthouse. I had planned on staying home. Why then was I driving the car? And where was CJ?

CJ, as it turns out, was the one at home, taking a nap on the

World's Most Comfortable Couch. He'd slaved on the property in the rain all morning with Titou and Gabby. After lunch, battered and exhausted, he came to me with a rather impassioned plea.

'Would you drive everyone to the coast instead?'

He's cute when he's tired. I'd had a relatively easy morning, so I foolishly said yes. It was only afterwards that I thought of how the road to Cape Palliser requires you to ford several streams. Normally the streams are a trickle and our Nissan Pulsar does fine, but what about in this rain?

'Maybe they got less rain out there,' CJ said. 'It might be fine.'

Around this time I should have remembered that one of my nicknames for CJ is 'Tom Sawyer' — the boy who famously fast-talked his friends into doing his chores. But alas, I didn't remember this until we were out on the road, driving toward the sea, as the rain got worse and worse.

The farms to the right were lost in grey watery sheets and the Aorangi mountains to the left were covered in mist. In the back seat Titou and Gabby were talking to each other in English, their only common language. Their thick accents filled the car. Aunt Charlie was busy staring at the landscape, soaking it all in.

'Oh, just look at those mountains,' she cried out, to nobody in particular. 'They look like Chinese paintings!'

Not even a drive in torrential rain towards certain doom could stop Aunt Charlie from having a good time.

There's a point on Lake Ferry Road where a sign points to the left, to *Cape Palliser*. This is where you leave the good flat roads behind and the madness begins. At first the road seems fine, but that's just to lull you into a false sense of security. Before you know it you're turning and twisting through the hills that edge the coastline like a fortress wall.

There's a particular point where the view opens up and you catch your first glimpse of the sea in the distance. On this summer day, however, the only thing we saw at that point was a vast, thick blanket of grey.

It was as we descended the hills that we came across the first rock slip. A tumble of enormous boulders lay across one side of the road, and I carefully drove around them.

'It would not be good to be under those rocks when they fell,' Titou said.

Everyone heartily agreed, and from then on we watched the cliffs carefully. At the second slip we came to, the rocks totally covered the road, but they looked smaller. I slowed and drove towards the spot where the rocks looked smallest. As we passed over them there was a loud *CURR-RUNCH* from underneath the car. I imagined a hole in the petrol tank, causing us to lose fuel in a slow and insidious way, so that we'd become stranded. I was certain we were going to die.

I considered turning around, but doing a U-turn in the rain on that narrow, curving road — with a rock face on one side and a sheer drop-off on the other — would have been impossible. I drove on. Just then the view finally opened up, and Aunt Charlie screamed, 'The sea! The sea!'

Titou and Gabby craned their necks from the back seat. 'Where? Where?'

Directly in front of us, down a steep precipice, the wide expanse of Palliser Bay threw giant white waves at the shore. The churning seabed had turned the water brown. The wind and rain swept the coast from the east and pushed at our faithful and determined little car.

We descended further, and suddenly the sea was to our right, thick and angry and close. Waves crashed on rocks and threw foam to the sky.

'Why would anyone build a road so close to the sea?' Titou asked.

Nobody answered.

NEAR THE ENTRANCE TO the Putangirua Pinnacles scenic reserve a car approached us from the opposite direction. It was a huge four-wheel-drive ute clearly built for conditions like these. The driver rolled down his window and yelled out over the sound of the wind and the sea.

'Tourist or local?' He had a brown beard and tousled hair.

Although I'd been living in Martinborough for just over two years by then, we were out on the coast, and it was a very different world out there.

'Tourist,' I said.

After all, who else would be out there on a day like that, driving a two-door hatchback?

'The road's gone,' the bearded man said. 'You should turn around.'

'Can we get at least to Ngawi?'

He looked down at the wheels of our car and shook his head. 'That car will never be able to cross those streams.'

Our trip was over. We hadn't even made it to Ngawi. I thanked the man and he drove on. In order to salvage something out of our outing, I pulled over at a place where a gravel access led down to the sea. Out of fear of getting stuck, I stayed up near the road. I turned off the engine and all four of us sat in silence, watching the sea as it raged. The wind rocked the car.

It was Aunt Charlie who said, 'Can we go outside?'

'Outside?' I said.

'Please?' she added. 'It's just so beautiful.'

I looked back at Titou and Gabby.

Titou smiled. 'Why not?'

Gabby nodded and shrugged.

That was how we ended up, moments later, standing out by the sea on a remote stretch of rocky coast at the bottom of the planet, wearing gumboots and raincoats that did absolutely nothing to keep us dry as we laughed and shouted at the sky. The rain and sea foam hurtled towards us like tiny pellets of sand.

We stayed a respectful distance from the water. Nobody wanted to be swept away. But even at that distance, the power of the crashing waves reverberated in our chests. It was so ridiculous to be there. So fantastic and so ridiculous. Aunt Charlie's grey bob blew across her face. She flicked back her white scarf and it trailed alongside her in the wind. She leaned into a strong gust and screamed. Gabby nearly fell over and Titou held her. We all howled and laughed some more.

Later, on the way back to Martinborough, we would take a detour to the Lake Ferry Hotel, where we would sit and drink hot chocolate, feeling our soggy socks squish disgustingly between our toes as our cold, wet jeans stuck to our legs.

But for now, we were out there in the elements. We were wild, and we were happy. And we were utterly and totally free.

Chapter 36

Egg delivery gone wrong

The train pulled into the station at Featherston, and I stepped up into the carriage carrying two dozen farm-fresh eggs. It's not what most people carry during their morning commute, but when you live in the country and work in the city as we do, you start doing strange things.

I HAD ALREADY TAKEN a capsicum plant to the office. It was growing beautifully in a pot next to my desk. I wondered if I was on a slippery slope. Soon I'd be taking in live chickens and setting up chicken runs in the meeting rooms.

But on this particular day I had a very good reason to take two dozen eggs to work. Our hens were in full production — the Fat English Ladies, the aristocratic South Americans, and the surly Barnevelder Sisters. Those six hens were giving CJ and me more eggs than we could possibly eat. Even the Communist Egg Collective had enjoyed more than their fair share. So I was taking some to my co-workers. But alas, things didn't exactly go according to plan.

I found a seat on the train, placed the eggs on the overhead shelf, and settled in for the 55-minute train ride. Before I continue, allow me to admit to something of a character flaw. I can be forgetful. CJ says that even Old Man Henry has a better memory than I. So it should come as no surprise that I was already sitting at my desk reading my first emails of the day when I remembered the eggs, which I'd left on the overhead shelf.

I turned to my co-workers. 'I brought you farm-fresh eggs today.'

They ooh-ed and aah-ed appropriately, craning their necks to see where I might have put them.

'And I left them on the train.'

They moaned loudly together as though on cue. Lucky for me there were no farm-fresh tomatoes lying about at that point, or they would have surely thrown them at me.

Then someone said, 'Why don't you call Lost Property?'

I ended up speaking to a man named Ed who works at the Wellington Railway Station. He was in charge of lost property. He had a heavy, rumbling voice, and when I told him I'd left two dozen eggs on the train, he audibly guffawed.

'That's a first,' he said.

'Do you have them?' I asked.

'No. What train were you on?'

'The Wairarapa line.'

'Huh. That explains it.'

In Wellington city, 'Wairarapa' is synonymous with 'the country'. It seemed that, at least in Ed's mind, someone leaving two dozen eggs on the Wairarapa train made much more sense than someone leaving them on, say, the suburban Johnsonville train. After all, you never knew what those crazy country people got up to. You just might find a herd of cattle in the luggage car.

'What were they in?' Ed asked abruptly. 'Box? Bag?'

I described my eggs: four egg cartons of a half-dozen each, all inside a white plastic grocery bag. For some reason — perhaps to distinguish these two dozen eggs from any others that might have been left on the train that morning — I added the fact that some of the eggs were blue.

'Blue?' Ed barked. 'You can eat those?'

'Sure. They're delicious. In some light, they look sort of green.'

Ed harrumphed. Then he quickly explained that the cleaners hadn't cleaned the Wairarapa train yet. 'Call back later. See if they handed them in.'

When I called that afternoon, Ed recognised my voice immediately — something I've noticed happens a lot more here than back in the States, no doubt because of my accent.

'It's the egg bloke,' Ed said warmly, as though he were greeting an old friend.

I was surprised by his friendliness. 'That's me. Any luck?'

'Got 'em right here,' Ed said. Then he paused. 'Those blue eggs —

they're quite nice, aren't they?'

Something had changed in Ed. Perhaps he'd been charmed by the sight of blue eggs. They are pretty magical, really.

'Yep,' I said. 'They're from a South American breed called Lavender Araucana. The chickens are grey with tufted feathers on their heads.'

'Well, you learn something new every day.'

That evening I went to the train a couple of minutes early so I could stop by the Lost Property desk and talk to Ed. He was an older man, with buzz-cut grey hair. His uniform sleeves were rolled up, revealing thick forearms. I imagined he must have been a labourer on the tracks years ago, before he took this desk job.

'Hi, I'm Jared. I'm here for the eggs.'

He smiled as he got up slowly and turned to a table behind him. He grabbed my white plastic grocery bag and handed me my eggs. As he pulled out a ledger for me to sign, he said, 'I told my mates if you didn't show I was going to have a fry-up. Never ate blue eggs.' He was all laughter and warmth, jokes and smiles.

I considered giving Ed some of the blue eggs. I really wanted to. But I was afraid he would think it was odd. I signed the ledger, thanked him and left the office.

And yet, as I walked onto the railway platform and toward the Wairarapa train, I kept thinking about Ed. My moment with him felt like a little failure. I should have given him some eggs. I would have been a nice 'country' thing to do. I suppose that when you've lived in large cities like I had been doing for years, you start to learn strange, unwritten rules — things you don't even realise you're learning until they're already a part of your psyche.

Keep to yourself on the streets. Don't nod hello to people you don't know. Be aware of your wallet at all times. Be careful never to look like you're lost, even if you are. And of course, never, ever give eggs to strangers. Especially if those eggs are blue. It's as though in urban places we build small walls around us. Perhaps I had lived in large cities for too long. It takes a great deal to unlearn these things, even after you've moved to the country.

When I got to the train, CJ was saving me a seat. As I went to put my two dozen eggs back on the overhead shelf, just then Katy walked by. Katy is the ticket clipper that CJ and I really like. She's got four or five large silver hoops in each ear, and her hair has a fantastic burgundy-purple tint to it. She's the friendliest ticket clipper you'll ever meet on the Wairarapa line.

Katy saw the egg cartons through the bag. 'Cooking omelettes for fifty?' she asked me.

I laughed and explained why I had the eggs.

'Ooo, farm-fresh eggs,' she said, and then she continued walking down the aisle.

WHEN SHE WAS OUT of earshot, CJ whispered a wonderful thing to me.

'Let's give Katy some eggs.'

I smiled. It was the perfect idea.

When the train arrived in Featherston, I pulled the eggs down off the shelf, took two of the small cartons out, and handed them to CJ. As we stepped down off the train, he ran up to the front to find Katy. She was on the platform, making sure everyone was off before she shut the doors.

'For you!' CJ said.

Katy broke into a wide, surprised smile. 'Oh, thank you!'

'Some of them are blue,' CJ said, as he waved goodbye.

'Blue? Fantastic.' Katy waved back as she hopped up on the train with a big smile on her face.

After that, we were on a roll. As CJ and I walked towards the Featherston–Martinborough bus, we bumped into Jane. She lives in Martinborough and sometimes gives us a ride so we don't have to take the bus.

'G'day!' she said. 'Want a ride?'

We climbed into her car and I immediately said, 'Hey Jane, want some fresh eggs? Some of them are blue.'

How can you not smile when someone says that to you? She laughed and said, 'Sure.'

And I handed her the rest of the eggs myself. As I did, I thought of Ed. I felt like a wrong had been righted, and everything was okay again. We had given away all of our eggs. The co-workers would have to wait another day.

Chapter 37

Shovel
and axe

I had just hopped back over the fence after visiting Kiwi Bronwyn and Jim the Mad Welshman when I saw CJ walking towards the chicken coop with a shovel in one hand and an axe in the other. The evening light was bright on the far hills, up where the two noble pine trees stood together, but the paddock we were in was drenched in shadows.

I knew what CJ wanted to do. In fact, I'd agreed to it a couple of weeks earlier, but all of a sudden I had reservations.

I CERTAINLY HADN'T EXPECTED to be doing it now, on a peaceful evening after visiting the neighbours. I wasn't prepared.

As CJ came closer I said, 'Why now?'

He set the axe down on the ground near a weathered log. 'We should do it before we go. Get it over with.'

He walked with the shovel over to a spot alongside the chicken coop, and he started to dig. We were about to go to Sydney for a holiday, and we'd be gone for a week. Still, I didn't want to do it now. But I just stood there watching CJ dig.

The ground by the chicken coop was hard and dry. It was the middle of summer. CJ struggled to get the shovel in. But after only a couple of shovelfuls of dry soil, the hole was deep enough. CJ walked around and opened the chicken coop door. All the chickens had settled down on their perches for the night, and CJ reached over and grabbed Natasha.

She was right next to Françoise, as always. Having survived the Chook House Race Wars against the Fat English Ladies, Natasha and Françoise had become the best of friends. Natasha started screeching and squawking horribly. Soon the entire chicken coop was in an uproar.

'I'm not wearing clothes I can get blood on,' I said to CJ.

'I'll do it. You just hold her head.' He was carrying her towards the log and the axe.

'Wait. That log's not right. Let me get another.'

I went into the hay shed to find another log to go under the axe, but none of them was right. When I came out of the hay shed, CJ was watching Natasha run away.

'What happened?' I asked.

'She got out of my hands. She just ran around the back of the hay shed.'

Secretly, I was pleased.

THE YEAR BEFORE, during our time when Monday night had become Scaly Leg Mite Night, Natasha had at first made significant improvements. Her legs became less grey and bumpy. Her dark scales started to grow back. We thought we were in the clear. But as soon as we stopped the treatment, her legs became worse than ever. Soon they were covered with grey, deformed bumps and dying leg scales.

One day during winter, CJ took Natasha to the vet, but the vet just said to use Vaseline. As a result, we'd started up the treatments again. That time, instead of the month-long, weekly treatments that the vet had recommended, we were out there greasing our birds' legs with Vaseline every Monday night for three solid months. We'd also begun cleaning out the chook house more regularly, and we'd treated the entire place with generous doses of mite powder several times.

Again Natasha made progress, but even after those three months of regular treatment, her legs quickly descended into a grey and bumpy mess again. The mite-carrying sparrows were still visiting our pest-proof Chicken Palace as though they owned the place. Fortunately, through some miracle, none of the other chickens had become infected. At least, not yet.

When spring came and Natasha was still sick, I of course called the High Priestess of Chicken Wisdom.

'Well, well,' Aussie Bronwyn said over the phone. 'That *is* a problem. I've heard that some hens are just prone to it. Sounds like you've got a real Typhoid Mary on your hands.'

It was after that phone call that CJ first said it. 'We should cull Natasha.'

I was horrified. There is an antiparasitic drug called Ivermectin on the market, although it's not approved for chickens. Aussie Bronwyn had told me about it. I mentioned it to CJ. The vet wouldn't give it to us, as it wasn't approved for chickens, but it was approved for sheep. Aussie Bronwyn had said she could get me some.

CJ looked at me. 'Let me get this straight. You want to go to the black market to get drugs for our sick chicken.'

'I guess that's what I'm suggesting.'

He sighed. 'Even if we did that, even if we got rid of Natasha's scaly leg mites, she'll just get them again.' He looked away. 'Eventually she's going to give it to the others. Then we'll have a real mess on our hands.'

I said no to the culling idea for months. But in the end, I gave in. CJ was right. Natasha was prone.

NOW CJ FOLLOWED NATASHA towards the back of the hay shed, where she had run. I walked around the other way to head her off. When I got there, CJ was staring into a thorny patch of blackberry.

'She went in there.'

I felt horrible. She was hiding for her life. Who knew how long she'd stay in there? We gave up. CJ opened the door to the chicken coop so Natasha could get back in later. It was late. Natasha would live to see another day. She might even live until we got back from Sydney.

CJ and I started walking over to the shovel and the axe, ready to take them back to the garage. And just then, a terrible thing happened. Natasha came running around and back into the coop. She went right up to her perch next to Françoise and settled in.

Stupid bird, I thought. You should have stayed in the blackberry patch.

CJ went over and grabbed her again. He held her tightly and carried her to the log. Françoise and the others were making terrible noises now. CJ laid her out on the log. 'Grab her head.'

I reached down and held the tip of her beak, the way I had seen Aussie Bronwyn do.

'Don't hit my hand,' I said.

Then CJ brought down the axe.

Natasha's body fell down to the ground and twitched and flopped. CJ and I watched in silence. When she stopped moving, CJ picked her body up and dropped it in the hole he'd dug, along with her head.

'God bless you, Natasha,' he said.

Later that night, when we were reading in bed, I set down my book and stared at the ceiling.

'Don't make me feel bad,' CJ said. 'I was the one who took her to the vet.'

'Don't feel bad,' I told him, but I could tell I sounded robotic. 'She was putting them all at risk.'

CJ closed his book. 'I can't do that again. You have to do it next time.'

I didn't answer.

We rolled over and turned out the lights.

Chapter 38

CJ wants a pig

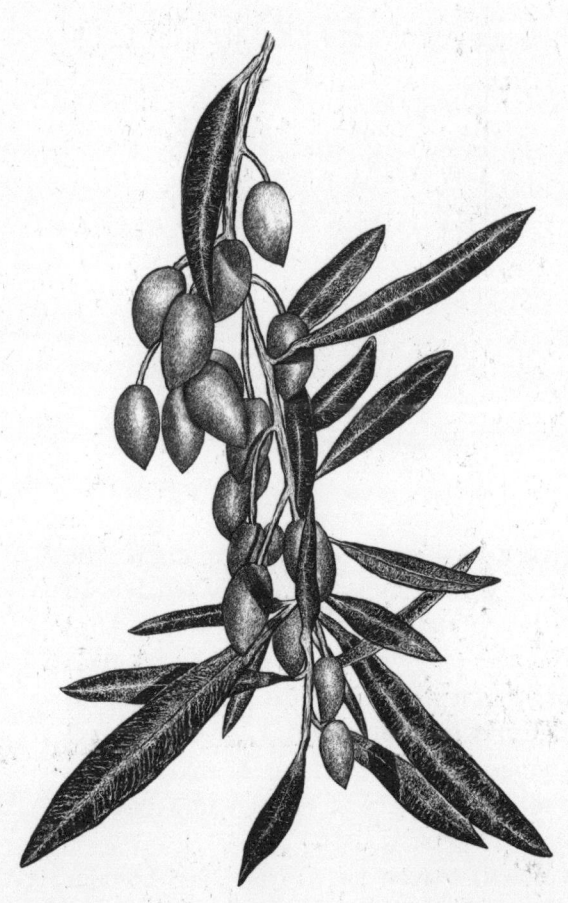

'You want a what?' I said.

CJ smiled. 'A pet pig. A kunekune.'

I paused, then laughed. 'For a second I thought you were serious.'

CJ looked at me blankly. 'I am serious,' he said. Suddenly his voice changed pitch, like he was talking to a baby. 'They're just so darn cute.'

I knew right then I was in trouble.

KUNEKUNE PIGS are a New Zealand pig of uncertain origin. The general consensus is that they were brought here by whalers in the early nineteenth century and used for trade with Māori. After that, Māori took to farming the pigs because they graze on grass and produce a lot of meat and fat from very little food. The word 'kunekune' means 'fat and round' in te reo Māori.

As pigs go, kunekunes generally are good-natured, enjoy human contact, and aren't prone to wandering. As a result, some mad pig lovers say kunekunes make good pets.

I immediately sat CJ down. Maybe he was still upset about Natasha so he wasn't thinking clearly. Whatever the cause, anyone could see we needed some kind of intervention.

'CJ, you're a city boy,' I said. 'Remember? Think about Chicago. Think about Tokyo. Think about the packed trains and the noisy streets. You loved that. So did I. It's embarrassing enough that we've actually become fond of our chickens, but now here you are actually wanting a pet pig? What is happening to us? This has got to stop.'

CJ just stared at the ground and shrugged. I sighed. 'Clearly we're both in need of a good dose of Chicago bus exhaust. All of these clean-living, rural Kiwis around us are a very, very bad influence.'

By then we had met two pet pigs in Martinborough. Our friends Leelee and The Wolf had their pet kunekune sow, which was named Squiggles, and our neighbour Patricia down the road had a boy kunekune named Sammy. CJ had fallen in love with them both. He was constantly wanting to go visit those pigs. He was like a man obsessed. It wasn't long before he was telling everyone he wanted a pet kunekune — friends, neighbours, even strangers in cafés. But the worst thing was when I caught him secretly eyeing unsavoury, seedy websites such as Pig Breeders and the New Zealand Kunekune Association. And at night he'd say romantic things like, 'I want a cute little kunekune pig — don't you?'

Over and over I tried to talk some sense into him. 'Those nasty beasts are by no means cute and little when they grow up,' I'd say. 'They are big, fat and ugly. And they'll eat you alive if you trip in front of them.'

'That's not true,' CJ insisted. 'That's just blatant pig-phobia. I'm surprised at you.'

After that, I tried taking a different approach. 'Raising a baby pig is a lot of work,' I would say. 'They have to be fed with a bottle on a regular basis. With our day jobs and our commute into the city for work, we're not home enough for a baby pig.'

CJ nodded slowly. 'You're right. Baby pigs are a lot of work.'

Finally he was listening to common sense.

'So we're not getting a pet pig,' I said. 'And that's final.'

A few months went by, and all was quiet on the pig front. Then one day CJ came home from his day job in Wellington with the most horrifying news I had ever heard.

'I found us a kunekune pig,' he said.

'We agreed we can't take care of a baby pig,' I said.

CJ smiled broadly. 'This one's not a baby.'

IT TURNS OUT THAT CJ's manager's manager, Grant, had a 13-year-old pet kunekune named Lucy. She had been a childhood pet for Grant's two young sons years ago, along with another pig named Lily. But the boys were grown and gone now, and Lucy's pig-friend Lily had died as well. Old Lady Lucy was sad and lonely.

First let me just say that there are very few modern, Western countries where two office workers in the capital city could be found discussing pet pigs. New Zealand is one such country. Probably the only one.

'Grant said we can have Lucy,' CJ said proudly. 'We just have to go over and pick her up. Since she's old, she's calm and docile. She's perfect for us.'

At this stage in the game, the approach I decided to take was one of sheer denial. Whenever CJ spoke about this beloved Lucy, I simply ignored him.

'Looks like rain today,' I'd say. Or, 'We need to pick the tomatoes in the greenhouse.' Maybe, I hoped, it would all go away.

It didn't. CJ started talking about Lucy over and over and over. Two months later he was still rattling on about it, and I finally broke down. It was like some kind of bizarre psychological torture, and I just couldn't handle it anymore.

'Okay, okay. You can have your damn pig, but you have to take care of her. And there's one unbreakable rule: no pigs in the house.'

CJ smiled. 'Patricia down the road lets her little pig Sammy come inside by the fire when it's cold outside.'

'No. Absolutely not. Never. I swear to God if I ever see that pig in our house, I'll call the home-kill guy and have her turned into bacon.'

'Well, you don't have to get nasty about it,' CJ said. 'We're picking her up in three weeks.'

'What? You already scheduled it?'

'I knew you'd give in,' he said.

He'd arranged for Leelee and The Wolf to help us out. The Wolf had a lot of experience transporting pet pigs, and Leelee of course is the Martinborough Pig Whisperer. What's more, they had a ute with a large trailer that was perfect to hold a 13-year-old pig.

'Lucy lives over on the Kapiti Coast,' CJ said. 'I can't wait to go get her.'

I resigned myself to the fact that soon, whether I liked it or not, our top paddock would be home to a very large, hairy pig.

———

Chapter 39

Last of the Horse Paddock Pinot

S ummer was coming to a close. The days were getting shorter and the nights were growing cooler.

On a dark, rainy evening the neighbours were gathered around the dinner table over at Jim and Kiwi Bronwyn's house. John pulled out an unlabelled bottle of red wine and set it down right in the middle of the table. Everyone sat and stared.

'IS THAT THE GOOD STUFF?' Jim asked, pointing at the bottle.

Just about everyone was there. Jim and Kiwi Bronwyn had invited John and Aussie Bronwyn, Suzanne and Murray, and CJ and me. Kiwi Bronwyn had made a beautiful roast lamb, bought from the local butcher. It was rolled and stuffed with an olive tapenade that included basil and feta. It looked and smelled heavenly. John's unlabelled bottle of wine was sitting right next to that steaming lamb now.

'Yes, it's the good stuff,' John said. Then he sighed. 'It's my last bottle.'

Suzanne gasped, Kiwi Bronwyn shook her head in horror, and Jim cried out, 'No! It can't be!'

All of us at the table knew the story of that wine, and we knew that the last bottle of it was a kind of tragedy.

MY FIRST EXPERIENCE with that particular wine was back during our first summer in Martinborough, when CJ and I had the neighbours over for dinner. It was our first country dinner party ever, and we were nervous. But somehow we managed to pull it off. John and Aussie Bronwyn showed up that night with a bottle of this same unlabelled red wine.

'This is a special wine,' John explained. 'You can't buy it anywhere.'

Something about the unlabelled bottle made it seem vaguely illicit, as though a dodgy liquor-store owner had started whispering to me about his secret stash. I hadn't seen a full, unlabelled bottle of wine since I was a boy, when we lived in Minnesota and my mom decided it would be a good idea to make 'dandelion wine' in the basement. It must have been horrible, since I only remember picking the dandelions for it once. I don't think she ever repeated the experiment.

I eyed John and his unlabelled bottle suspiciously. 'What kind of wine is it?'

'Good wine,' he said, and then told me where it came from.

An award-winning winemaker who worked for one of the large Martinborough vineyards owned a relatively small, private vineyard next to his house. It was in a secluded valley not far from us, and it was planted with pinot noir. John managed the small vineyard part time and did the pruning himself. This wine was from that private vineyard, given to John by the winemaker.

My suspicion eased. Certainly this wine would have to be better than any weed-infused home brew concocted by my mom in our Minnesota basement. When I told John about my mom's wine, he tipped back his white beard and laughed.

'I promise you,' he said, 'this wine contains no dandelions. The man who made this wins awards.'

It wasn't unusual for Martinborough wines to win awards, especially the pinot noirs, although it's a notoriously difficult grape to cultivate and turn into wine. In 2007 alone, 12 medals were given to various Martinborough vineyards for their pinot noir at the prestigious Romeo Bragato awards in Auckland. The hot summers, cool nights, long, dry autumns, and free-draining soil combine to make this area ideally suited to the grape. The name pinot noir means 'black pine' in French, and it comes from the fact that the dark purple grapes are tightly clustered in a pine cone shape. It's an ancient grape, still very closely related to its wild forbears.

That night, at our very first country dinner party, as John stood in our kitchen, he opened that unlabelled bottle of wine and poured me a glass. I lifted the glass to my nose, inhaled, and lifted the glass to my mouth. I tasted dark cherries and spice, with something like cranberries in it, too. The flavour was rich and deep and came to me in layers. Honestly, it was incredible.

John then told me the story of how he'd once taken that wine to a winemakers' dinner. Everyone brought expensive bottles of French wine, which would have cost $100 or more. The bottle John brought was the only one unlabelled, and it was one of the first bottles emptied.

In the months that followed my first taste of that wine, I had the good fortune to drink from a few more of John's precious bottles of it. That first summer passed, the grape harvest came and went, and when it was time for John to prune back the vines in the winemaker's vineyard during the winter I asked if I could help. John, apparently unaware of how absolutely useless I still was at any agricultural activity, said yes. Early on a Saturday morning he picked me up in his ute and we drove off to that secluded valley.

The winemaker wasn't home, and John and I got straight to work. The sun was bright, the sky was blue, and the pine trees on a distant hillside were a rich dark green. The rows of vines supported by long wires made geometric patterns against the rolling contours of the land.

All the grape leaves in the winemaker's vineyard had fallen by then, so there was nothing left but empty vines climbing up and out from their woody trunks, and the wires running back and forth. It looked large and barren and beautiful, almost like an enormous art installation, something by Christo.

I liked being there in the vineyard that had produced the pinot noir I'd enjoyed so much all summer. The winemaker's historic wooden house just beyond the vines was charming. The spot was a slice of heaven.

John showed me what to do. I had to select two good leaders for each vine and tie them to the wire, one leader heading off to the left and one off to the right. All the other leaders I had to snip off. Each vine ended up in a neat and tidy 'T'. The difficulty was in the tying.

We didn't use rope, or string. Instead we used soft, round, elastic things that looked like something my nieces would use to tie back their hair. There was a very complicated and important way of turning and looping these silly little hair-ties so they held the vine firmly yet didn't constrict growth in any way.

'First you do this,' John said, moving his hair-tie around the vine. 'Then you do this, and then—' Suddenly his hands spun in a wild and incomprehensible blur. 'You do that and you're done.'

There, in front of me, his vine was tied back as if by magic.

'Not too tight, not too loose,' he said, pulling at the vine.

I was confused. 'Sorry. Could you show me that again? I missed a step.'

John took out another hair-tie. 'First this, then this, then—' Once again his hands spun and blurred. 'You're done.'

I had to ask for several repeat performances before I was able to replicate the magical spinning part. But in the end I got it. Still, all day long I struggled to keep pace. John was amazing. Every time he tied a vine, the speed of his hands caused sonic booms to ring out across the valley. Then he was quickly on to the next. We worked near each other, talking here and there. The sun felt fantastic. John never said a word about how slow I was.

When the year's harvest was ready, John procured for himself half a case of that amazing pinot noir, at a good price. Jim managed to wrangle half a case as well. Somehow I missed out on the high-level negotiations and ended up wineless, but John and Jim assured me there would be plenty of those nice bottles showing up at neighbourhood dinner parties, so I took heart. I also put my hand up for buying half a case the following year.

Shortly after that, the winemaker sold his vineyard. An American bought it. The American had a horse. There was one problem. The paddock in front of the house was full of pesky grapevines.

Yes, you know what he did. He pulled them out. I don't really understand why somebody would move to a winemaking region and pull out established, beautiful vines. But that's what he did. Suddenly the wine that John and Jim held in their possession was priceless. And the name of it, at least in my mind, became Horse Paddock Pinot.

SITTING AT JIM AND KIWI BRONWYN'S table on that dark, rainy evening, staring at John's last bottle of Horse Paddock Pinot next to Kiwi Bronwyn's steaming roast, nobody knew what to say. For a moment the only noise was the sound of the rain on the roof and the fire crackling in the woodburner. Everyone was thinking the same thing. Did we dare open that bottle of wine?

It was Jim who finally broke the silence. He stood up and said, 'No. Not your last one. You take that home. I have three bottles left. We'll open one of mine.' He picked up John's bottle and carried it over to the door, setting it down on the floor. Then he pulled out one of his own bottles and set it on the table.

'John,' he said, 'you do the honours.'

John picked up that precious bottle and opened the screw cap, which I'd discovered practical Kiwis love using on their fine wines. He poured everyone a glass, and soon, crisis averted, we were all talking and laughing, eating Kiwi Bronwyn's deliciously tender lamb, and drinking that beautiful wine. It was as amazing as the first time I tasted it — the cherry and spice, the hints of cranberry, the multiple and complex layers. I remembered the vineyard, the winemaker's old house, the sun in the pine trees nearby.

Although that wine was precious, and although there would never be any more, Jim and John clearly were not wine hoarders. Horse Paddock Pinot was such good wine that it almost demanded to be enjoyed with friends. I counted myself fortunate that my neighbours were so willing to share.

At the end of the evening, we took score again, or we counted down, as the case may be. John had his one bottle left. Jim had two. I quickly offered to help drink them at some future date.

'That's very kind of you,' Jim said.

I shrugged. 'Well, you know, I believe in helping out my neighbours. I'm good that way.'

Kiwi Bronwyn's Marinated Lamb Stuffed with Olives, Feta and Basil

This delicious blend of East and West goes well with a good bottle of pinot noir.

Ingredients

1 cup kalamata olives, stones removed
5 cloves garlic, crushed
2 tablespoons olive oil
1.75 kg butterflied lamb leg
100 g feta cheese, chopped
12 basil leaves, torn
freshly ground black pepper, to taste
2 cloves garlic, crushed
1 tablespoon minced ginger
¼ cup hoisin sauce*
2 tablespoons soy sauce
2 tablespoons chopped hazelnuts

*Note: For gluten-free, replace the hoisin sauce and soy sauce
  with the following:
2 teaspoons gluten-free flour
1 teaspoon sesame oil
4 teaspoons honey
2 teaspoons white vinegar
4 tablespoons gluten-free tamari sauce
To mix: Add the sesame oil to the gluten-free flour and blend until
  all lumps are dissolved, then add other ingredients.

Preparation

Put olives, 5 cloves garlic and olive oil in a food processor and blend
until smooth. Place the lamb, opened out flat, on a board. Spread the
olive mixture onto the lamb. Spread the feta and basil over the mixture.
Season with black pepper. Roll up the lamb and tie tightly with kitchen
string so the mixture cannot fall out.

Combine the 2 cloves garlic, ginger and sauces (or their gluten-free
alternatives) and then spread over the meat. Transfer the meat to an
oven dish and marinate for at least four hours in the fridge, or overnight.

Heat oven to 170°C. Remove the meat from the dish and drain off
excess marinade. Return meat to the oven dish and cook for approximately 2 hours, depending on the weight. (The *Good Housekeeping Cookery
Book* recommends 25 minutes per 450 g plus an extra 25 minutes.)

Remove the meat from the oven and rest it for 15 minutes before slicing.
Serve with an Asian-flavoured rice dish (or, if not gluten-free, couscous)
and a green salad. Place the rice or couscous on the plate then top with
the sliced lamb, and sprinkle chopped hazelnuts on top.

Chapter 40

Bringing home Old Lady Lucy

'**I** still don't want this pig,' I said to CJ. It didn't matter that I was already sitting in the back seat of Leelee and The Wolf's ute on the way to get it. As we drove out of Martinborough, we passed one vineyard after the next with gold and red leaves in rows. The grape harvest was done. The olive harvest would be soon.

CJ was sitting next to me, practically bouncing with glee. 'I know you. As soon as we have her, you'll love her.'

FROM THE FRONT SEAT Leelee and The Wolf yelled almost in unison, 'Pigs are great!'

'Leelee,' I asked, 'how long do kunekune pigs live?'

'Oh, somewhere between fifteen and twenty years,' Leelee said. 'Because Lucy's thirteen years old, she's definitely an old lady.'

I shook my head. 'You mean we're going to be stuck with this fat pig for at least two years? And maybe as long as seven?'

CJ jabbed me in the side.

As we drove through the tight curves and past the precipitous drop-offs of the Rimutaka Hill Road and then the Haywards Hill Road on our way to the Kapiti Coast, I watched the empty trailer we were towing behind us sway and bounce.

'CJ, your precious pig's going to have a heart attack in that trailer and die on the way back,' I said. 'Then you'll be sorry. You'll have a fat, old, dead pig on your hands. Not even good for bacon.'

'No bacon jokes,' CJ said.

When we arrived at our destination, we were greeted by Grant, who works with CJ in Wellington, and Grant's wife, Sarah. They'd been looking for a good home for their old pig for months, and they had finally found a sucker in CJ.

We all put our gumboots on and headed down to the paddock where the pig lived.

Sarah said, 'We brought Lucy home thirteen years ago in a little shoebox, and she's been in this paddock ever since.'

As we neared the paddock, the pig's back end was towards us.

'There's the pig,' The Wolf said.

My jaw dropped. It was huge.

'I see the cow,' CJ said. 'But where's the pig?'

The Wolf paused. 'Um. That *is* the pig.'

CJ's eyes grew wide. This was the biggest, blackest, hairiest pig any of us had ever seen.

Grant set to work right away. I suspect he wanted to get the pig into the trailer and get us out of there before CJ had a chance to change his mind. Waving a hotdog bun in front of the enormous Lucy, Grant tried to entice her up into the trailer. Lucy tried desperately to move up the sloped trailer to get the hotdog bun. But the slope was steep and it took several tries. In the end Lucy managed to pull her back feet up into the trailer and get her well-deserved treat.

The Wolf and CJ quickly put the tailgate back on the trailer.

I whispered to CJ, 'That's no pig. It's a brontosaurus.'

Leelee called out from over by the pig house, 'Is this where she sleeps?' There was a pile of hay and old netting inside.

'Yes,' Sarah said. 'Lucy gathered that herself and made her bed with it.'

Leelee smiled. 'We have to take that with us. It'll give her comfort.'

Sarah got an old, empty wool bale to put it in. Then CJ actually got down on all fours, climbed into the pig house, and gathered Lucy's bedding. It was his very first Selfless Act of Pig Love.

We put the wool bale full of bedding in the back of the trailer with Lucy, along with a bale of hay that The Wolf had thought to bring to make sure Lucy didn't get knocked about on the roads. Lucy immediately tried to push open the wool bale with her snout to get at the bedding.

'See? It's her blankee,' Leelee said.

With the pig secured in the trailer, we thanked Grant and Sarah and drove off, up the long driveway.

I looked over at CJ. 'I still don't want this pig.'

Just before pulling out onto the main road, we stopped the ute and got out to check on Lucy. She was making strange squealing noises, and behind her was the most enormous turd I have ever seen.

'That's going to stress her,' Leelee said. 'Pigs don't like to have poos where they're lying. Jared, you have to get it out.'

'Me?'

'Yes.' Leelee forced a tissue into my hand. 'Reach through the bars and pick it up,' she said.

I looked at the turd. The turd looked back.

'It won't fit out through these bars,' I said. 'It's just too big.'

CJ quickly grabbed two tissues. Then he climbed up onto the side of the trailer, reached over the top of the open cage and — gripping the colossal Turd from Hell with both hands — threw it to the side of the road. Selfless Act of Pig Love Number 2.

ALL THE WAY BACK over the curvy roads, CJ kept trying to see Lucy in the trailer behind us. 'I hope she's okay,' he said. Then he glared at me. 'You'll feel bad if she's dead.'

At the summit of the Rimutaka Hill Road, we pulled over and got out to check on her. What we saw wasn't pretty.

Poor Lucy had diarrhoea running down her backside, all over the wool bale, and across the trailer. My cold heart started to melt, just a little bit. I felt bad for the pig.

'She's so frightened,' Leelee said.

'I don't blame her,' I said. 'If you put me in the back of a trailer and dragged me over the Rimutaka Hill Road, I'd crap all over myself too.'

'We have to clean it up,' Leelee said.

'Now?' I asked. 'Here? How? We're on top of a mountain.'

We piled back in the car and got Lucy home to Martinborough right away.

The Wolf drove the ute into our top paddock, but when we opened the back gate of the trailer and tipped it down to let Lucy out, she wouldn't budge. Not even offers of food tempted her. The poor thing was still so scared.

It took only a couple of minutes before our resident Pig Whisperer realised that Lucy didn't want to leave her bedding, which was still in the wool bale at her side. Leelee reached into the trailer and dragged the wool bale out. Then at long last out came Lucy.

As Leelee got the hose and cleaned the diarrhoea off the pig, The Wolf sawed a bigger opening in the old side-by-side double dog kennel near our hay shed, so that Lucy could fit inside. Yes. She's that big. She takes up two dog kennels.

CJ carefully pulled the still-clean bedding out of the poo-covered wool bale, and put the bedding inside Lucy's new home. He was so grateful to Leelee and The Wolf for their help that they now have the official title of Pig Godparents.

Within a month it felt as though Lucy had always been with us. She grew on me somehow. She quickly established her own routine. In the morning she would linger in a wallow at the edge of the pond behind the hay shed. In the evenings she would wander down to the culvert in the paddock in front of the house and munch on watercress. Every night she would lie in her customised, double-wide dog kennel, her head on her familiar old netting.

Given that we'd already adopted a geriatric rooster, and now we'd adopted a geriatric pig, CJ and I began to joke that we should put a sign out front: *The Martinborough Twilight Home for Geriatric Farm Animals*.

Every evening, when CJ and I visited Lucy to give her a pat, she would lie down slowly — like a fat, old lady — and plop down onto her side so that we could rub her belly. It was incredibly cute. I decided that having a pet pig wasn't such a bad idea after all.

Chapter 41

Olive harvest on a misty day

We were going to have an olive harvest, and I couldn't wait.

It was May, and the willows down at the river had already lost their leaves, exposing the bright orange tips of their branches to the sky. I walked through the grove and inspected the olive trees.

There were, of course, no olives on the Nabali, but I didn't care. *Leave them be*, Andrew-of-the-Olives had said. The rest of the grove looked fantastic.

THE BARNEA TREES WERE so heavy with their long, pointed olives that the branches leaned down from their tall space in the sky. The Manzanillo were covered with their fat, round fruit, and the young Leccino and Frantoio were laden with their smaller, oil-rich, oval-shaped ones. Our pruning and organic spraying regime was working wonders. There were over 450 trees offering up an abundance of olives to harvest, and the fruit would be ripening soon.

Right — The olive grove when we moved in. The grass was chest-high in places, and the trees hadn't been properly cared for in years.

Bottom left — Dave's Carrot Cake. It's the most heavenly carrot cake on the planet, and one of the first things I learned how to bake gluten-free.

Bottom right — Manzanillo olives ripening. Olives need sunshine to ripen, and Martinborough summers have sunshine in spades.

JARED GULIAN

JARED GULIAN

JARED GULIAN

JARED GULIAN

The harvest ready to go to the press, picked by our friends and neighbours, packed into Helen's crates, and sitting on the back of John's ute. It takes a village.

Sunshine the Tractor in our grove. John has let us borrow that tractor more times than I can count. Notice the short exhaust pipe sticking up at the front — one of CJ's infamous 'improvements'.

The olive grove feels like a magical, sheltered place. It's part hedge maze, part grassy meadow and part tree-lined reserve.

Blossom, Aussie Bronwyn's cow. Blossom has supplied cream for countless homemade scones with homemade strawberry jam over at Aussie Bronwyn and John's house.

Above — Sweetie the pet sheep, who has a dangerous addiction. Don't let her charming demeanour fool you. She just wants you to give her chicken feed.

Right — The river at the bottom of our property. This place is a sanctuary. Summer afternoons spent along its banks seem to last forever.

Left — Our two extra virgin olive oil blends. The Crescent Blend has beautiful green tea and butter flavours, from Barnea and Manzanillo olives. The Full Moon Blend has a gorgeous, grassy opening with a peppery finish, from Frantoio and Leccino olives.

Below — The Christmas gingerbread boys and girls. Nothing says Christmas like Santa, snowmen, green aliens, and ladies with pecan brassieres.

I did everything in advance that year. I had already talked to Helen the Olive Angel of Olivo about borrowing her hand rakes and nets and crates. I had also arranged to borrow John's ute again, invited and confirmed the city friends, attended a pre-harvest meeting of local growers, booked in with Diane to drop off our olives at Pressing Engagements, and even decided on what bottles to order.

That year we were going to put our oil into something that looked professional, rather than the random recycled wine bottles we'd used our first year. CJ and I had also purchased our first, ridiculously expensive, 50-litre, stainless steel olive oil container. A local company imported them from Italy, and when it showed up on our front deck, we tore open the packaging and stared at the shiny container for quite some time. We'd never owned anything like it in our lives.

The city friends arrived on the Friday night of Queen's Birthday weekend, just as they had two years before. Everyone was talking about the horrible weather that had been forecast for the weekend. All week long CJ and I had been nervous about the weather. The last thing we wanted was to have our friends out harvesting our olives in nasty, miserable rain. After all, we hoped that when the weekend was over we'd still be able to count these people as friends.

There was less of a chance of rain on Saturday than there was on Sunday, so we decided to start working early on Saturday and hopefully finish everything that day. Our plan was to harvest just the Frantoio and Leccino — about 150 trees. We'd actually arranged to sell our Barnea and Manzanillo fruit to Olivo that year. Helen was going to take care of that harvest herself, so we didn't have to worry about them.

Before dinner on Friday evening we drove John's ute over to Helen's to pick up the equipment she was letting us borrow. When we got there she said, 'Take the mechanical rakes, too.'

I looked over at those rakes. They were the expensive Italian ones that ran off the air compressor. We hadn't borrowed them our first year. I remembered how Helen had said that they were fragile and it was impossible to find replacement parts for them in New Zealand.

'Are you sure?' I said.

'Absolutely. I know you'll take good care of them.'

I felt incredibly grateful, but I was also filled with a heavy sense of responsibility. Helen hadn't harvested yet, and if we broke those rakes it could easily threaten her business.

'Thank you so much.' With those mechanical rakes, our harvest time would be cut in half.

We packed the mechanical rakes, hand rakes, compressor, nets, and crates into the back of John's ute. With all this borrowed equipment, it felt like the entire neighbourhood was behind us.

On Saturday morning I woke early and peeked out the front windows. The olive trees down in the grove were shrouded in mist. Thankfully there was no rain, yet.

We were out in the grove by 8 a.m., starting the harvest with the Frantoio. The morning crew was an international team of friends that year — two Kiwis, one Aussie, one Argentinean, and CJ and me as the two Americans. Later that day we were expecting another Kiwi and a Brit. I felt incredibly grateful to those people for showing up to help us.

We worked hard all morning. The mist swept and swerved on the hills beyond the bottom paddock. Old Lady Lucy sniffed around on the other side of the paddock fence, wanting to get into the olive grove to see what was going on.

I knew from our first year that I'd be remiss if I didn't offer the harvesters something for morning tea. We took a break at 10:30. I brought thermos flasks full of hot coffee and tea into the olive grove, and we ate the delicious homemade granola bars that our city friend Nate had brought with him.

Then we got back to work. More raking, more netting. I kept a careful eye on the two mechanical rakes. Everyone was taking very good care of them.

It was only then, after morning tea, that I realised there was something wrong with some of the fruit that had been coming in among the morning crates.

Some of the Frantoio were not exactly green, as I'd expected them to be. Some of them were an odd shade of brown.

The weather that autumn had turned cold and rainy earlier than usual. In the two weeks before our harvest, we'd had incredible amounts of rain, low temperatures, and a couple of frosty mornings. The Frantoio ripen late, and there had been a frost at a point when the fruit was vulnerable. I wondered if I was looking at frost damage.

Standing there beside the crates in the grove, I immediately pulled out my mobile phone and consulted with some other Martinborough growers. I called Leelee, and I called Helen. I was still learning, and I'd never had to deal with frost-damaged fruit before. I described the situation. Yes, it was frost damage. Yes, we had to get rid of that fruit.

The Wairarapa has been noted for its excellent olive oil, and that doesn't come from pressing bad fruit. Mike Wilkinson of Ruakokoputuna Olives, not far from us, once said, 'You can grow olives in warmer places but the oil hasn't got the intensity of flavour like we have here in Wairarapa.' This is due to the combination of cool nights and hot days. At the beginning and end of the growing season, however, those cool nights can mean frosts, and frost-damaged fruit can ruin the taste of your oil. I was determined that none of our damaged fruit would make it to the press.

One of the city friends started sorting through the crates of Frantoio to pull out the frost-damaged fruit. There wasn't actually a lot, so you had to look for it. We dumped the bad fruit onto the ground.

While the sorting continued, I took a position in front of the rakers to check each tree before it was harvested. I gave the nod to harvest or not. Usually only a small part of a tree was affected by frost, or it was just the odd olive here and there, which I'd pull off by hand and discard before the rakers got there.

By the time we stopped for lunch at 1 p.m., we'd only finished about 35 trees.

As we sat down at the big wooden dining table back up at the house to eat — stuffed peppers, salami, ham, cheeses, dips, and several kinds of bread — everyone looked tired.

THE AFTERNOON WAS THE HARDEST. The weather was cold and our energy was waning. Fortunately, when we moved on to the Leccino, there was no frost damage as there had been on the Frantoio. I breathed a huge sigh of relief.

But there were still crates of Frantoio from the early morning that needed to be sorted for quality. It was a long, tedious job. Thankfully, with the afternoon arrival of our friends Biscuit and Anne, we got a new burst of energy and more hands on deck.

Time passed quickly, and before we knew it we were losing the light. It also began to rain, but only in light and periodic sprinkles. We still had one long row of trees to do. All the city friends were keen to keep going and everyone kicked into overdrive, skipping the trees without much fruit and concentrating on the good ones.

As the last of the light slipped out of the olive grove and off to its place behind the hills, we loaded the final crate of olives onto the back of John's ute, along with the compressor and mechanical rakes.

We never would have finished on Saturday if it hadn't been for the blessing of Helen's magical rakes. And they were still working perfectly, not broken at all.

CJ drove the ute out of the grove and up to our driveway. It was about 7:30 p.m. by then. We had to have the fruit to the olive press by 8:30 p.m. at the latest.

But in the final push to finish the harvest, we'd stopped sorting for quality, and now we saw that there were still crates of Frantoio that had yet to be picked through.

We unloaded the crates in the garage, pulled up old chairs, and used the next hour to get out all the frost-damaged fruit that we could. I'd been told that having 'a little' frost-damaged fruit would not compromise the quality of the oil. But just how much was 'a little'?

IN THE END WE ran out of time, and we took the olives to the press as they were, a few crates still unsorted. Would it ruin the taste of our oil? I had no idea.

We got to the press at 8:15, and Diane greeted us with a smile. From the back of John's ute we unloaded our 30 crates of olives, our shiny new stainless steel container, and the containers Helen the Olive Angel had given us two years before.

Diane said she was so busy that we wouldn't be able to pick up our oil until Monday. She was working 13-hour days and was pressing as fast as she could. I showed her our crates of unsorted fruit.

'Do you think the taste will be okay if we press this?' I asked.

She stuck her small hands into the crate and picked up a handful of olives. She looked tired. 'Well, you harvested it. It should be fine.'

'Really?' I asked.

She looked again. 'Should be.'

I decided to have it pressed, hoping all along that I wasn't making a mistake. Was I being greedy, just to have more oil? Was I risking the taste of the entire batch?

When we got home from the olive press, I reached into the fridge and took out the three lasagne trays I'd prepared the day before — one beef, one veggie, one gluten-free, all of them heaped with ricotta, mozzarella and fresh basil. I had made these without any help from anyone. For me — someone who three years ago barely knew how to make microwave popcorn — this was a kind of quiet miracle. I quickly popped the lasagne into the oven, and dinner was on its way.

By the time we sat down, the table was nearly overflowing with food. Everybody had made or brought something special. Kumara cooked with garam masala. Fresh crusty breads. Potato, green bean and pesto salad. And for dessert I had made the famous carrot cake.

That evening, after we'd feasted and toasted to the harvest and talked and laughed about the day, we all finally turned in. I closed up the house for the night, happy to have our city friends down the hall. I locked the front door, turned down the damper on the woodburner, and shut off the lights.

Finally I fell into bed beside CJ with the kind of pleasant collapse that comes only after a long day of arduous, satisfying work. Before I drifted off into sleep, I lay there for a moment thinking about our oil. How would it taste? Would it be okay?

It killed me that I was going to have to wait to find out.

Chapter 42

Hand-picking for pickling

T
he day after our big olive harvest, the weather took a turn for the worse. It didn't matter. Four of us in the harvest gang were determined to do something new that year. We wanted to hand-pick some olives for pickling and preserving. We weren't about to be put off by the weather.

EVERYONE WAS SORE FROM the day before. Inside the fire was going, and outside the temperature had plummeted. The mist across the hills had thickened. But we four intrepid olive harvesters put on winter coats and gloves, left behind the others who were reading by the fire, and headed down into the grove with a couple of old plastic buckets.

Although the coldest days in Martinborough are nothing compared to the serious, snow-filled winters of my native Michigan, it seemed that after a few years living here my body had adapted. I was so incredibly cold that day. It was weather that would have made most Michiganders laugh and say 'You call this winter?' But I was absolutely chilled to the bone. Perhaps I was becoming soft.

We walked along through the rows and rows of trees until we came to a row of Manzanillo. 'These are the ones for pickling,' I said, and we gathered around our first tree.

Olives for pickling have to be harvested by hand so they don't get bruised or damaged in the process. I suppose some big commercial growers overseas must do it with machines, but not here. The quality of eating olives depends on the care they get from tree to table, and we just wanted good olives.

The city friends and I quickly realised how hard it was to hand-pick with gloves on, so the gloves came off. Each person picked only the best olives, careful to avoid those that the birds or the frost had damaged.

It was quiet. We talked about the trees, the olives, each other. The mist surrounded us. Our conversation was dotted with the pleasant and rhythmic sound of fat, round olives hitting the inside of plastic buckets.

When we'd harvested one tree, we moved to the next. There was no hurry. We had no particular quantity of olives in mind. We just wanted enough for all four of us to have fun with some pickling. The silvery-green leaves were wet, and our hands grew colder and colder.

After about an hour we decided we'd had enough. Our hands had become red and stiff, and picking had become increasingly difficult. We put our gloves back on and wandered up to the house.

The city friends who'd had the good sense to stay inside also had the good sense to prepare us lunch. We ate steaming hot, home-made pumpkin soup, which one of the city friends had made for the weekend. Another city friend had run into the village and brought back loaves of fresh bread. Because I can't eat gluten, for me they sliced up some of the fresh gluten-free bread I'd baked for the weekend — full of delicious cornmeal and amaranth flour.

THE FOLLOWING DAY, BEFORE everyone left to drive back over the Rimutaka Hill and into the city, we divvied up the Manzanillo olives among the four of us who wanted them (and who'd made the commitment to pick them in the cold).

I made quick photocopies of the pickling recipe a friend of a friend had given us. All the picklers headed off carrying a plastic grocery bag full of olives and a small white piece of paper with the recipe.

Years ago, my old friend Becca back in Michigan told me a story about her first trip to Greece. She and a friend rented bicycles and were riding through the Greek countryside when they came across an olive grove. They got off their bicycles and ran over to the grove, yelling 'Olives! Olives!'

Being from Michigan, they'd never actually witnessed olives growing on trees. They decided they were going to experience fresh olives for the first time. They each picked an olive and popped it directly into their mouths. What they experienced then was the most bitter, foul taste they'd ever known. They shrieked and spat the olives out on the ground immediately.

Becca and her friend didn't know about oleuropein, the phenolic compound that makes fresh olives bitter. Neither did I until I landed in an olive grove. The only way to get rid of the bitterness is through pickling, preserving or curing the olives in some way.

I have no idea how the first person discovered that olives, which actually taste terrible raw, could make such delicious fruit when pickled and such delicious oil when pressed (the oleuropein doesn't get transferred to the oil). It's one of the world's mysteries.

On Monday afternoon, after all the city friends' cars had pulled away after the long harvest weekend, CJ and I strolled back into the house. The fire was burning brightly, and we curled up together on the World's Most Comfortable Couch. We felt the deep satisfaction that came from having had such a fantastic weekend with our friends as well as having our second olive harvest under our belt.

Noah's Olives

This is a very easy way to pickle olives. It takes 40 days and 40 nights.

Ingredients

raw olives
rock salt
sliced lemons
whole garlic cloves
fresh thyme, rinsed in boiling water
extra virgin olive oil
vinegar

Preparation

Put the olives in a bucket of water. Leave for 40 days, changing the water every 2 days.

After 40 days, drain the olives and cover with rock salt. Leave for 2 days.

Wash the olives well in cold water and pack them into clean, sterilised jars with the washed lemon, garlic and thyme. Use sterilised utensils to handle all of the ingredients. Cover with a ⅓ vinegar ⅔ olive oil mix. Seal and leave for 2 weeks before eating.

These olives will keep for approximately 6 months.

Chapter 43

Picking up the oil

CJ and I drove up to the olive press and looked in through the ornate metal gate. It was dark out, and the lights were still on inside. Diane of Pressing Engagements was still inside pressing olives. It was the Monday night of Queen's Birthday weekend. Diane had just called to tell us that our oil was ready, and we wanted to get it home to taste it right away, in order to see if the frosts had affected the taste. Had our efforts to remove the damaged fruit been enough?

DIANE SMILED WHEN SHE SAW US. 'Your oil is beautiful,' she said immediately, and then waved us in through the gate.

She gave us a piece of paper, which reported on our pressing. In total we had 383 kilos of olives. It had taken Diane about 11 hours to press them all. We got 48 litres of oil out of it.

Our yield was 12.6 per cent — much less than the 16 per cent we'd got from the Frantoio and Leccino in our first harvest.

'In the past two weeks, everyone's yield has dropped,' Diane said.

'I talked to the press up in Masterton, and the same thing's happening there.'

'Why?' I asked. I'd been running figures based on 400 kilos of olives at 16 per cent yield, so I was expecting 64 litres of oil, not the 48 we had in front of us.

She reached over and touched a blue bucket full of someone else's olives waiting to go into the pressing room. 'All this rain,' she said. 'The olives soak it up, and it makes them heavier. Your yield is a measure of the weight of the olives compared to the amount of oil they give off, so olives that are full of rain give a lower yield.'

She picked up an olive out of the bucket and turned it in her fingers. It was smallish and dark. She moved slowly, no doubt exhausted from her 13-hour days.

'The low yield doesn't necessarily mean your olives had less oil,' she said. 'It means they had more water. That's all.'

From a grower's perspective, the main problem with pressing rain-soaked fruit is that it's extremely expensive. Olive presses charge per kilo of fruit pressed, so you're paying to press out a lot of heavy water.

Compared to our first harvest, when the weather was dry and our yield higher, this year's pressing costs were almost double per litre of oil obtained.

'But oh,' Diane said, 'the oil you have is gorgeous. So clear.' She smiled brightly. 'You'll have almost no sediment. You'll be able to drink most of it.'

She pointed to our report card. It read: *Oil colour: Vibrant rich green. General comments: Clear oil — stunning!*

Only later would we learn later that Diane was so impressed with the quality of our oil that she was even telling our neighbours about it. She told John, when he came in to press his fruit, that our oil was some of the most beautiful she'd ever seen.

'It's stunning?' I asked her.

'Stunning,' she said.

CJ AND I FELT like small children who'd received gold stars on our foreheads. The oil was clear and beautiful, but how would it taste?

We had to get it home.

Diane had filled only one of our four containers — the big 50-litre one. CJ and I lifted the heavy stainless steel container together and put it in the hatchback of our little, two-door, city-boy Nissan Pulsar. It felt silly putting such an industrial olive oil container in the back of such a wimpy car. Locals had begun teasing us about our car, telling us that we needed to get ourselves a ute. We figured we were probably in breach of some rural ordinance, driving that Pulsar.

We drove away from the olive press and the nearby town square and left the village of Martinborough behind us in the dark as we headed down the country roads that lead to our property.

CJ and I carried the oil inside the house and set it down in the guest lounge over on the B&B side of the house. In the winter, when we have fewer B&B guests, we tend not to use that room, and the oil was out of the way there. But that large silver container next to the breakfast table almost looked like another guest ready to pull up a chair.

We unscrewed the wide-mouthed lid and dipped in a ladle, poured some into a clear glass, then carried the glass to the kitchen.

Standing together at the large island counter in the centre of the kitchen, we held the glass to the light. It was true what Diane had said about the colour. This oil was such an intense, rich green that it looked almost luminescent.

Now, as CJ and I stood there in the kitchen, we each held a spoonful of our just-pressed olive oil. I looked at mine, shining green on the end of silver. CJ and I simultaneously opened our mouths and tasted our spoonfuls.

Ahh. There it was. The grassy opening notes, the mild and fruity middle, the powerful bang of pepper at the end.

Yes. We'd saved our oil from the frost. It was absolutely delicious.

Chapter 44

Zen and the art of pickling olives

I washed our pickling olives carefully, put them in a large black bucket, and filled it up with enough water to cover them. I had never pickled olives before. To my surprise, the olives floated.

FOR THE NEXT 40 DAYS, I changed the water in those olives every two days, just as the recipe required. I didn't need salt water; plain old tap water would do. CJ marked the water-changing days on the big wall calendar in our office, and he also wrote in the other steps on the days we needed to do them — packing the olives in rock salt, placing them in jars with lemon, garlic and thyme.

There was something Zen-like and meditative about changing the water so regularly for such a long time. It felt as though I was measuring time. I always did it in the evenings, just before going to bed. It became my new ritual, like feeding the hens in the morning.

Every second evening, I took the large plastic bucket from the empty guest room where it lived, and I brought it into the kitchen. I unclasped the black handles that held down the lid, then set the lid on the counter. I lifted the bucket to the sink and — slowly, so the olives wouldn't tumble and get bruised — poured out the contents into a large colander. Then I filled up the bucket with water and poured the olives back in. The water broke their fall.

I never knew what I'd find when I opened the lid. After just a few days the olives already smelled so fresh, fruity and — well, olivey that I was tempted to eat them there and then. Around Day 10 they began leaving bubbles at the top of the water, but by Day 16 the bubbles had stopped.

Gradually the olives began to sink to the bottom of the bucket, and the colours changed. We were pickling a mix of black and green olives together. Over time the dark ones turned a lighter shade of black while the bright green ones turned a darker shade of green. It was as though their colours were spilling into each other.

Every evening, when I had finished changing the water, I would put the lid back on and put the bucket back in the guest room. I felt like one person in a long line, doing something that people had been doing for centuries. Then I would shut off the lights, turn the damper down on the fire, and climb into bed next to CJ — the beautiful smell of olives still lingering in my head.

At the end of those 40 days, I packed the olives in rock salt for two days, just as the recipe said, and then I became a bit anxious. I had arrived at the part that could all go horribly wrong. I'd read that pickling olives can create botulism. I really didn't want to kill the village.

I stood at the island in the centre of the kitchen. It was a bright Saturday morning, and the light was streaming in the French doors that open out to the deck and the olive grove beyond. Above me the peaked wooden ceiling spread its wings. In front of me I had my canning jars, garlic, lemon, thyme, vinegar, and the olive oil fresh from our grove just a month and a half before. It was time to risk making botulism.

I brought the olive bucket into the kitchen and opened the lid. The white circle of salt at the bottom of that black, inky void looked like the moon. I poured the salt-covered olives into a colander in the sink and washed them. At all stages of the process I made sure everything — the colander, the sink, the counter — was immaculately clean. A little voice inside my head kept saying, 'Botulism, botulism . . .'

I didn't want anyone to die.

Various recipes I'd read said that to pickle properly you have to boil everything — the ingredients, the jars, the lids, the utensils. Everything.

First I boiled the jars in water, then boiled the fresh garlic cloves, lemon juice and freshly chopped thyme in the vinegar. I filled the sterilised jars with the dark olives and poured in the vinegar, complete with one or two of the garlic cloves, until the jars were filled halfway. Then I topped them up with our vibrant green olive oil. Finally I put on the lids and placed the full jars into a pot of — you guessed it — boiling water. No germ was going to survive my phobic sanitation regimen.

Everything was going fine. The only difficulty was that I had six jars full of olives and the pot could only fit three at a time. So when the first three had been in the boiling water for a few minutes, I tried to lift them out.

That was a mistake.

To get at the jars, I used the pair of overpriced, high-tech oven mitts CJ and I had bought last time we were in the States. They're rubber, and their selling point was that you can use them to put your hand in a pot of boiling water to pull out a lobster.

I have never once needed to pull a lobster out of a pot of boiling water. Neither, I can say with some certainty, has CJ. Yet that minor point escaped us both when we saw those gleaming red mitts in the store.

Now it struck me that those oven mitts were the perfect thing for pulling jars of pickled olives out of a pot of boiling water. I could pull the jars out and put the second batch in without missing a beat.

I slipped both gloves on and reached in. The gloves, thankfully, didn't leak. I picked the jars up by the lids. Out came the first jar. Out came the second.

As I was lifting the third and last jar out, the screw-top ring came off. I suppose the hot water had made the metal expand and become loose.

I watched as the jar fell from my hands and hit the countertop next to the oven with a thunk. Miraculously, the glass didn't break. What's more surprising was that the lid stayed on, even though there was no longer any screw-top ring to hold it in place.

But the jar, unfortunately, had not yet come to rest.

It rose up in an odd bounce, and I reached out to stop it from falling onto the floor — both of my hands still encased in thick red rubber. It was like trying to catch an active grenade while your hands are shoved inside a pair of shoes.

I hit the jar wrong. The lid let loose its tenuous grip and came off. Suddenly hot vinegar, olive oil and olives came flooding out. I jumped back.

IT IS A SCIENTIFIC fact that the crack between the stove and the kitchen counter serves as a kind of voracious black hole, sucking in all falling objects within a metre radius. I pondered this particularly fascinating phenomenon as I watched the contents of that jar pour directly down that crack.

Any liquid that managed to escape the grip of the greedy Stove Meets Counter Vortex spilled out gracefully along the countertop, cascaded lovingly down the cupboard doors, and flowed swiftly across the terracotta tiles of the floor.

And olives rolled like marbles everywhere.

I wish that I could say that I responded with a calm, Zen-like equanimity, but I did not. Instead those overpriced, high-tech, bright red oven mitts went flying across the room, along with a stream of obscenities.

I stood there and looked at the mess. There were splashes of garlic, lemon and thyme across every surface imaginable. In what was not my finest hour, I actually contemplated trying to save the olives on the floor, but the little voice in my head once again wisely whispered 'botulism', and so they went straight into the compost bin.

It was almost 45 minutes before I'd cleaned everything up — a herculean task, which of course involved moving the stove. Then I went calmly about boiling the last three jars. I can tell you this: when they were done, I did not pull them out with the red oven mitts.

The recipe says you have to wait two weeks after jarring the olives before you can eat them. The two weeks came and went, but for some reason CJ and I never opened a jar. These olives were special, and rare. After pressing most of our harvest olives for oil, and giving buckets of olives away to helpful friends — not to mention spilling that one jarful across the kitchen floor — we had just five jars of olives in our cupboard.

These were olives that needed an occasion.

Then three HelpX volunteers came to stay with us. They were in their late twenties, travelling the world — two young British women from Newcastle and a Japanese woman from Tokyo. The Brits had worked hard that day grubbing thistles out of the top paddock, and the Japanese woman had cleaned bathrooms and windows. We wanted to thank them.

It was dark already. Dinner was an hour away. Outside the moon was full. Inside the fire roared. I got out some cheese and crackers, offered our guests a beer. Then, out came the olives.

I checked the jar, top and bottom, to see if I could see any signs of mould. I shook it and checked again. All clear. Then I opened the jar and sniffed to see if the olives smelled putrid. They did not. They smelled absolutely delicious. Garlic, lemon and thyme soared around my head.

CJ and I tasted them first, just to make sure they were okay to serve, and because we deserved it. They were heady and strong with garlic and thyme, and absolutely wonderful.

I put some in a bowl and told an olive story to our guests. When they tasted them, they oo-ed and aah-ed. But most tellingly, they ate them all up.

The
Fou
Yea

rth

Chapter 45

Making olive oil labels at Wolfies

It was a sunny spring day when I knocked on the old wooden door and out came a giant pig, Squiggles, the pet kunekune pig that belonged to Leelee and The Wolf. I patted Squiggles on the head and laughed as she squealed a charming little hello. Then I stepped around her and gave big hugs to her human owners, who were standing right behind her. I was thankful that they were helping me out in such big way.

LEELEE AND THE WOLF are the brains behind Wolfies. Walking into their charming colonial cottage was a little like walking into Peewee's Playhouse. It was a fun-filled place full of love and a little bit of madness in the best possible way.

Just outside their door was a pile of heart-shaped stones that Leelee had collected over the course of years; the walkway up to the house was set with flower patterns, and the word 'Love' was the last thing my foot touched as I stepped up onto the front porch that had been recently rebuilt by The Wolf himself. Next to their house was the old barn they were refurbishing — half of it to become an art studio, and the other half to become a shop where they planned to sell their olive oil and their art.

I was there because I had a problem, albeit a good one to have.

Six months before, I'd started a blog. I was writing about our life on our little olive farm, telling stories about our hens, our neighbours and our olives. I'd called the blog 'Moon over Martinborough' after the moonlit nights in the olive grove.

Surprisingly, people started reading it. And it wasn't just my friends and family back in the States. People I didn't know from all over were reading it regularly and leaving comments. And they kept asking where they could buy our olive oil.

Buy it? Total strangers wanted to *buy* our olive oil?

Although I loved the idea of selling our olive oil in stores, the very thought of it overwhelmed me. For starters, how would I do the labels? I didn't know what the legal requirements were, what the nutritional information was, who could help me implement the design, or who we could get to print them.

So I did what I always do. I started asking the locals.

It turned out my friends at Wolfies had already designed labels for their own award-winning olive oil, researched the labelling requirements, and begun selling it in local shops. So when they said 'We'll help you,' I was overwhelmed again — this time with gratitude.

For a long time CJ and I had no idea what to even name the oil. We struggled with all sorts of names. We were missing the obvious, but eventually it hit me.

'Duh,' I said to CJ. 'We need to name the olive oil after the blog. Since people are asking to buy it on the blog, it makes sense.'

'Great idea,' CJ said.

Moon over Martinborough Extra Virgin Olive Oil was born.

I SAT DOWN ONE evening to scribble out exactly what I wanted on the label. I made a couple of different versions, but the one I liked the most had the moon at the top of the label and the words *Moon over Martinborough* beneath it. 'Martinborough' was such a long word that I figured vertical was the only way to fit it on a tall, thin olive oil bottle.

I had those scribbles in my back pocket as I walked with Leelee and The Wolf into Wolfies. Squiggles followed us. We passed an almost life-sized papier-mâché and canvas sculpture of the Virgin Mary, a row of pastel-coloured handmade glasses catching sunlight in the window, and several of Leelee and The Wolf's playful paintings.

As Squiggles settled down on her blanket next to the couch, we opened a bottle of local pinot gris, chatted a bit, and then settled down ourselves, in front of the computer. Outside in the paddock, daffodils were coming up through the grass and their three pet sheep were bleating and playing in the sunshine. We talked about colours that I liked and the kind of feeling I was hoping to capture in the label. I talked about how beautiful the olive grove was in the moonlight. When I picked a font I liked, we laughed at how appropriate it was that it was called American Typewriter.

Then The Wolf got to work. What would we end up with? What would it look like?

The Wolf drove Photoshop like a true professional, transforming my scratchy scribbles and the image in my head into something beautiful on the screen. Meanwhile Leelee helped me dream up more words for the label.

We went from a pale blue label to something that was even more lush and gorgeous, and it also met the legal labelling requirements. At the top of the label, a pale moon glowed on top of a dark purplish-black background. The words *Moon over Martinborough* appeared in a luminescent white underneath. I loved it.

When we were finished, they gave me advice on where and how to get the labels printed, and then Leelee made us a delicious meal of steak, chips and salad. We finished off the pinot gris and laughed as Squiggles backed her big bum into the large potted tree in the centre of the room, almost knocking it over.

I left that evening with the label on a USB stick, happy as a clam. Yet again, I had experienced another great act of kindness from the locals. I couldn't wait to try to get our olive oil into the very first store.

Chapter 46

Old Man
Henry fades

It was early in the spring of that fourth year that Old Man Henry started sleeping in the nesting box. At first I just thought that he was cold, as the nights were still chilly. I figured that as soon as summer arrived he'd go back to his low senior citizen's perch. Then I found him sleeping smack dab on top of three eggs, and I knew something was not quite right.

FROM THAT POINT ON, Henry was always on the eggs. Every morning I found myself in the odd situation of having to reach under our rooster to gather the eggs from the nesting box.

As I've said before, things are never normal at our place. I'd already had to deal with the world's first chicken-feed-addicted pet sheep, so I wasn't too surprised to find that we now had the world's first broody rooster. Because we're very accepting at our house, I was careful never to shame Henry for his unroosterly behaviour. I just reached under him each morning and said, 'Thank you for the eggs, Henry.' After all, if a poor decrepit rooster finds a last glimmer of joy in pretending he's a sprightly young hen, who am I to judge?

What was truly amazing was that, when Henry next began sleeping on the floor of the chook house, the hens started laying their eggs where he slept so he could look after them. It was clearly some kind of gender-bending chicken conspiracy.

Then, one Saturday morning in the middle of September, I went out a little late to feed the hens. I opened the door to the run and shooed out some sparrows, cursing under my breath as I did.

All five of our hens scolded me for my tardiness with loud squawks and squeaks. But Old Man Henry, rather uncharacteristically when food's involved, was nowhere to be seen. I did the first thing you do when you realise your rooster's missing: I checked to see if he was trying to hatch some eggs.

I looked inside the chook house and saw the old man back in a corner, sitting with his legs thrust out in front of him. I'd never seen him sit like that before. As I walked over to him, he began struggling, but it seemed his legs wouldn't go where he wanted them to. He flapped his wings and squirmed, and then I realised the problem. Henry could no longer walk.

I picked him up gently and took him out to the chicken run. As soon as I set him down in front of some chicken feed, he fell back on his tail feathers again. When he tried to walk, he just went scooting backwards until he was up against some chicken wire. He looked around strangely, as if to ask why his legs weren't right. I held him over the food and the water, but he wanted none.

Most people, I suppose, would have chopped off their rooster's head right then and there. But we're not most people. Even bloodthirsty CJ refused to do it. Instead I phoned Aussie Bronwyn.

'Oh,' she said. 'That doesn't sound good.'

'What should I do?' I asked.

'Does he seem to be in pain?'

'No. He's looking around and seems very alert. He's not frothing at the mouth or anything.'

Aussie Bronwyn sighed. 'It would be a shame to traumatise him by chopping off his head. I don't think you need to worry. I suspect he won't be here in the morning.'

That night, I set Old Man Henry up on a thick bed of extra pea straw in the corner of the chook house.

'Goodnight, Henry,' I said, and closed the door.

Early the following morning I went out to the chook house and opened the door, absolutely certain that I would find Henry dead. But there he was, exactly as I'd left him, looking around and blinking, perfectly alert. When I tried to give him food and water, he once again wanted none.

Surely, I figured, he'd be gone the next morning. After all, he hadn't eaten in two days, and the hens had started laying their eggs in the nesting box again. Surely it was some kind of sign? Had they given up on him?

ON THE MORNING OF THE THIRD DAY, Old Man Henry was exactly the same. I brought him an apple core, which I know he loves. He took one large bite, but then refused to eat any more. When I held him over the water, he took several sips.

That night I checked on him one last time before going to bed, and I found that our little grey Araucana hen, Françoise, was not in her normal spot on the top perch. She was sleeping cuddled up next to Henry down in the straw. The two of them were the oddballs in our flock. Françoise had been out of sorts since CJ and I had culled her sick friend, Natasha. Clearly Françoise had some kind of bond with Henry.

The next morning, on day four, I opened the chook house door to find that Henry — surprise, surprise — was still alive.

'This is getting ridiculous,' CJ said. 'He's like the fat lady in the opera, taking forever to die.'

That evening I got a call from Suzanne, our neighbour who'd given us Old Man Henry. She'd heard about Henry's plight. After I filled her in on the details, she said, 'He always was a stubborn bird. People don't normally have this problem. Roosters usually just drop off their perches and die.'

Suzanne offered to call the vet the next day to see if Henry could be put down. She even offered to take him herself. I was hesitant. The truth was that I wanted the old man to go quietly. I didn't want to terrify him by carting him off to the vet in a cardboard box. But Suzanne and I agreed to talk the following evening, after she'd spoken to the vet.

After I got off the phone with Suzanne, Leelee called. I'd told her Henry was sick. Leelee has very close relationships with animals, and she recommended that I sit down with Henry and tell him that it was okay to go, that it was okay to die. I didn't quite know what to make of this. I could imagine having such a conversation with a sick human, but not with a sick rooster.

As soon as I hung up the phone, it rang again. It was Aussie Bronwyn, calling to check on Henry. It was entirely possible that no rooster in the history of poultrydom had ever had so many people fussing over him.

THAT NIGHT I WENT out again to go check on Henry. Once again, little Françoise was sleeping next to him in the straw. I opened the door and stepped inside. Françoise squirmed, but she refused to leave Henry's side. I squatted down and, yes, I admit it, I spoke to Henry. I spoke to an old, dying bird.

The truth is, I had grown very fond of the old man. He had, after all, brought us peace. There was a slow, stubborn way about him that I admired. Even on his old, feeble legs, he did his best to keep up with the young hens. If you'd ever seen him eat an apple core, you'd know he had a serious lust for life.

'Henry,' I said. 'I know you don't want to go. I know you love life, but it's time. Your body is sick, and your spirit can't stay inside of it anymore. It's okay. You have to go.' Then I smiled and joked with him. 'In heaven you'll have a harem of young ladies, I'm sure. And you won't be impotent. Think how much fun that will be.'

I reached over and gently stroked his head, then I stood up, walked out and closed the chook house door.

When I went out in the morning, I opened that door and looked over at Henry's corner to find that he was still very much alive, blinking and looking around. He looked like somebody waiting for a party to start.

But when I came home from work that day, things had changed. Old Man Henry was leaning forward so far that his head was nearly, but not quite, touching his extra-thick bed of pea straw. He was still breathing, and his eyes were open, but there didn't seem to be much life left in him at all.

When Suzanne called that evening, I explained the situation. She said, 'Well, I suspect he won't be here in the morning.'

I checked on him again before going to bed, and his situation was the same — still leaning, still breathing. Little Françoise had faithfully curled up next to him on the ground for the night.

On the morning of the sixth day, when I opened the chook house door, Old Man Henry looked unnaturally still. Françoise was no longer next to him. I leaned down and touched him, and then I knew. His body was hard and stiff under his soft feathers. After many long and happy years on the planet, Old Man Henry had finally gone to the Great Chicken Palace in the Sky.

I whispered quietly to the stiff, dead tumble of feathers in front of me. 'Goodbye, old man.'

I buried him under the oak tree behind the hay shed, as I always said I would. There was a big grey stone nearby, and I placed it on top of his grave. Now CJ and I call that tree 'Henry's tree'. I point to the stone and I tell people that a stubborn old rooster is buried there.

I watched our fives hens closely after that. The Fat English Ladies remained close. The Barnevelder Sisters were as unfriendly and distant as ever. There was almost no change in any of their behaviour after Henry died. Some would say that's not surprising, that animals simply don't grieve.

But I have only this to say. For three solid weeks after Henry died, every night little Françoise slept in the same spot where she slept the last few nights of Henry's life — right next to the place where the old man died.

Chapter 47

Pinot speed dating

The room was dimly lit. There were candles glowing everywhere, red and white heart-shaped helium balloons floated across the ceiling, and an inviting fire burning in the fireplace. I stood talking to an energetic, grey-haired woman whose intricately beaded black necklace sparkled in the candlelight. She was telling me about her life as a vineyard owner.

'I DO ALL THE P WORDS,' she said. 'Plant, pick, prune and price!' Then she let loose with a delightfully mad, very infectious laughter. Her short hair flipped back as she doubled over.

I was speed-dating, and having a fantastic time. Of course, this woman was old enough to be my mother. But never mind. She was not my date. I was there to find my perfect pinot match.

Martinborough is a small wine region, responsible for less than three per cent of New Zealand's total wine production. But there's something about the combination of climate, soil, and human dedication that makes Martinborough wines punch well above their weight. A few weeks before, Martinborough wines had taken 20 per cent of the Top Twenty New Zealand picks in the prestigious British wine magazine *Decanter* for 'exciting producers and stunning wines'. How's that for a small community?

So when I had the opportunity to taste a wide range of local pinot noirs as part of the first ever 'Pinot Speed-Dating' event by Wines from Martinborough, I jumped at the chance.

That night CJ dropped me off at the venue, Brackenridge Country Retreat & Spa, so I wouldn't have to worry about drinking too much. Before he drove away he said, 'Have fun!' I suppose it's not often that your partner of 15 years tells you to have fun speed dating.

While waiting in the lobby for the event to start, I met some of the other 'daters' there — a married couple from the Netherlands, a young couple from Wellington. We sipped La Michelle from Margrain Vineyard, a very nice champagne-style wine of predominantly pinot noir grapes.

All of us were wondering if we were going to find the pinot love of our life that night, or just a brief viticultural fling. Then I bumped into Martinborough's local physician, Charlotte, who'd come along for the event. She and I joined one of the small tasting groups together. You know you live in a village when you team up with your doctor for a fun night out.

Suddenly a pair of double doors swung open and we were met with the sight of 10 winegrowers, each standing at a wine barrel table, ready to serve their wines.

The tasting groups were assigned a 'first date', and very quickly four or five people had gathered in front of each winemaker. In true 'speed-dating' style, we'd been encouraged to find out as much about the wine and the vineyard as possible in our allotted 10 minutes.

Each wine was matched with a canapé from Bar Saluté in nearby Greytown. There were delicious things like Moroccan spice wild venison croquettes with pinot jelly, and octopus and squid ink risotto with shaved parmesan. With so much good food and wine, my taste buds were in heaven all night.

Our first date was with Cambridge Road's pinot noir.

Just a few weeks before, our house had been burgled. Fortunately CJ and I didn't have much of any value at our place. Our television was as old as the hills, and the burglars had no interest in lugging the heavy relic away. They stole only one thing, a gift from a friend who had come to visit, a bottle of Cambridge Road pinot noir. They didn't touch the other bottles of wine nearby. Clearly, Martinborough burglars are a very discerning bunch.

Cambridge Road winemaker Lance Redgwell looked as organic as his wine, with his scruffy goatee and gentle demeanour. He wore a black suit and Converse sneakers, and could have passed for one of the band members from Blondie.

He poured us each a taste of his pinot noir, and I was happy to be able to taste at last the wine that had been stolen from me. It was delicious — young and balanced, with hints of berry and plum. We talked for several minutes to Lance about his approach to winemaking, which is biodynamic and stresses a holistic approach to the vineyard.

AFTER A PLEASANT CHAT, we heard the bell ring. Our 10 minutes were up. On we went to our next date. That was when I met Winifred of The Cabbage Tree Vineyard — she of the P words and the mad, infectious laugh. Winifred was there with her much more mild-mannered husband, David.

As soon as we'd gathered around, Winifred launched into a raucous version of the old tune 'Hey Big Spender' with the words rewritten as though The Cabbage Tree pinot noir itself were singing to us. Meanwhile, David poured us each a taste.

I hadn't heard much about The Cabbage Tree Vineyard, and I was taken aback by how good the wine was. It was wonderfully silky, with wild berry, aniseed and smoky bacon flavours. It was a mature, delightful and surprising wine. A bit like Winifred herself.

As Winifred told us about the wine, she explained that they don't do any 'fining' (adding substances to filter out the solids and proteins). Instead they rely on time, which is the traditional approach used in the Burgundy region.

'That's why the 2006 is our current release,' Winifred said. 'Other wines of the same quality sell for nearly twice ours. David tells me I'm a socialist to price it so low!'

At one point Winifred began looking very intently at Charlotte, who was standing next to me. 'You look familiar,' Winifred said. 'Do I know you?'

Before Charlotte had the chance to speak, Winifred screamed, 'Oh! You're my doctor!' She immediately threw her arms around Charlotte and gave her an enormous hug.

The entire evening went like this — meeting delicious wines and fantastic characters in quick succession. Some of the wines and people were subdued, some refined, and some were larger than life. As we moved from one date to the next, it struck me over and over again what an amazing opportunity the night was — not only to taste 10 different pinot noirs from one small winemaking region, but also to meet the winemakers themselves and learn about their individual approach to wine. I was amazed at what a vast range of tastes I found in those wines, considering they were all Martinborough pinot noir.

After the dates were over, we all had a glass of Muirlea Rise's Après Royale, which was an amazing dessert pinot.

When CJ drove up at the end of the evening to give me a ride home, I fell into the car seat feeling very happy indeed. As I told him about the evening, we drove down the dark rural roads, past open paddocks where cattle slept, and right towards the heart of the village. I felt a flush of small-town, local pride.

My 10 pinot noir dates

Ata Rangi, Crimson pinot noir Serious date material. Forty-something. Just mature enough. Humorous, witty, sexy, nice on the eye. Sweet red plum and black cherry.

Big Sky Wines, pinot noir A masculine bloke wearing muddy gumboots and a spotless tux. Sophisticated but very down to earth. Ripe cherry and dark plum, a nice touch of thyme and cinnamon.

Cambridge Road, pinot noir Young, organic and very natural. Balanced with hints of berry and plum. Burglars love it.

The Cabbage Tree Vineyard, pinot noir A surprise win and a great date. Wild berry, aniseed and smoky bacon. A mature, delightful wine.

Escarpment Vineyard, pinot noir Definitely someone to take home to Mom. Sophisticated and complex. Rich and lush.

Hudson Vineyard, pinot noir The girl next door who's a pleasure to be with. Cherry aroma. Vanilla and cloves.

Margrain Vineyard, Home Block pinot noir A multifaceted woman. Sleek and stylish. Tangy cherry bouquet. Juicy, dark fruits.

Martinborough Vineyard, pinot noir Dashing and full of finesse. All class. Dark chocolate to the nose, dark fruits to the tongue.

Murdoch James Estate, Fraser pinot noir A cultured partner who's a bit feisty. Spice and leather. 'Not a pinot for wimps.'

Nga Waka, pinot noir A lovely young lady ready for long-term commitment. Nice and fruity. Will still be a great date after eight to 10 years.

Chapter 48

Jack the baby lamb

I knew I was in trouble when I received a text from CJ that said: 'We have a new baby.' When I got home I found CJ sitting on the front deck, holding a very small lamb in his arms. Its head was resting peacefully on CJ's shoulder.

CJ LOOKED UP AND SMILED, 'Isn't he just the cutest thing you've ever seen?'

I sighed. 'And just how did this lamb end up in your arms?'

Earlier that day a fencer named Jack had come over to work on our fences. Finding a sad little two-week-old lamb suckling from its dead mother, he pounced on the lamb and brought him up to the house.

Even though all the sheep on our property belong to Hamish, the farmer who leases our paddocks, CJ took one look at that lamb and decided it was his.

'He's a ram lamb,' Jack told CJ. 'And he'll need to be bottle-fed if he's going to live. Three times a day to start.'

'I don't care,' CJ said. 'I'll do it. And we'll call him Jack.'

Jack the Fencer smiled and said, 'Well, that's a fine name.'

CJ immediately called Hamish to make sure he could keep the lamb. Hamish must have heard the desperation in CJ's voice, because he said yes.

There was one minor flaw in CJ's clever plan. Being a city boy, CJ knew absolutely nothing about taking care of a lamb. They don't have many orphan lambs wandering the streets of his hometown Chicago. But if there's one thing you can say about CJ, it's that being ignorant of an activity has never stopped him from doing it.

CJ called everyone we know in Martinborough, asking just what you do to take care of a lamb. Then he zipped off to PGG Wrightson's to buy rubber teats and powdered sheep's milk.

By the time I got home, he'd already given the lamb its first feed since its mother had died. You would have thought CJ had given birth to the little woolly beast, the way he carried it around. And during the rare moments when he set it down, the lamb followed him like a lost puppy.

'No sheep in the house,' I said, clearly delusional that I had any say in the matter.

'Don't be cruel,' CJ said. 'It's too cold. There are still frosts.'

And so I woke the next morning to the sound of a bleating lamb coming from a large box in the laundry.

Over the next week, Jack slept in our laundry every night and spent his days (thankfully) outside. CJ fed him diligently every morning and every evening. We had friends staying with us at the time, and they fed Jack lunch when we were off at work. With so many caregivers, Jack was becoming highly social. And when we invited 20 people over for a sausage-making party the following weekend (doesn't everyone have sausage-making parties?), Jack the Lamb was perhaps the only guest milling about on the front deck who didn't have a glass of wine in his hand.

There must have been murmurings of the madness going on at our house, because the neighbours began stopping by to meet the new member of our household. One by one they showed up, took one look at CJ carrying Jack around, or CJ sitting in front of the fire with Jack in his arms, and shook their practical farming heads and left.

IT WAS ABOUT THEN that our neighbour Aussie Bronwyn staged an intervention. She called up and gave CJ a stern talking to.

'You can't keep a ram lamb as a pet,' she said. 'They may be cute when they're little, but ram lambs grow up to be a horrible nuisance. We've got a pet ram in our paddocks and I don't ever turn my back on him. He'll head-butt you as soon as look at you. And if you castrate them and turn them into a wether, they serve no useful purpose whatsoever. It's far more sensible to raise a ewe lamb as a pet, since at least eventually she can be bred to earn her keep.'

'But he's just so adorable,' CJ said.

'Mark my words, if you keep him, you will regret it.' Then Aussie Bronwyn delivered the coup de grâce. 'Besides, what are you going to do with him next week when you go on holiday? He still needs to be bottle-fed.'

It was true. CJ and I had planned a trip away. Who would take care of him when we were gone?

Aussie Bronwyn and her husband, John, offered a solution.

They would take Jack and care for him until it was time to turn him into Christmas roast. Then they'd give us the meat from one of their lambs, so CJ wouldn't have to eat Jack. They'd also help to find a ewe lamb for CJ to raise as a pet next season.

I told CJ it was up to him.

It took him a couple of days, but eventually CJ said to me, 'Well, I guess we could rename the lamb "Jack Chop".'

CJ had decided to give Jack over to Aussie Bronwyn and John.

The day before we left for our trip, we dropped the lamb off. We put him in their paddock, and I wandered back up to the house with Aussie Bronwyn and John.

Then I looked back and saw CJ. He was still at the fence, leaning over and giving Jack Chop an ear rub. He stood there petting that little lamb for a very long time.

Chapter 49

The very first store

I took a deep breath and walked up to the counter at the Martinborough Wine Centre. All around me, bottles of gorgeous wine and olive oil stood sparkling on the shelves. I was there to try to sell our olive oil for the very first time, and I was nervous.

Would a Real Live Store actually want to put our little labour of love out on display with all those bright shiny things?

IN THE THREE YEARS that led up to that moment, CJ and I had worked hard. We'd kept the grass down, cut out the suckers, attempted to prune the trees, finally hired contractors to prune and spray when we just couldn't manage to do it ourselves, harvested the olives with our amazing friends, pressed the fruit to extract their precious oil, designed the labels, selected and ordered the bottles, and filled every single bottle by hand. We were ready for the next step.

I found that I had begun to approach olive oil in the same way I had always approached writing. It comes out of a love for doing it, out of a deep-seated desire to create something good, to send something out into the world that hopefully people will enjoy. But the flip side of that love is fear — fear that it will be rejected, that the thing you've put your heart and soul into is really, in the end, just a small, shabby thing that nobody likes.

I stood at the counter of the Wine Centre and pushed away the fear. I cleared my throat. 'Hi. Um, we have some olive trees here in Martinborough. And, um, would you like to sell our olive oil?'

That was, I'm afraid, my entire sales pitch. I said nothing about the boutique olive grove with nearly 500 trees at the edge of a sparkling river. Nothing about the artisan olive oil, where the emphasis was on quality not quantity. Nothing about the beautiful grassy flavour and the fantastic peppery finish. Not even the basic facts — like my name.

Let's just say I probably did not amaze the woman behind the counter with my sales finesse. But it turns out that was okay. After all, I had come to the Martinborough Wine Centre first because it was a safe place.

The Martinborough Wine Centre is a smallish shop that shares a charming red building with the Village Café. Many times I've sat in that building eating wonderful food and sipping coffee with friends, and I've often wandered through the racks of wine and olive oil and thumbed through the small section of books on the region.

The shop and café feel comfortable. It's a spot frequented not only by locals but also by urban Wellingtonians who drive over the hill in search of laid-back rural weekends and Wairarapa wine and olive oil. It was one of the shops that CJ and I had looked at on our first trip out to Martinborough, when CJ brought me to see our property. Now there I was, trying, however pathetically, to sell our own olive oil.

In response to my woeful sales pitch, the woman behind the counter said simply, 'Hi. I'm Amanda.' Thank goodness someone had the sense to introduce themselves.

'Sorry.' I laughed. 'I'm Jared.'

Amanda had a gentle and steady demeanour. It turned out she ran the Wine Centre. She asked a few smart questions about our grove and the olive oil. In the end, even though I hadn't thought to tell her, she figured out the stuff that mattered. The boutique grove. The artisan oil. At her prompting, I even thought to tell her about the amazing taste. Then I mentioned the little blog I'd started.

'Oh,' she said, 'you're "Moon over Martinborough"? There was a woman in here last week asking for your oil. So that's your blog?'

In fact, a really kind reader named June had sent me an email saying she'd looked for our oil at the Wine Centre. It must have been her. Now Amanda asked, 'Do you have some of your oil with you?'

'Um. No,' I said. 'But I can run home and get some.' (Professional. That's me.)

Amanda smiled. 'Bring some in when you can. We'll sample it. If we like it, we'll stock it.'

Later that day I returned to drop off a bottle, and Amanda said she'd call me. A day went by. Then two. Then three. Every evening I came home from my day job and eagerly checked our answering machine, but there was never a message from the Wine Centre.

CJ kept asking, 'Are you sure she said she'd call? Maybe you're supposed to call her?'

'No. She said she'd call.'

By the fourth day I figured out what had happened. It was obvious. Amanda hated our olive oil. She'd probably gagged and spat it out on the floor. She probably cursed the day our olive trees were spawned. Clearly she was avoiding the call. She just didn't know how to break it to me that our olive oil was not fit to grease her bicycle chain.

Another day went by. And another. After a solid week there was still no news. So I decided to face the music. I had to be put out of my misery. On a summery Saturday afternoon I walked into the Wine Centre, my head hung low, fully prepared to have Amanda tremble with disgust at the very sight of me.

But as soon as she saw me, she smiled. 'Hi, Jared. You're on my list of people to call today. Your oil is beautiful and the label's stunning. I'd like to place an order.'

I looked behind me to make sure there wasn't a smarter, more skilled olive-grower named Jared standing there. Nope. Just a few relaxed shoppers, milling about happily.

'Um. Are you sure?'

She nodded.

That day Martinborough Wine Centre ordered six whole bottles. Six. Okay, so I knew that wouldn't turn CJ and me into Olive Oil Barons anytime soon, but honestly those were the best six olive oil bottles I have ever sold.

Two weeks after that first order, Amanda got in touch saying she needed more oil. And the comments and emails kept coming. One day I got a fantastic message from a nice guy named Mark on the blog Facebook page. He said, 'We called into Martinborough on a family visit to NZ specially to get your oil . . . As of Sunday 1 bottle of oil left on the shelves at the Wine Centre — better stock them up.'

I immediately stopped in and asked Amanda if she needed more.

'Absolutely,' she said. 'It's selling well.'

Sometimes, it seems, the thing you put your heart and soul into can actually end up being something that people really like.

Chapter 50

Behind the scenes at Toast Martinborough

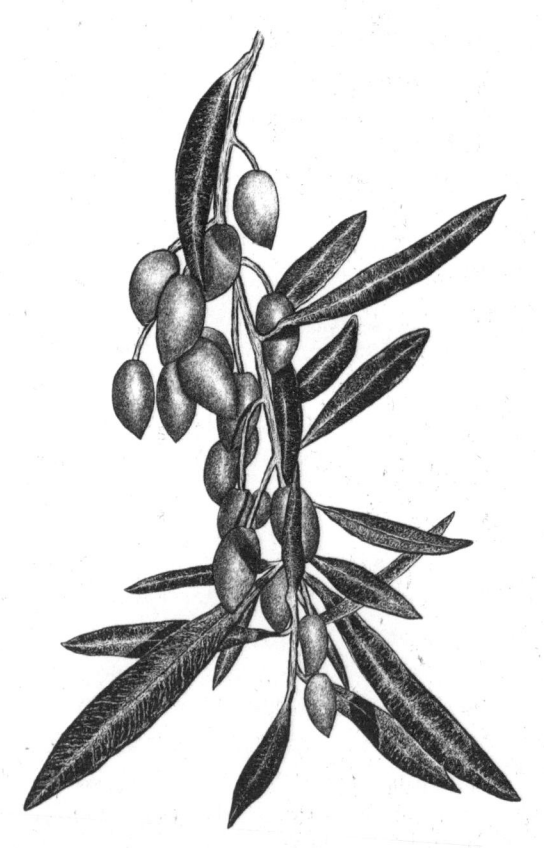

It was almost 9:30 a.m. and the floodgates were about to open. Thousands of wine lovers would soon be swarming around the large white festival tent and the outdoor stage at the Escarpment pavilion of Toast Martinborough.

I had already received my red Escarpment Vineyard T-shirt, and I was waiting to talk to a woman named Cath to find out what my duties for the day were going to be. Based on my chats with the other volunteers, it seemed the responsibilities varied widely.

THE PEOPLE WHO'D DRIVEN down from the Manawatu Wine Club were all going to be 'pourers' — serving fine Escarpment wines and helping people match their wine choices to the amazing food offered by Wharekauhau on the other side of the tent. A couple of other people I'd talked to were going to be on 'rubbish duty'.

What would I end up doing? Would I be one of the wine pourers — who got to wear swanky-looking black aprons — or would I end up emptying rubbish bins and picking dirty napkins off the ground all day?

Back in 1992, little old Martinborough decided to set up a wine and food festival to celebrate what was then a relatively new local wine industry. According to New Zealand's *AA Travel*, Toast Martinborough is now the biggest wine and food festival in the country.

Although the population of our town is only 1300, on the day of 'Toast' it swells to over 10,000. Busloads of people are carted over the treacherous Rimutaka Hill Road from Wellington and dropped off at our charming town square.

From there they wander from vineyard to vineyard, wearing wine glasses on strings around their necks (their 'ticket' into the vineyards), eating food from the best restaurants and caterers in the region, listening to great live bands and, most importantly, drinking fabulous Martinborough wines. Not a bad way to spend a day.

Although Toast is a large-scale and smoothly run operation, it's also a kind of community event. The local Rotary club pitches in, and people from the region often help out at the various vineyards.

I had met the winemaker of Escarpment, Larry McKenna, on Twitter. I'd offered to help and he'd said yes, so there I was. I walked up to him while I was waiting for Cath and introduced myself. In person he came across more like a humble high-school wrestling coach than one of the most noted winemakers in the Southern Hemisphere. Larry and I had a brief chat, and then Cath came over.

Cath had long, blonde hair and was clearly highly organised. In the short time she spoke to me she was interrupted by at least three other people. Everyone had questions for Cath, and she answered them all calmly and graciously. Now she looked at the clipboard which held my destiny. 'You're on security,' she said.

Let me explain that I am no six foot two, muscle-bound bouncer. I'm five foot 10 inches tall on a good day, and just the week before I had walked into a shoe repair shop to get another hole punched in my quickly shrinking black leather belt. (The shoe guy smiled and said, 'Keep it out of water.') Very few people would look at me and think, 'That guy could keep the drunken masses in line.'

Obviously I had misunderstood Cath. Although I had been in New Zealand about six years by then and had adjusted to Kiwi accents, every once in a while I still met someone I had a little trouble understanding. Cath probably said something like, 'You're on cellar keys.'

I asked for clarification. 'Um, did you say "security"?'

'Yeaaah. It's easy.' She tilted her head back and waved her hand in the air. 'You just walk around and make sure everything is okay. If a tent flap needs to be tied down, you see to it. If there's somebody's passed out in front of the toilets, you make sure they're okay. Get them a glass of water. That kind of thing.'

'And if a drunk guy starts a fight?'

'Oh, we've got real security for that.'

Clearly Cath had noticed my lack of muscle. In two seconds I'd gone from feeling surprised I was on security to feeling slighted. Cath explained. 'If someone's had too much to drink and they're out of line, you just go find one of the guys in the bright yellow vests.' She pointed across the way at two huge men with dark sunglasses, thick arms, and day-glo vests.

In the end, I breathed a sigh of relief. I was basically a nark. All I had to do was tug on the sleeves of the big guys and say, 'That one. Over there. You go get him.' This was a security job I could handle.

I had heard stories about how drunk some people got at Toast Martinborough, but that's not what I saw that day. Of course people are drinking wine, but I can testify, as a kind of an undercover cop, that the security guys on that particular day at the Escarpment pavilion of Toast Martinborough had surprisingly little to do. The bottom line was that the crowd was incredibly well behaved. Everybody was too busy having fun to cause any trouble.

OVER THE FIRST COUPLE of hours I opened up some canvas sides to the festival tent, secured other tent flaps in the unusually ferocious wind, walked around the back of the stage to see what was there, and then had a long, pleasant chat with the one other 'security' volunteer — a really nice farmer from Gladstone.

In fact, I had so little to do that I eventually ended up helping out with a million other things. I carried in case after case of wine from the refrigerated truck out back, took a dizzying number of empty bottles over to an enormous wooden skip, kept the water bottles filled up at the pouring tables, made a run with Escarpment's viticulturist to pick up a trailer for rubbish bags, and chatted briefly with the assistant winemaker when it was slow.

Throughout the day, festival tents at two other vineyards actually lifted off the ground under the force of 120 km/h gusts. Fortunately nobody was hurt. No such excitement happened at Escarpment. If it had, at least the guys on security would have had something to do.

Then, around 2:30, when the crowd was at its peak, one of the pourers came over to me. Her name was Kristina and she was part of the Manawatu Wine Club.

'I hear you're on security,' she said.

I considered denying it, but eventually said yes. She explained that there were two young men who were 'pissed' and who had been repeatedly denied alcohol by the pourers. But these guys kept going up to different pourers trying to get more wine.

'They're getting a bit stroppy,' Kristina said.

I asked her to point them out to me in the crowd, and she did so from a safe distance. I then marched right over to those two hooligans, picked both of them up at once, and carried them — one under each arm — out the front gate.

No I didn't. I went and got the big guys.

The big guys went over and talked to the young men quietly, and suddenly the young men were leaving. It was all very civilised. No fuss. No muss.

What amazed me was that, with the thousands and thousands of people who walked in and out of the Escarpment gate that day, there were only two people who'd had too much to drink and got a bit messy. Two. That's all.

What I saw was people having a really good time with friends, laughing, dancing, eating and drinking. The band at Escarpment was Sola Rosa, and they were fantastic. And those Escarpment wines, aaahhh! There's a reason Larry's got the reputation he has.

All in all, I was very impressed. I went home with two bottles of Escarpment wine in my hands, and I was a happy, exhausted man.

Chapter 51

Toyboy for Old Lady Lucy

It was a warm, summer afternoon when I noticed Old Lady Lucy standing in the middle of the top paddock covered in mud and screaming. She was not a happy pig. Clearly something was wrong.

I went over to check on her, but she was irritable and aggressive, and didn't want to be touched. So I did what one does when your pet pig turns psychotic. I called the Martinborough Pig Whisperer.

'I'm on my way,' Leelee said. Ten minutes later she was in our top paddock, asking Lucy what was wrong. Then Leelee announced, 'She's in heat. That's all.'

'HEAT?' CJ SAID. 'BUT she's an old lady.'

Leelee laughed. 'You think old ladies can't still get their ju-ju on? She's not that old.'

I just stood there shaking my head. How had this happened? Once upon a time I had a busy, bustling life in big-city Tokyo — now I had a hormonal pet pig.

Much to my dismay, the next day CJ had a new plan. Nothing is as troubling to me as when CJ gets a plan. He'd been talking to James the Sprayer, who not only manages the organic spray routine for our olive grove but also generally knows a lot about farming and the local community.

'There are some Alaskans that live out Longbush way,' James told CJ. 'They've got a kunekune boar they loan out for breeding. Kunekunes make excellent meat.'

When CJ explained to me that he thought breeding Lucy for meat was a perfectly sound idea, I was horrified.

'Do you really want to eat Lucy's babies?' I asked.

I'd grown very fond of Lucy by then. She is adorable when she lies down to get a belly rub.

CJ shrugged. 'Sure. We're not going to eat Lucy.'

'I don't know,' I said. 'There's a real moral dilemma when it comes to eating your pet's babies.'

Two weeks later Jeremy and Naya of Longbush Free Range Pork were unloading their kunekune boar, Kowhai, off the back of a trailer and onto our driveway. While Naya and Jeremy farm a heritage breed of pig called Large Black under their Longbush Free Range Pork label, they like keeping kunekune pigs as pets on the side.

As Kowhai came off the trailer, it struck me that he was one of the most incredible living creatures I had ever seen. He was large and brown and hairy, and he had tusks that gave him an odd, bemused expression. He had the 'tassles' typical of kunekunes, which hung down as hairy bits of skin on either side of his jaw. His short nose was almost comical. He looked like he was part Ewok and part *Where the Wild Things Are*. You could have cast him in a movie as an alien life form and you wouldn't even need special effects.

Naya began leading Kowhai out into the paddock by enticing him forward with some bread. None of us knew how Lucy would respond. She had never been bred before, and she'd been a loner pig for a long time. What's more, Kowhai was also considerably younger than Lucy. She was 13, he was only three. It was practically scandalous.

When Old Lady Lucy laid her eyes on that strapping young boar, she went directly over to him and sniffed. Then she freaked out. She squealed and turned and ran. Suddenly she was as nervous and flustered as a young schoolgirl.

Only after several minutes did she finally settle down and approach him again. Then they stood nose to nose for a long time. It looked suspiciously like a pig's first kiss.

'She likes him,' Jeremy said. 'She's a real cougar.'

Naya, who is a vet and saw right away that CJ knew nothing at all about pig breeding, kindly explained pig ovulation, pregnancy, and the signs of heat. CJ counted out 21 days from the last time Lucy was in heat and realised that his beloved pig would be in season in just a few days.

'Good,' Naya said. 'If she doesn't cycle the time after that, then she's pregnant.'

Let me just say that never before in the history of our household have we had ovulation cycles marked on our calendar. There truly is a first time for everything. Soon we couldn't even glance out into our paddocks without witnessing illicit pig love. It was shocking.

In the weeks that followed, we noticed a distinct change in Lucy's behaviour. Previously, she was always grazing over by the sheep. But now that she had her young toyboy to keep her company, she forgot all about her woolly-faced friends. Lucy and Kowhai were always together, grazing side by side.

Lucy was very quick, however, to put her young lover in his place. Whenever food was involved, she just pushed him out of the way. At first he pushed back, but it didn't take long before he finally accepted that Lucy was in charge.

CJ and I both grew fond of Kowhai. He was surprisingly friendly. When we went out into the paddocks, Kowhai would grunt and come over for a scratch. He would lean into your leg and rub his head against you like an affable, oversized alien dog.

It wasn't long before I overheard CJ saying to a friend on the commuter train, 'I don't know. Kowhai's so cute, and Lucy's so cute. I'm beginning to think maybe I can't eat their babies after all.'

Meanwhile, CJ continued checking the calendar, wondering whether Lucy was pregnant or not. One day, as I was petting Lucy, it seemed as though her belly had become surprisingly swollen and tight. It didn't feel like fat to me, but what did I know? Then I noticed that she had a new waddle to her walk. CJ agreed. It looked suspicious. Was she pregnant? And if she was, would we really eat her babies?

Chapter 52

The gingerbread boys

When Christmas came that summer, I thought of gingerbread. No matter where I've lived in the world, if I couldn't get back to Michigan for Christmas, then a little bit of my boyhood Michigan Christmas has always come to me — in the form of a box of gingerbread men.

WHETHER WE'VE BEEN LIVING in provincial Japan or crowded Tokyo, central Wellington or out here in our rural paradise of Martinborough, the gingerbread men have always come. That is, until that fourth year in Martinborough. Things had changed, and the only way we were going to get them this year was to make them ourselves. We'd never done that before, in any country.

'I don't know if we can get molasses here,' I said to CJ. We were standing in our kitchen and reading the list of ingredients just two days before Christmas.

'Are you serious?' CJ said. 'No molasses?' There was a slight tinge of panic in his voice.

Long ago he had come to love these gingerbread men as much as I do, and the thought of a Christmas without them — the first in the many years we'd been together at that point — struck terror in his butter-and-sugar-loving heart.

'I don't know,' I said. 'I've never seen molasses here, but I've never looked. The recipe calls for it.'

CJ looked at me. 'We must get molasses. We have to make them exactly according to that recipe.'

When I was a boy in Michigan, it was my Auntie Olive and Uncle

Herby who showed up every year at Christmas with a tray of home-made gingerbread.

Even in my adolescence, what struck me about Olive and Herby was how generous and loving they were in all aspects of their lives. They were adopted family, not really blood relations at all. Herby was the minister of the Methodist church my sisters and I grew up in.

My entire family appreciated Olive and Herb's gingerbread men, which were always soft and delicious, but in me that ginger, cinnamon and molasses combination brought about a state of profound and heavenly bliss. After I ate more than my fair share, I'd start grovelling in front of my sisters. 'Just an arm off yours, please? Maybe a leg?'

Every single gingerbread man that came out of Olive and Herby's kitchen was meticulously decorated. They produced everything from traditional red-suited Santas and white snowmen to more original creations with purple lederhosen and bright yellow bikinis.

Each cookie was always carefully placed in plastic wrap and tied up with a red ribbon. It took hours and hours to make them all, and they always did it as a team.

Back in 1998, when CJ and I moved from the States to Japan, it was the first time we were too far away at Christmas to make it back to visit family. In response, Auntie Olive and Uncle Herby shipped off a box of their precious gingerbread men to the other side of the planet. It was addressed to both CJ and me. Opening the front door and seeing that box on our concrete doorstep in Yamagata filled me with a kind of love and gratitude that went far beyond ginger, cinnamon and molasses.

Every year after that, a box came. It was like a constant in the universe. In spring, flowers bloom. In autumn, leaves fall. And at Christmas, gingerbread men arrive from Michigan. Doesn't that happen for everyone?

When I was diagnosed with coeliac disease in 2006 and could no longer eat wheat, rye, barley or oats, I decided that Herby and Olive's gingerbread men would be my one annual dose of food that I would eat even though I shouldn't. They were that good.

Because CJ and I had only really started learning how to cook and bake since arriving in the country, we didn't know about alternatives to molasses. So, before driving the 45 minutes to the grocery store in Masterton to hunt for molasses, our friend Will consulted an expert about alternatives just in case we couldn't find any.

Will was visiting from Chicago. Many years before he'd spent about five years in Malawi with the Peace Corps, and he knew an American woman from those days who was an expert baker. She'd had years of experience converting ingredients in American recipes to whatever was at hand.

Will sent her an email saying, 'Need quick response. It's two days before Christmas. What can we use in gingerbread if we can't find molasses?'

She replied immediately, saying, 'I know an emergency when I see one.' She gave us a list of alternative ingredients. Treacle. Cane syrup. Honey.

Off CJ and Will went to the grocery shop. When they returned, they had about them an air of victory. They had found molasses. Turns out, it's as common in New Zealand as it is in the States. In fact, cattle farmers here feed it to their stock.

Right away we began baking — two batches, one regular and one gluten-free. Each batch was supposed to make between 12 and 15 gingerbread men. I don't know what we did wrong, but somehow the dough multiplied. We ended up with over 60. There were so many gingerbread men in our house that they covered the stove top, the kitchen counter, and the dining room table.

Will looked around and said, 'Holy cow. It's like an army of terracotta warriors.'

The last batch came out of the oven at 11 p.m.

The next morning, Christmas Eve, we woke early and started with the frosting. I mixed red and green and blue and yellow and purple and something that turned out black.

It took us all morning and some of the afternoon to decorate our army, but we laughed and had a fantastic time. Will made a Cyclops, I made a lady with a pecan bra, and CJ perfected the art of cavorting green elves.

'Did you know,' Will said as he frosted, 'that molasses has very wide range of non-culinary uses? It can be used to remove rust, for example. And a small amount can be added to help make better mortar.'

As Will rattled off more random facts about molasses, we finally frosted the last of the gingerbread army. Then we immediately started eating. They were delicious.

Of course we spent the next several days taking them by the truckload over to our friends and neighbours. Because that's what you do at Christmas.

THE YEAR BEFORE, on 19 December 2008, my Uncle Herby had died at the age of 84. A month later, a box of gingerbread men showed up in Martinborough. It was the very last batch of cookies Herby and Olive had made together.

What does it mean to eat gingerbread decorated by a man who has already passed over to the other side? What sort of connection does it give us with the dead?

I wrote Olive telling her how much Herby had meant to me and I tried, as best you can at times like that, to tell her I was sorry for her loss. Our loss. I thanked her again for all the gingerbread men over years. And then I asked her for the recipe. I didn't want her to feel obligated to continue sending them every year. She was 83 herself. And her gingerbread partner was gone.

So the recipe I held in my hand, as I was standing in the kitchen with CJ two days before Christmas, was written in Olive's handwriting.

Gingerbread Boys, it said across the top, in bold letters. This is how traditions are passed down.

Auntie Olive's Gingerbread Boys

This is my aunt's old recipe from years ago, originally from an old copy of a Betty Crocker cookbook.

Ingredients

1½ cups black molasses (or treacle)

1 cup brown sugar

⅓ cup butter or lard, softened

½ cup cold water

7 cups gluten-free flour (Bakels Gluten Free Health Flour works well,
or Orgran Gluten Free All Purpose Plain Flour. For a wheat version,
replace with the same of quantity wheat flour.)

1 teaspoon ground ginger

1 teaspoon cinnamon

1 teaspoon allspice

1 teaspoon ground cloves

1 teaspoon salt

2 teaspoons baking soda

Icing

2 cups icing sugar

1 tablespoon water (approx.)

Preparation

In a large mixing bowl, beat together thoroughly the molasses, brown
sugar and butter or lard.

Stir in the cold water.

Sift together the next 6 ingredients, then stir into the mixture.

In a teacup, dissolve the baking soda in 2 tablespoons cold water,
then stir into the mixture, which should now resemble a dough.

Chill the dough 1 hour, and heat the oven to 175 °C.

Roll out the dough to a thickness of 12—15 mm on a floured surface.
Cut out shapes (to prevent sticking, dip the cutter in flour). Place the
shapes on a baking tray that is lightly greased or lined with baking
paper. Bake 15-18 minutes.

To make the icing: Add water, 1 teaspoon at a time, to the icing sugar
reach the desired consistency.

Ice shapes when cool.

MAKES 12-24 GINGERBREAD BOYS, DEPENDING ON THE SIZE
OF THE CUTTER

Chapter 53

Is the old lady pregnant?

'So, is she pregnant?' CJ asked. Naya looked over the fence at Old Lady Lucy. 'She does look a bit more plump, doesn't she?'

Naya was wearing a thick knit cap and an old jacket that was tied closed with a bit of twine wrapped around her waist. There was a bit of hay stuck to her left shoulder.

CJ AND I HAD asked Naya to come over to give us her professional opinion. Although CJ and I suspected Lucy was 'in pig', as they say, the simple truth is that city boys like us wouldn't know a pregnant pig from a bar of soap.

'I swear Lucy's getting bigger every week,' I said. 'There must be a whole pile of tasty bacon babies inside her. Yum, yum.'

'Jared!' CJ scolded. 'Don't say such mean things about Lucy's babies.'

I sighed and looked at Naya. 'Forgive him. CJ failed pig farmer school.'

Ever since Kowhai had arrived I'd been mulling over the value of raising your own meat. I came to the conclusion that eating animals you know, and that you have raised yourself, is actually more ethical than buying anonymous meat in the supermarket where you don't know how the animals were treated. So I had decided that eating Lucy's offspring was a great idea. This decision was no small thing given that I have a history of dabbling in vegetarianism.

For CJ, however, having Kowhai on the property was a very different experience. When Kowhai turned out to be the friendliest,

Ewok-faced creature we'd ever met, and when Lucy and Kowhai became inseparable, CJ began feeling a bit conflicted.

I should take a moment to point out that CJ is someone who loves eating pork almost as much as life itself. One of his favourite sayings is, 'Everything tastes better wrapped in bacon', and he finds pork crackling so addictive that he refers to it affectionately as 'pork crack'.

Nevertheless, slowly CJ's love for Lucy and Kowhai grew to overshadow his love of eating pork. One day he announced, 'There is no way I'm going to eat Lucy and Kowhai's babies. I can only eat pigs I don't know.'

It was like some kind of Home Farm Freaky Friday. CJ and I had completely changed places. The former vegetarian was ready to rip into piglet flesh, while the mad carnivore had suddenly become sensitive.

Now Naya turned to CJ and asked, 'If you don't want to eat Lucy's piglets, what do you want to do with them if she's pregnant?'

CJ smiled in a way that I have come to associate with serious trouble. It's an impish smile full of mischief and clever plans. He looked at Naya and blurted out one word, and one word only: 'Pets!'

I shook my head in disbelief. 'CJ, Lucy could have up to 12 babies. We can't keep all those piglets as pets. We'd be overrun with pigs.'

'No, we'll just keep some,' CJ said. 'The others we'll sell as pets on TradeMe.'

'Exactly how many is "some"?' I asked, wanting clarity.

CJ just shrugged and gave me that worrying smile again.

'Has Kowhai mounted Lucy recently?' Naya asked.

'I don't think so,' I said. 'Why?'

'Well, if she were pregnant, she wouldn't let him mount her.' Naya smiled. 'She'd be like, "Young man, you keep that thing to yourself!"'

Naya then stepped forward and pressed down with her hands on either side of Lucy's back. Lucy stood still. 'You push like this to test to see if they're ready to accept a mate. If they're in heat, they stand still.'

CJ laughed. 'You mean she thinks you're about to mount her?'

'Well, yes,' Naya said. 'And I'm afraid she's going to be terribly disappointed. But the only way to know for absolute certain if she's pregnant is to scan her. Do you know if any of your neighbours have scanning equipment for their sheep?'

'We could ask around,' I said.

What happened next is difficult for me to describe, since it may be slightly offensive to some. I suspect that if you're a city person, you might think it's just Too Much Information. If you're a farmer, you'll probably not even bat an eye. Lucy turned around and evidence of Pig-on-Pig Action came dribbling out of her nether regions.

'Oh,' Naya said, in her most practical veterinarian's voice. 'Look at that. Well, guess what, Lucy is most definitely not pregnant.'

'Really?' CJ said.

Naya nodded. 'Kowhai has clearly hit the bull's-eye, and Lucy would definitely not let him do that if she were pregnant. No way.'

The fact that CJ and I weren't disgusted by seeing things dribbling out of Lucy was a clear indication that we had been in the country too long.

'But then why is Lucy so fat?' I asked.

'I bet it's the bread,' CJ said.

Ever since Naya and Jeremy dropped off Kowhai, they had been leaving us weekly rations of the day-old bread they collect from bakers to feed their pigs. Kowhai has an incredible underbite which causes him to have a little trouble grazing. So Naya and Jeremy thought he should get a good supply of bread.

The problem was that every time we fed Kowhai bread, Lucy pushed him out of the way and ate it all.

Naya nodded. 'Yes, that would explain it. I suspect Lucy has a Bread Baby. And Kowhai's been here for three cycles. If she's not in pig now, she probably never will be. She's just too old.'

CJ and I looked at each other. We were both, for our separate reasons, surprisingly disappointed.

'No pets?' CJ said.

'No pork roast?' I said.

Naya shook her head. 'I'm afraid not.'

Suddenly CJ looked horrified. 'You're not going to take Kowhai away from us, are you?'

Naya laughed. 'He seems pretty happy here. And Lucy seems to be enjoying her late-life fling with the strapping young boar, although she needs to go on a diet.' Naya looked at CJ. 'I suppose you can keep Kowhai as long as you want him.'

CJ's face lit up, and he yelled out into the paddock. 'Did you hear that Kowhai? You can stay! You hear that Lucy? Kowhai's staying!'

Both Kowhai and Lucy looked over and expressed their satisfaction with deep and resounding grunts.

I shook my head. Yes, CJ had definitely failed pig farmer school.

Chapter 54

The Spiritual Leader

'**T**urn up Te Muna Road,' I told Russ. 'It's up there.' I was in the front passenger seat, and Russ was driving. Joel, Louise and Karen were squished together in the back seat. They were friends of ours visiting from Chicago, and we were heading to one of my favourite Martinborough wineries, Escarpment Vineyard, for a private tour.

DRIVING ACROSS THE CATTLE STOP at the entrance to Escarpment Vineyard, you'd never know you were entering the domain of a man who has been called 'the spiritual leader of New Zealand pinot enthusiasts'. There was no imposing gate, no angelic music from on high. Just a small brick wall with a stylised 'E'.

Russ drove us up the long driveway through the vineyard, and we passed a blue truck with a long mechanical arm that was jutting out over the vines to dispense netting. Men were walking behind the truck, pulling the nets down around the grapes. It was late summer. The fruit was ripe enough to be enticing for the birds, but it would be weeks before it was ready for harvest.

At the end of the driveway stood a modest building surrounded by vines. Like the cattle stop at the front gate, the building was immensely practical, and it was all part of the no-nonsense charm there. This place is not about pretentiousness. It is about making exceptionally good wine.

The 'spiritual leader' at Escarpment is winemaker and director Larry McKenna, and he's credited with putting New Zealand pinot noir on the global wine map. On the day we were there, Larry was in the UK. But he had put my friends and me in the care of his viticulturist, Dave Shepherd, and his assistant winemaker, Huw Kinch. I'd met both of them when I volunteered at Toast Martinborough. It was Dave who greeted me when I entered the building. He is a rugby-playing wine lover with a solid six-foot frame and a sturdy handshake. He had high-tech hearing aids on both ears. At one point I thought he was talking to unseen spirits, but it turned out he was just using the hidden Bluetooth cellphone connected to his hearing aids.

I introduced Dave to my four Chicago friends, and we wandered off together into the vineyard.

There is always something vaguely awe-inspiring about talking to someone who knows a lot about a specific subject, and talking to Dave about vines that day was no exception. He told us about the vines, about the different spaces between the varieties. They had planted the pinot noir vines for their flagship Kupe wine closer together than their chardonnay vines. More densely planted vines give less fruit per vine, but more intensely flavoured grapes. The closer row spacing meant they had to keep the grapes closer to the ground — to cut down on shading and to hold the day's heat longer.

Dave walked over to the vines, touched them, and talked about how the relatively cool summer had meant the grapes were ripening later that year.

'What's this?' Russ asked, pointing to a bushy thing by the chardonnay vines. Near the bush was something like a tiny roof.

'It's manuka,' Dave said. 'It attracts parasitic wasps.' The tiny roof, Dave explained, was for a wasps' nest. There were holes up inside it. The parasitic wasp was there to kill the pesky light brown apple moth, which did damage to the vines. The set-up was a clever alternative to spraying, and no doubt it was part of the reason Escarpment had been accredited as a sustainable winegrower.

After our walk through the vines, Dave took us over to the edge of the steep escarpment for which the winery is named. There the ground dropped away dramatically, and we were suddenly looking out over miles and miles of gorgeous pastureland. There were rolling hills in the distance, and we could see the line of the Huangarua River. Below us a local farmer had recently felled a stand of pine trees, and he was now burning off the remains. Smoke rose into the air.

Then we walked down to the wine cellar to meet Huw. At the very edge of that steep escarpment was a large concrete pad in the open air. It was a working area, and Huw was busily washing out wine barrels as we came down the steps. There was drainage below our feet, and the water ran red with wine.

I introduced Huw to my friends. He was at least as tall as Dave, with a peaches-and-cream complexion. Being a young twenty-something, he had to be very good at what he did. After all, it was no small thing to be chosen as the assistant winemaker to Larry McKenna. Huw was just as friendly and unpretentious as Dave, and I suspected that was part of why Larry had picked them both.

Now Huw turned and led us into the wine cellar. The space was high and dark, built into the edge of the escarpment itself. To my left was a countertop with bottles and clear tubes. It looked like the lab of a mad scientist. To my right, rows and rows of wooden barrels were stacked high. Against one far wall stood tall silver vats, which nearly reached the ceiling.

'How much time do you have?' Huw said. These words were music to my ears. He then proceeded to take us through every single one of their yet-to-be released 2009 pinot noirs. I felt I had died and gone to heaven.

DAVE IMMEDIATELY STARTED PASSING out the wine glasses. Huw climbed up on top of the barrels. He was carrying a large wine glass and something that looked suspiciously like a turkey baster. He was opening barrels and sucking out wine, blending the wine from different barrels to the correct mix in the glass.

Dave slapped down a blue plastic bucket in the middle of the group.

'For spitting out your wine,' he said.

'Spit it out?' Louise said. Her eyes were wide. 'We're not allowed to drink it?'

Dave laughed. 'Of course you can.'

Joel piped in. 'You spit it out if you don't want to get drunk.' Joel and Russ were wine lovers to the core. They knew the rules.

'Seems like a waste,' Louise answered, smiling.

When Huw came down from atop the barrels, he poured wine from the large glass he was carrying into each of ours. We started with the Escarpment pinot noir, and it was very good. I liked the dark taste of plums. But from there, things only got better.

We moved up through what they call their Insight Series — wines each from a single site around Martinborough. The idea was that each site offered distinctive characteristics. It wasn't just about the Escarpment brand but about the exact plot of land the wine came from.

The Insight Series sites were all around Martinborough:

- Pahi — The McCreanor Vineyard, Princess Street; 25-year-old vines.
- Kiwa — The Cleland Vineyard, Cambridge Street; 25-year-old vines.
- Te Rehua — The Barton Vineyard, Huangarua Road; vines over 20 years old.
- Kupe — The young, densely planted vines on the main Escarpment site.

All of these locations were places I passed and had come to know. As I stood there underground, tasting all these incredible wines, I felt as though I was drinking in my village, tasting the way the grapes had pulled the soil up into their hearts. I was learning so much from this place.

My favourite wines of the day were the Te Rehua for its bold black cherry flavours, and the Kupe, which was subtle and sophisticated and unbelievably delicious.

When we had tasted the last wine and Huw and Dave had answered the last of our many questions, we thanked them repeatedly and headed up the steps to the main building again. Piling into the car and heading back down the drive, I felt like Dave and Huw had taken care of me and my friends incredibly well. Russ, Joel, Karen and Louise were all going on about the enchanting setting and one-on-one attention we received.

I was left with only one unanswered question, which bottles of Escarpment wine were we going to buy at the Martinborough Wine Centre? Because that was where we were heading right away.

Chapter 55

Françoise and the return of the silver monster

'**K**ill them all,' CJ said. 'We'll start over.'

'What?' I was horrified. 'We can't simply cull all of our chickens because they couldn't learn how to use a chicken feeder!'

For over a year we'd been hearing stories from Aussie Bronwyn about how easy her life was with her collection of Grandpa's Feeders — how she didn't have to go out and feed her chooks every day, how the sparrows never ate the feed anymore, and how even her clever young hatchlings had learned how to use the feeder.

SHE LAUGHED GOOD-NATUREDLY when she told us this, knowing how our hens had failed miserably at using our Grandpa's Feeder.

CJ and I were sick with envy. But kill our chickens?

'If we get new chickens,' CJ said, 'we can raise them using the Grandpa's Feeder, and our life will be easier.'

I shuddered at the thought of killing all our chickens — the domineering Fat English Ladies, the unfriendly Barnevelder Sisters, and our one lonely aristocratic Araucana, little Françoise.

'Let's give them one last chance,' I said. 'Let's try using the Grandpa's Feeder again. If they don't learn to eat from it, then you can have your way. We'll cull them all.'

CJ, who has become surprisingly good at thinking like a chicken, thought that we should borrow Aussie Bronwyn's smaller Grandpa's Feeder, as it was less scary than our large one. I set down the smaller silver monster in the run and gave the hens a serious talking to. 'Listen, if you don't learn how to use this thing, CJ is going to come after all of you with an axe, just like he did Natasha. Consider yourselves warned.'

When they looked at the feeder, they were obviously still terrified. The Barnevelder Sisters twitched nervously, the Fat English Ladies squawked so loudly I could almost make out the words 'It's back! The killing machine is back!', and little Françoise cowered in the corner by herself, peeking out from under her tufted head feathers.

I had become increasingly fond of Françoise, and I couldn't blame her for cowering. She'd had a difficult life, first losing her sister, Natasha, and then losing her secret love, Old Man Henry. Now that Françoise had no allies, the Fat English Ladies had gone back to seriously harassing her and keeping her away from food. Nevertheless, Françoise had laid our very first egg on this property, and her eggs were that amazing blue-green, which to me always indicated that there was something very special about her.

I left the chicken feeder in the run and shut the door. Over the next couple of weeks, what happened was terrible, and I felt cruel. The hens started losing weight. They begged and squawked for food every time I walked by. They were starving, but they wouldn't go near the feeder. They were that scared.

Meanwhile, the evil sparrows were having a grand old time. Because I'd set the feeder in the half-opened 'training' position, the sparrows were jumping in and gorging themselves.

'The little bastards,' Aussie Bronwyn said, when I told her about the sparrows. Then she added, 'Maybe carpet would help.'

'Huh?' I asked.

'I think your chooks are afraid of the noise when their little claws hit the metal step. You should carpet it.'

By that point I was desperate, and no idea was too absurd. I found an old scrap of indoor/outdoor carpet and duct-taped it to the step.

I also set up two large rounds of firewood on either side of the feeder to block the hens from reaching into it without stepping on the step. Finally, I put the lid in the closed position to stop the sparrows. All in all, my improvements to our Grandpa's Feeder looked like the work of a slightly deranged mind. Alas, while the sparrows stopped coming, the chickens continued to get thinner and thinner. Soon even the Fat English Ladies looked like anorexic supermodels. They were positively emaciated.

I felt so horrible that I decided to give the hens some mercy bread. However, in light of the fact that their lives depended on eating from the feeder, I put the broken up bits of bread inside the silver monster. I also sprinkled some on the step to tempt them. The next day when I looked in the feeder the bread was entirely gone. It was like a miracle. 'You ate from the feeder!' I yelled to the hens. 'Fantastic!'

AS THE DAYS WENT by, the feed levels started dropping. Soon I was having to fill the silver monster regularly, and the hens seemed to be gaining weight. But still, I had never actually witnessed them eating from the feeder, and I was apprehensive. Were all of them eating from it, or only some? Was poor little Françoise getting any food? To solve the mystery I did what any dedicated and obsessive chicken owner would do. At long last, I truly did perform a stake-out. I loaded the feeder with bread again and hid behind the chook house. What I saw was absolutely astonishing.

The Fat English Ladies approached the feeder first, but they were clearly too afraid to tread on the step to open the lid and get the bread. When their backs were turned, Françoise marched up and stepped directly on the step. *Clank.* The lid opened, and she started scoffing bread. Now that the lid was opened, the Fat English Ladies turned around and, still careful not to step on the step, grabbed some bread. Then the Barnevelder Sisters came over. When everyone got too pushy, Françoise stepped away and the lid came crashing down.

In the days that followed, over the course of many stake-outs, I watched this happen over and over. No other hen seemed to understand how to open that terrifying lid, or they lacked the courage to do it. Little Françoise was feeding the masses. As a result, the lives of the entire flock were spared.

It took months before the other chooks finally got over their fear and learned to use the feeder on their own. My admiration for Françoise grew. She was small, and she was lonely, but she was very, very brave.

The disease-carrying sparrows looked down from the trees at the Chicken Palace. They were not laughing. Clearly they were longing for the days when chicken feed was strewn about the ground for their consumption.

I looked back up at them and grinned. 'Hah!' I yelled. 'I told you I would win!'

Chapter 56

One sick pig

It wasn't until CJ went away to the States and I had a week off that CJ's beloved pet pig, Old Lady Lucy, started having trouble.

The first sign was when she showed no interest in a piece of bread. This is a bit like a fierce lioness losing interest in a limping wildebeest. Lucy's previous owners regularly fed her day-old doughnuts, but at our place stealing bread from Kowhai was as close as she got to the glory days of her misspent, doughnut-eating youth.

AS A RESULT, she usually snatched bread up. When she wouldn't even lift her head to eat the bread I'd laid next to her, I was worried. It was unusually hot for late summer, and the following day Lucy collapsed by the pond behind the hay shed. In spite of the expression 'sweat like a pig', pigs don't have functional sweat glands. Wallowing is how they keep cool. Yet Lucy had fallen awkwardly about two metres away from the water. When she tried to move closer, her legs buckled. Although she was under shade, she was burning up, so I sponged her down to cool her. Lucy was 14 years old by then, which is very old. I leaned over and whispered in her ear. 'Look, Lucy. If anything happens to you while CJ's away, I'll be in serious trouble. So pull it together.'

The next morning I was relieved to find her back up in her pigsty, sleeping happily next to her young, studly toyboy, Kowhai. But then she got worse again. Later that morning I found her flailing in the hot sun, suffering from diarrhoea and unable to use her hind legs. Flies were swarming around her mouth and eyes. She was seriously heat-stressed. I sponged her down again, but how do you move a giant pig out of the sun? Even without the doughnut diet, Lucy was well over 150 kilogrammes. I felt utterly helpless.

Of course, in my world when you don't know what to do, you call the neighbours. Before I could say 'extreme pig emergency' John and Aussie Bronwyn were in the top paddock putting a temporary shelter around Lucy to keep the sun off her. John carefully sprayed Lucy with a fly repellent you use on sheep.

Shortly after they left, Lucy stumbled out from under the shelter and collapsed again in the sun. I moved and rebuilt the shelter on my own. This happened five times over the next several hours. Jim the Mad Welshman and Kiwi Bronwyn also showed up to help, but I was at my wits' end. That's when I called Naya. I needed a trained vet and pig farmer. She came swooping down like a superheroine, brandishing magical white powders and pink liquids.

Under Naya's wise instruction, we used two old towels to create a sling and heave Lucy into the hay shed. Next Naya gave me intricate instructions on the over-the-counter treatments she'd brought, and told me I had to call the official vet to get prescribed medications — an anti-inflammatory and an antibiotic.

Thus began a long saga involving three more vets with differing opinions and several after-hours consultations. When I got the drugs, they involved needles. Thankfully Aussie Bronwyn came back to shoot Lucy up. Then Leelee the Martinborough Pig Whisperer came by, with molasses and glucose to put in Lucy's water. Several other local pig lovers showed up, too. We practically had a team of specialists working around the clock to care for that old sow. I can only hope I get such good treatment when I'm old and decrepit.

Let me remind you that getting a geriatric kunekune was CJ's bright idea. I was opposed. And where was CJ now? On the other side of the planet. That's where. Typical.

LUCY SPENT THE NEXT two days lying around the hay shed, barely eating or drinking. Kowhai kept watch just outside the hay shed gate, even in the rain, always near her. Twice a day I gave her oral medication by syringing it into her mouth, and I mixed all sorts of things into her water.

Then, one afternoon, I found her shaking with terrible spasms. I sat down next to her for a while, petting her. She moaned. The following morning she was even worse. She'd been spasming for nearly 24 hours, and had been terribly sick for a total of five days. I called the vet. I had to put Old Lady Lucy down.

As I waited for the vet to arrive, I told Lucy I was sorry that she was suffering, but it would be better where she was about to go.

'Just think of it,' I said. 'You'll get doughnuts every day.'

It's always a heartbreaking thing to lose a pet, whether it be a dog, cat, pig, or aardvark. Pets have a mysterious way of bringing us joy. We learn things from their wholehearted and unselfconscious way of being in the world. I was very sad to say goodbye to that old girl.

Lucy picked up her head and started sniffing the air.

'What's that?' I said. 'Is Death here?'

At that moment my cellphone rang. Liz the vet was up at the house and couldn't find me. In the time it took me to walk to the house and back to the hay shed with Liz, Lucy was up and moving, grunting through the gate at Kowhai and sniffing around for food.

'I'm not ready to go yet,' the old girl seemed to be saying. 'You keep that vet away from me.'

'She seems so well, I'd hate to put her down', Liz said, and we agreed to wait.

Lucy was a miracle pig. Over the next two days, she got better and better. By the time CJ got back from the States, she was up and about and acting as though the entire episode had never happened.

'What's all the fuss about?' CJ said. 'Lucy's fine.'

It was all I could do not to slap him. Nobody knew what had made Old Lady Lucy sick. The heat? Something she ate? Pining for CJ? And nobody could say just how much longer she would be with us.

Chapter 57

Buying firewood is a sin

A
utumn was on its way. CJ and I were talking with our neighbours at a dinner party about getting firewood for the coming winter.

WHEN YOU HEAT YOUR HOME with a woodburner, getting wood in for the winter becomes an annual event, like the changing of the leaves and the onset of shorter, cooler days. Every year since CJ and I moved to Martinborough, we had picked up the phone to have firewood delivered.

When I admitted to this at the dinner party that night, I received some strange looks from around the table. I didn't understand. Had I said something wrong? After somebody very quickly changed the topic of conversation, Suzanne leaned over to me and said, 'Surely you've got downed trees on your land. Why are you *paying* for firewood?'

She said this in such a hushed tone that it was clear that paying for firewood was an unspeakable act — something that should not be discussed at full volume in polite company.

I felt compelled to deny everything, but it was already too late. Our terrible secret was out. For the past three winters we'd been unwittingly breaking the First Commandment of Rural Living: 'Thou shalt not pay for firewood.'

On a bright autumn morning a week later, John stopped by. We didn't know it, but he was on a mission to save our rural souls.

'You haven't ordered any firewood yet, have you?' he said, scratching his Santa Claus beard with a worried look in his eyes.

'No,' CJ said. 'We're about to. Would you like to order some together?'

John let out a shocked, insulted laugh and shook his head. 'I'm here to see if you want to collect some free firewood. I'll help you.'

It turns out that a local farmer had cut down a large crop of pine trees for export to China, and he'd left behind a huge tangle of trunk rounds and twisted branches. He'd given the nod to John to collect it.

'Opportunities like this hardly ever come around,' John said. 'Only a bloody fool would say no.'

CJ and I didn't want to be fools — bloody or otherwise — so of course we said yes.

IT WAS EARLY ON A SATURDAY MORNING a week later that CJ and I drove out to meet John at the spot where the trees had been felled. John's big white ute was parked nearby and he was already out among the tree debris, chainsawing his way through a large trunk. Although he's in his sixties, he's a workhorse and has more endurance than most men in their twenties.

When we climbed out of our little Nissan Pulsar still sleepy-eyed, John turned off his chainsaw and began laughing at us.

'You're late,' he said. 'It's already quarter past seven. I've almost finished loading up the first ute full of wood.' Then he waved his arms at the wood around us. 'Grab the small bits and throw them in the back of the ute. The bigger bits I'll cut up.'

CJ and I got to work right away. We quickly discovered that the 'small' bits were not small at all. They were thick, massive rounds of trunks. It was hard work, and we were at it all morning. In fact, in the end we spent *two* Saturday mornings gathering firewood that way. We unloaded all of it next to the shed on John's property. But even those 'small' bits were still too big for a typical woodburner.

Then one weekend John borrowed a log splitter, and CJ and I showed up early for our third Saturday of work. We were originally scheduled to start at 7 a.m. as usual, but the day before John had discovered that the borrowed log splitter wouldn't function in the early morning. It needed a couple of hours of sun on it before it was warm enough to start.

John called to tell us. 'The log splitter runs on city time. Don't come until ten o'clock.'

Now that's my kind of log splitter.

The machine was a home-made job, mounted on a trailer. It

was rusty and had tubes and pipes and hydraulic things I didn't understand. I had expected a swift, guillotine-like thing that would chop off your fingers in the blink of an eye. But this machine operated with a kind of mulish determination. The metal wedge came forward at a snail's pace, stubbornly pushing through even the most knotty rounds of trunks.

We fell into a pattern where I lifted the chunks of wood up to the log splitter, John operated the machine, and CJ and I would then toss the split pieces into the ute. Once the ute was full, CJ drove over to our place, unloaded the firewood into our hay shed, and returned again for more wood.

On one trip back CJ brought an old log that had been sitting by our chicken coop. When John and I split it we found it was full of life — earwigs, big black spiders, tiny burgundy spiders with bulbous bodies, orange fungus, centipedes, and slaters.

'This is a hardwood,' John said, as the insects went scurrying. 'Throw one of these on the fire when you go to bed, it'll still be burning in the morning.'

It was around then that CJ began bemoaning the fact that he had the hardest job. 'Unloading this truck single-handedly is exhausting,' he said. 'You two are just standing there watching bugs run around.'

John said, 'Jared's picking up these heavy trunks. Your job's easy.'

'Um, I don't think so,' CJ said.

When we went inside to eat lunch, CJ continued to gripe. Neither John nor Aussie Bronwyn gave CJ any sympathy. I kept my mouth shut because I was grateful he was driving the ute.

Perhaps motivated by a sense of injustice, CJ's search for pity continued well into the evening, when we all gathered for dinner over at Jim and Kiwi Bronwyn's. As soon as we arrived that evening, CJ launched into his great tale of log splitting and how he'd had the hardest job.

'Unloading the ute?' Kiwi Bronwyn said. She's a small woman, and she looked up at CJ. 'Oh, that's my job. Those big trunks are too heavy for me to lift, so Jim does that.' Everyone started laughing. And CJ finally shut up about who had the hardest job.

But it didn't matter. As we sat down to dinner with our neighbours, CJ and I both knew we had a hay shed full of firewood we had gathered ourselves. We were incredibly grateful to John. That wood was enough to last us two winters. And we hadn't paid a cent.

Chapter 58

Lucy gets doughnuts every day

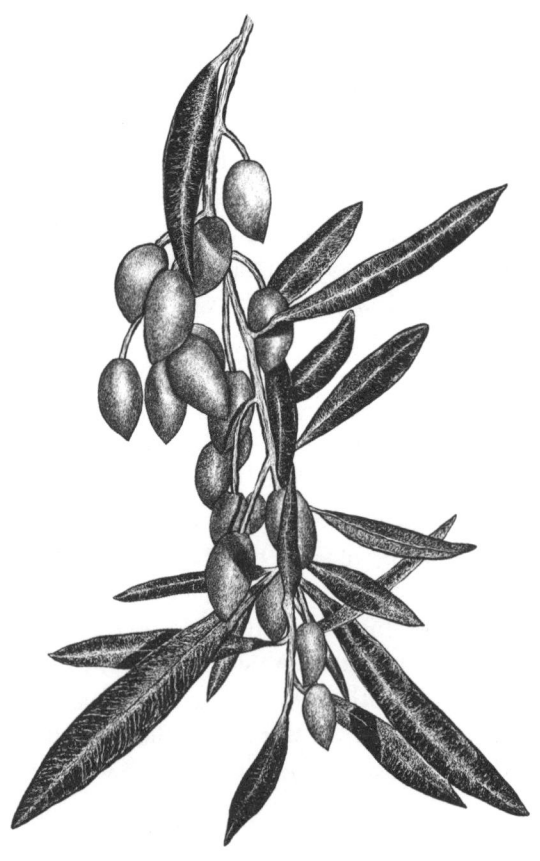

S uddenly one day Old Lady Lucy lay down and stopped eating. She had never been quite right after her late summer sickness, and we'd been worried about her. Now she was taking a turn for the worse.

I IMMEDIATELY WENT BACK into emergency treatment mode, but when I syringed water into her mouth, she let it fall out the other side. CJ and I quickly moved her back into the hay shed hospital. We called Liz, the vet, and got Lucy a new round of anti-inflammatories in a powder form, but we couldn't get the drugs into her. Poor Lucy wasn't even interested in the lovely, drug-infused jam sandwiches I made. She began whimpering in a new way.

We had been taking some days off for a long weekend when this all happened, so we were able to fuss over Lucy constantly for four straight days. At the end of that weekend, and after several conversations with Liz, CJ and I decided to have Lucy put down. She was a very old pig, and she'd had a good run, but now she was suffering.

It was our first day back at work when I called Liz in the morning and asked her to come put Lucy down. 'Could you come over after CJ and I get home from work tonight?' I said. 'I know it's out of hours, but it would break my heart to not be there when Lucy goes.'

Liz, being a kind vet, said yes.

On the way home that evening, CJ and I stopped and bought a dozen mini doughnuts. We wanted to give Lucy a last meal we knew she'd love. Surely she wouldn't say no to doughnuts?

When we got home, we immediately went out to the hay shed to say our goodbyes before Liz arrived. We called out to Lucy, but she didn't answer with her usual grunted hello. She was silent. I stepped in through the gate and walked over to her. I put my hand on her side. She was still warm, but the dear old pig was already dead.

When my grandmother was dying, she asked everyone to leave the room just before she passed away. It was as though having everyone there with her, loving her, was somehow keeping her in this world. She had to be alone to die. Maybe CJ and I, without knowing it, had been holding Lucy back the same way.

I said a small prayer over Lucy's large hairy body. I asked the pig god to take care of Lucy's enthusiastic pig soul. Then I called Liz to tell her that she didn't need to come anymore.

That's when the real work began.

I WAS RAISED IN cotton wool. Before coming to Martinborough, other people had always taken care of the bodies of the people and animals I loved. Doctors and vets and funeral directors. It wasn't until I moved out to the country that I learned true death is a physical thing. It involves moving and lifting and burying. It hurts your back as well as your heart.

The hole CJ and I dug was large and deep. A grown man could have lain down inside of it, if he curled up his legs.

We moved Lucy's 150 kg body in fits and starts, with two towels wrapped underneath her in a sling, as Naya had taught me. We took five steps and rested, then five steps more.

I don't know why we didn't ask friends and neighbours for help. I suppose it was something CJ and I wanted to do together. A private, sacred act. The last thing we would ever do for our Lucy.

She started out being CJ's pig. In the end, she was definitely *ours*.

We wanted to get her body into the hole with dignity, but we failed. We could only hold her at the edge and drop her in. I still feel bad about that. She landed with a tumble and thump, her feet sticking up into the air. It was horrible.

'We have to put her on her side,' I said. 'We can't leave her like that.'

I climbed down inside the grave. There wasn't much room for my feet. The walls of the earth came to my waist. I tried to turn her, but I couldn't. She was too heavy, too big. I gave her one last belly rub, down there with her in her grave, and then I climbed out.

CJ and I stood with one foot on either side of the grave, reached in, grabbed her legs, and tried to turn her again. If it wasn't so sad, it would have been funny. Two incompetent city boys trying to bury an enormous pig.

We stood and looked down at Lucy, now lying peacefully at the bottom of her grave.

CJ said, 'Thank you, Lucy, for all of the joy you brought us.'

I opened the box of doughnuts and placed them in the grave with her, around her mouth.

'In heaven you'll get doughnuts every day,' I said.

Then, reluctantly, as carefully as we possibly could, we shovelled the dirt down over her poor, sweet head.

Chapter 59

Giving back Kowhai

'**W**e have to give Kowhai back,' I said.

CJ looked horrified. 'What? Get rid of Kowhai? How can you say such a thing?'

I shrugged. 'Well, he doesn't really belong to us.'

Kowhai had done very well serving as Old Lady Lucy's strapping young boarfriend and companion in the last year of her life. But now she was gone.

AFTER CJ AND I buried Lucy, I let Kowhai inside the hay shed so he could see she was no longer there. He wasn't convinced, and for three days after her death he continued lying in his spot at the gate, as if waiting for her return. It was heartbreaking. Pigs need company, and we had to do something. He'd been moping around the paddocks by himself for some time.

I said to CJ, 'Maybe Naya and Jeremy can come pick up Kowhai this weekend. He still belongs to them. They can take him home.'

'Stop saying things like that,' CJ said. The thought of being rendered pigless really upset him.

Then he got that look in his eye. It was his 'I have a plan' look. 'I've been thinking,' he said. 'We need a new pet pig.'

I sighed deeply. I was afraid it might come to this. 'Remember we agreed we're not home enough to raise a piglet.'

'I know, I know.'

Then CJ looked off towards the far hills. I could almost see the gears turning inside his head.

CJ knew a few things. He knew that Naya and Jeremy's Longbush Free Range Pork label was taking off. Their Large Black pigs were so delicious that their farm had been growing by leaps and bounds, making Naya and Jeremy very busy pig farmers indeed. CJ was also keenly aware of the fact that they had precisely two more pet kunekune pigs on their property — Dougal the Dim-witted Eunuch and Dougal's sultry sister, Mrs D.

CJ has two basic philosophies in life. The first is, 'Never let nap time pass you by', and the second is, 'Don't be afraid to ask.' This second philosophy is based on the belief that people can always say 'no', and it means that CJ generally never shies away from asking anyone for anything.

But not even CJ could bring himself to ask Naya and Jeremy if he could 'borrow' their last remaining pet kunekune pigs.

As luck would have it, one afternoon CJ found himself sitting next to Jeremy on the train home from Wellington. Jeremy has hands made rough from farming. He and CJ immediately began discussing the dilemma of Kowhai's loneliness.

Jeremy said, 'Maybe we can come by with the pig trailer and pick Kowhai up.'

'No! Please?' CJ begged. 'I can't give up Kowhai.'

'Well, he needs company,' Jeremy said.

'I know.'

At this point I suspect CJ used some sort of Jedi Mind Trick on poor Jeremy.

Jeremy said, 'There's always Dougal and Mrs D.'

'Really?' CJ said, as though this possibility had never crossed his mind. 'What do you mean?'

'Well, Naya and I already talked about it,' Jeremy said. 'We could bring Dougal and Mrs D over to your place to keep Kowhai company. We've been so busy lately that we don't have much time to give them a lot of attention.'

CJ smiled from ear to ear. 'Well, I suppose if you need help caring for them, we'd be happy to lend a hand.'

Jeremy laughed. 'Why do I feel like I've just been set up?'

When Jeremy opened the gate to our pig paddock that weekend to let in Dougal and Mrs D, Kowhai came galumphing over with his ears and tongue flopping wildly. He looked like the happiest pig on earth. All three pigs started grunting hellos and sniffing each other. They had grown up together, and it was clearly a happy pig reunion.

Mrs D had dark black lines around her eyes and puffed-up, white-blonde hair. She made me think of a very fat, 1960s housewife with heavy mascara and a big bouffant. The rings in her nose added a modern, punk-rocker quality to the look.

Dougal was black and white and shaggy, and just as incredibly fat as his sister. You practically had to pull back their fat cheeks just to see their eyes. Kowhai looked positively athletic in comparison.

'If Lucy was Kowhai's girlfriend,' Jeremy said, 'Mrs D is his wife. I think she missed him. She was getting friendly with the Large Blacks.'

'Will she get pregnant?' CJ asked.

Jeremy shook his head. 'She's never had a litter. Apparently she can't.'

VERY SOON AFTER THE new pigs arrived, they settled in. It became clear to CJ and me that Mrs D was an assertive sow, just as Old Lady Lucy had been. And just as Lucy did, she kept Kowhai in line.

Dougal had the personality of a loveable chump. He was so dim-witted that he made young stud Kowhai seem like a rocket scientist.

Kowhai suddenly had a spring in his step. With his plump harlot of a wife and his dopey brother-in-law to keep him company, he was clearly no longer lonely.

Even I had to admit that when I looked out across our property towards the olive grove and saw three big hairy pigs grazing in the top paddock, it made me smile. I hoped kunekune pigs would be grazing in our paddocks for a very long time.

Chapter 60

The olive muse and Moore Wilson's

As I looked up at the enormous building and the huge green sign that said *Moore Wilson's Fresh Market*, I felt like Dorothy at the gates to the Emerald City. In my arms I held a heavy cardboard box full of olive oil bottles that I'd carefully labelled by hand the night before.

At my side was our good neighbour Kiwi Bronwyn, carrying another box, which contained more olive oil, a tablecloth, a bread knife, and some plates and bowls.

CJ STOOD RIGHT BEHIND US, next to our little Nissan Pulsar. He'd just driven us over the Rimutaka Hill Road and into Wellington city for the day.

'Do you have everything?' he asked.

'Um, I think so,' I answered, still looking up at the sign.

If you are a foodie in the Wellington region, Moore Wilson's Fresh Market is basically Mecca. They have aisles and aisles of fresh, gorgeous produce, seafood, baked goods and gourmet food products. What's more, on Saturdays they have tastings and you can nibble your way through from one end of the store to the other.

'Well, then,' Kiwi Bronwyn said, 'let's get started, shall we?'

I swallowed hard. 'Uh. Okay.'

In a flash CJ wished us good luck, hopped back in the car and sped away. Then Kiwi Bronwyn and I marched forward into the bright and shining interior of the most spectacular grocery store on the lower North Island.

TWO MONTHS BEFORE, I had picked up the phone and cold-called Moore Wilson's to ask them if they'd like to carry our Moon over Martinborough olive oil.

'I'm sorry,' the man on the phone said, 'but we just don't have the shelf space. There are hundreds of small producers of olive oil in the Wairarapa, and we just can't carry them all.'

'Oh,' I replied.

I hadn't even thought about what I was going to say if they said no. Selling our oil the first time had been so easy that I didn't even think to prepare a snazzy marketing speech this time.

'But thanks for calling,' the man said. 'Best of luck to you.'

Something happened then. I'm not sure what. It seemed some sort of beneficent, other-worldly spirit invaded me and temporarily occupied my body. An olive muse, perhaps. One with a marketing degree.

'But this olive oil's different,' I heard someone say. It sounded like my voice. 'Not only is it absolutely delicious, but it's got a blog. People can buy the oil and then jump online to read about the growers, how the olives are harvested and pressed, even about how the labels were made. Everything.'

The man on the other end of the phone said, 'Really?'

Suddenly I heard myself rattling on about blog traffic, awards, radio and magazine spots, and newspaper articles like there was no tomorrow. I talked about how the Martinborough microclimate gave our oil an intensity of flavour that was astoundingly beautiful, and about how much care we give to producing our oil. I have never been such a blatant and shameless self-promoter in my entire life.

'Well,' the man said. 'Why don't you bring your oil in? We'll taste it and see what we think.'

The little muse had worked her magic.

The next day I dropped off one of our 250 millilitre bottles at Moore Wilson's, along with some of our bookmarks with the blog address. A week went by. Then two. Then three.

Finally I got a call back. 'Your oil's delicious and the label is beautiful. We really like the blog tie-in. We'll take 16 bottles right away, but we need you to do tasting support.'

Once again, I felt that olive muse take possession of my soul. I heard myself saying 'yes' before I even knew what 'tasting support' was. It was only after I hung up the phone that it dawned on me I'd committed to showing up at Moore Wilson's Fresh Market on a Saturday morning to do an in-store tasting. I was going to peddle our product live and in person. I am an introvert. The thought of standing in public and asking total strangers if they would like to try some olive oil absolutely struck terror in my shy and retiring heart.

When I told CJ about it, he rather diplomatically said, 'I'm a back-of-house person. I'll mow the grove, I'll prune, I'll pick, I'll drive the olives to the press, but I'm not doing any in-store tasting. You're the one who said yes.'

Clearly there was no room for bargaining there.

Not long after that I offhandedly mentioned to Kiwi Bronwyn that I was nervous about doing the tasting at Moore Wilson's.

'Oh, it's easy,' she said. 'I'll help you.'

'You'll what?'

'We used to sell our hazelnuts at Moore Wilson's,' she explained. 'I love doing in-store tastings. It's good fun.'

Once again, God bless our neighbours.

SO THAT'S HOW I CAME to find myself walking into Moore Wilson's with Kiwi Bronwyn, carrying everything we needed for an olive oil tasting. Kiwi Bronwyn is focused, and we quickly set up our table at the end of the olive oil aisle, right next to a tank of live lobsters. On the table we had a loaf of fresh bread cut into bite-sized pieces, and a shallow bowl with some of our beautiful, bright green oil. The Moon over Martinborough labels looked stunning.

Thank goodness Kiwi Bronwyn was there with me. She not only gave me courage, but she also taught me things. Kiwi Bronwyn, it turns out, is a saleswoman extraordinaire. In her previous life, before moving to Martinborough, she worked as a pharmaceutical rep, travelling up and down the North Island. Years ago she traded in her high-powered sales job for a lifestyle block and hazelnut trees.

'Don't just tell people about your olive oil,' she said. 'Ask them questions.'

The shoppers in Moore Wilson's are passionate about food, and within half an hour I realised it was actually very pleasant talking to people about how they use olive oil, what their favourite recipes are, and what tastes they look for in an olive oil. Before I knew it, we'd sold 10 bottles. And I was having a fabulous time.

What amazed me most was that somehow, when people asked me questions about olive oil, I knew the answers. Over the past four years I had slowly built up a surprising amount of knowledge. I could talk to them about how to harvest, how to take care of the trees, and what you need to look for in a quality olive oil. It felt good.

One woman, who initially assumed I was staff at Moore Wilson's, suddenly said, 'Oh, this is *your* olive oil. You're an olive farmer!'

I smiled. It was at that moment I realised that, somewhere along the way, that was exactly what I had become. 'Yes,' I said. 'I guess I am.'

After Kiwi Bronwyn and I had been there for a couple of hours, I noticed a blokey guy walking around the store with a small group of people following him. Moore Wilson's staff were scurrying about, bringing him things and answering his questions.

He passed by our table and Kiwi Bronwyn called out to him, 'Would you like to try some fresh olive oil?'

She seemed a little more insistent than she had been with most people that day, but I didn't think that much about it.

The blokey guy called back, 'Yep. As soon as I check out the seafood.'

When he came over a couple of minutes later, I was in the middle of helping another customer. When I was finished, I turned towards the blokey guy.

Kiwi Bronwyn had been talking to him, and she said, 'It's Jared's oil.'

'Hi,' he said, and he shook my hand. Then he nodded enthusiastically and pointed to our oil. 'Mmm. That's nice oil.'

I thanked him and we chatted for a couple of minutes about locally produced olive oil and what kinds of trees we have in our grove. He seemed vaguely familiar, but I couldn't place him. After a while he told me, 'Keep up the good work', thanked us, and then headed over to the baked goods.

As soon as he was out of earshot, Kiwi Bronwyn said, 'You know who that was, don't you?'

'Um, no. Should I?'

She started laughing. 'Jared, you're hopeless! That's Al Brown! The celebrity chef!'

'Oh, I thought he looked sort of familiar.'

'And he liked your oil,' Kiwi Bronwyn said. 'That's fantastic!'

'But he didn't buy any,' I said.

'He's got his own brand! What does he want with your olive oil? He's probably swimming in the stuff. But the fact is, he thought yours was good. You should be thrilled!'

Kiwi Bronwyn was right. Al Brown's opinion meant a lot. CJ and I had never bothered to enter our olive oil into any competitions due to the costs involved. But now the words of one of the country's top chefs felt like the only gold medal I'd ever need.

The next thing I knew, our city friends were wandering through the doors — first Debbie and Cody, then Paul and Alejandro, Biscuit, Anne, Steve and Nate, and others. CJ had joined several of them for yum cha earlier, and they'd all come over afterwards to say 'good on you' and buy some oil. Even one of my co-workers showed up. It was great.

The city friends asked about the upcoming harvest, and I told them how the olive grove was laden with fruit. We were going to have our biggest olive harvest ever. We had at least 16 people planning to help, and Aussie Bronwyn herself had volunteered to make the morning tea. I couldn't wait.

That was when Helen the Olive Angel of Olivo came walking up to me, smiling. She was at Moore Wilson's on business that day, talking with the manager, and she had come over to say how proud she was to see me doing a tasting of my own.

'You're borrowing our harvest equipment again this year, aren't you?' she said.

'Well, yes, if that's okay.' I answered.

Helen nodded. 'Of course it is.' She touched my arm and leaned forward, 'You're a friend.'

More and more people kept coming up to the table and tasting our oil. When they asked about how to use fresh olive oil, I told them how good it is over a plate of fresh mozzarella and ripe tomatoes from the garden, topped with cracked pepper. I talked about how I love using our olive oil to cook greens such as silverbeet and cavolo nero with fennel seed and chopped garlic. And I told people how great it is to slather it over a pork roast before cooking, along with rock salt.

In what seemed like a very short time, we had sold every single bottle we had brought in with us, plus we made a significant dent in the stock of our bottles that they had on the shelf.

AS WE PACKED UP and left Moore Wilson's that day, I thanked Kiwi Bronwyn for all her amazing help. Then, as we were walking out to the car where CJ was waiting, I quietly addressed the spritely little olive muse who had helped me get my foot in the door — the same muse, perhaps, who had made me fall in love with an olive grove years before.

'Thank you,' I whispered. I couldn't help but smile.

I was an olive farmer.

Acknowledgements

I AM GRATEFUL TO MORE PEOPLE than I can name here.

To the city friends, for helping us move house, harvest olives and cook meals.

To the country neighbours, for teaching us stuff, inviting us to dinner and giving us recipes.

To Vicki and Paul Taylor, for doing more than anyone on the planet to help make our experience in Martinborough absolutely incredible. To my family back in the States for their love and encouragement.

To the contractors Andrew Taylor and James Walker, for helping to get our olive grove on track. To the people at the organisations that have been so supportive: Martinborough Wine Centre, Moore Wilson's, Ingredient Café, Piccolo Café, *Martinborough Star*, *Wairarapa Times-Age*, Wairarapa Archives, and Hedley's Booksellers.

To Victoria University's International Institute of Modern Letters, for that amazing Iowa Workshop. To my instructor Curtis Sittenfeld, for saying, 'You should write about this place.' To my various writing groups, especially 'The Sittenfelds', for their invaluable feedback.

To Chris Else, for helping me learn that I didn't have to write so seriously. To the readers of the 'Moon over Martinborough' blog, for being so enthusiastic.

To Leanne French and Greg Keith at Wolfies (www.wolfies.
co.nz), for their creativity, graphic design and wordsmithing skills,
and advice on everything from olives to pigs to marketing. Greg is
also the artist behind the book's great illustrations.

To Helen Meehan of Olivo (www.olivo.co.nz), for teaching me
how to harvest olives and letting us borrow equipment.

To Naya Brangenberg and Jeremy Wilhelm of Longbush Free
Range Pork (www.longbushpork.co.nz), for giving us their delightful
kunekune pigs on semi-permanent loan.

To Raewyn Watson of *Wairarapa Lifestyle* magazine (www.
wairarapalifestyle.co.nz), for plucking my stories out of cyberspace
and including them in her magazine.

To Vicki Jones (www.allkiwiscancook.co.nz), for teaching me
how to do a tasting and offering her marinated lamb recipe.

To Nicola Legat and all the good people at Random House New
Zealand, for being a dream to work with.

And most importantly to CJ, for being my most critical reader,
my most generous subject, and my most precious companion.

Thank you.

For more information about our titles visit
www.randomhouse.co.nz